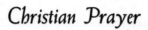

Christian Prayer

Cross and Crown Series of Spirituality

LITERARY EDITOR
Reverend Jordan Aumann, O.P., S.T.D.

NUMBER 23

Christian Prayer

By FRANZ M. MOSCHNER

&

Translated by

Elisabeth Plettenberg

B. HERDER BOOK CO.

15 & 17 South Broadway, St. Louis 2, Mo.
2/3 Doughty Mews, London, W.C.1

A translation of *Christliches Gebetsleben*, third edition, published by Verlag Herder Freiburg, 1953.

NIHIL OBSTAT

J. S. Considine, O.P.
Censor Deputatus

IMPRIMATUR

✠ Albert Cardinal Meyer
Archbishop of Chicago
August 10, 1962

Author's Preface

THE following thoughts are especially dedicated to my numerous friends whose desire for greater perfection in their lives as Christians has either brought them together in working groups or has prompted each one in his own individual way to make the solitary ascent to the summit. After many years of teaching and instruction, preaching and correspondence, I felt induced to try and summarize what, by these diverse means, had been said in a somewhat scattered fashion, and thus provide an approximate guide which would both outline the most significant and essential aspects of the interior way to God and give some pertinent practical advice. Although theoretically teaching had to take the first place—since this is a question of clearly defined basic concepts—the final objective of this book is eminently practical. It would help those of good will better to attain the fulfillment of their deepest longing: that they may grow and mature in the love of God and with God.

Hence this book should not be taken as mere reading matter to be perused more or less haphazardly and noted with nodding consent or doubting disapproval. Rather, it stresses the eminent importance of the faithful practice and the actual application of its suggestions. Reading is no substitute for action, and by mere reading no one will ever reach sanctity. To know the way is a good thing, but it is no more than a preliminary; the goal can only be found by walking the whole length of the road.

This is what this book would, again and again, impress upon the reader.

People nowadays so often and so urgently inquire about the way to greater depth and perfection in their life of prayer, that it seems indicated to set out a few generally valid statements to answer these questions. Quite deliberately we have not dealt with extraordinary phenomena—visions and the like—except in a negative way. They, more than anything else, oblige the soul to seek and to comply with that individual and immediate spiritual direction which written guidance—that is, generally applicable rules and explanations—cannot replace. All the greater has been the emphasis with which the positive aspects have been stressed: the way toward God and the life with Him. This is what really matters, and if in the last few pages the attempt has been made to transmit some of the radiance of this life itself, it should be remembered that its riches are beyond description. At best one can talk of them as of the impressions gained on a vast and wonderful journey which each would necessarily experience in a highly personal manner, and each would therefore describe differently. Yet all will recognize the beloved country even if but few words are said.

May a prayer to the Holy Ghost, for His guidance and for the strength of His love, precede each opening of these pages.

Preface to the Second German Edition

THE chief purpose of the book has been correctly noted: to describe and interpret those more advanced and intimate modes of prayer of which too little is normally said. There are far more people than one thinks who are called to these higher forms of interior life, and who earnestly desire to follow the call in which there is still much which they do not clearly understand. It is chiefly for them that this book has been written; not merely to be read, but to be practiced, if it is to bear fruit.

The central theme has been the love which exists between God and the soul. One might also have used the word "friendship" or "service," as has been suggested. But when we treat of these ultimate realities, we naturally fall back on the most highly charged expressions of our language, knowing that behind their differences the ineffable essence remains the same, and that they are all inadequate anyway. In the final analysis, words are never more than pointers to the Word, and he whom grace has helped to find the Word has left words behind.

Contents

Chapter 1

In Sancto Sanctissimo

A WELL-KNOWN painting of the early fifteenth century by the Russian artist Andrej Rubljow, generally described as *The Angels of the Holy Trinity*, shows three sublime forms seated at a table. The angels, whom we interpret as representing the Most Holy Trinity, resemble each other closely; in fact, only the different coloring of their garments, and their movements, faint and restrained, seem to afford them individual distinction. Their joint presence at the table emphasizes an intimacy of intense coordination, single-minded in action and essence, recollected in mutual awareness. A chalice, the only object on the table, contains some clearly discernible substance—pieces of bread, no doubt.

A wondrous stillness and repose pervades the whole scene. Evidently, not a word is spoken. Not, though, as if there were nothing to say, but because here is sacred silence itself become perfect discourse. No need for one to converse with the other, for each partakes fully and deeply of the other's being. Their resemblance is not one of repetition or uniformity; rather, it signifies plenitude, a plenitude which can bear witness to its undivided nature only in such threefold self-evidence. The table with chalice and bread reveals yet further how each one of the three partakes of, lives with, and exists in the other two; each to each is food and drink; each lives for, by and within the other.

Here is a mode of existence which is not a static accomplishment but a continuous operation. Whatever happens in God is not subject to time; it does not occur as a successive coming into being as we know it, but is at once an utterly complete and most perfect reality. Thus it is beyond both accomplished being and coming into being, since it is both of these in one. All divine being and acting belongs to each Person of the Trinity, in that it passes from one Person to the other in the complete giving of each one. And as one Person gives, so He receives anew in that very "instant," never to break this mysterious circle.

This is the supreme and all-perfect life of the absolute Spirit in which He reveals His ultimate being in the eternal discourse within Himself. And there is an equality of being in God's Word of self-expression, in which He is both Father and Son, and an equality of being, too, in His unbounded love—the Holy Ghost—in whom He embraces and recalls unto Himself the Word, His Son. Then the Son answers the call by a total surrender to that same love, the Holy Ghost, who proceeds from Him and the Father. This is the completion of the discourse within the unutterably lovable and loving Divine Spirit, in Himself the most translucent, the purest, the sweetest harmony. And as it culminates in ultimate offering and ultimate embrace, the discourse comprehends the divine essence, and in wordless unity of being there is unity of life.

This is the prayer beyond all prayer. God Himself, in His triune life, is substantial prayer: joy, thanksgiving and fulfilled desire.

Prayer is here perceived and understood in its most majestic comprehensiveness and depth: as concord within God Himself, unstinting current of life, boundless serenity and supreme action, ultimate manifestation and reality of the divine being, felicitous harmony of love in which three are one God in an endless stream of life from, by and for each other.

Chapter 2

Creation and the Priestly Race

LIKE the body, which is mute except for the reasoning head and the mouth that speaks, so God's creation is mute but for its head which is man. True, there are plenty of sounds and voices in the universe, and they may well be of a deeply stirring force or an enchanting sweetness. They certainly have their significance, their meaning and object, yet they are mute in the spiritual or intellectual sense. They exist, but they have no knowledge of themselves, they do not understand themselves, and therefore they cannot explicitly relate themselves to their Creator. They point to Him, they "sing the praise of the Most High," and they tell of the power and wisdom of His hands, but all this unknowingly. Only in man is there a sense of being, alert and conscious of itself. He alone knows that God is, and that He is "above all beings, through all, and within them all." He alone is capable of lifting his mind above himself to acknowledge God as the Creator, the Lord and Father of all beings. And man alone can, on the strength of such recognition, direct all his powers toward God in a definite act of the will and do so by virtue of that almost incomprehensible freedom by which, on the other hand, he can also refuse all recognition, relation and solemn praise in thought, word and deed, and turn them to perversion.

As the head of creation which is subject to him, man is the spokesman of all the other beings of this visible world and stands before God as the leader of their choir. He must elevate their mute voices to the spiritual and in his own mind must raise them in adoration. In him their nescience and their helpless stammer become transfigured. For man is the microcosm, and in him all the levels of creation are fused into one whole, their special properties as matter, plants or animals merging into one. Thus, in him they serve and worship, and he serves and prays in their name. What they blindly do in bonded submission to the divinely implanted principle of their particular order, man can and must do with awareness and freedom. Thus in man and through him creation attains to spirit and freedom, just as by the power of man's spirit the limbs of his body are the first to be lifted out of the apathy of their natural confinement to share in the service of the sublime. Thus, the knee, moved by the intellect and will to bend before God, is indeed at prayer.

Every interior gaze of man ought to be at once a gaze on God, a gaze together with God and a gaze from God to one's tasks. All man's actions should be performed in union with God, whose works he certainly sees, so that they become works of God Himself. He would thus stand in closest communion with God and become an apt mediator between Him and the universe. Moreover, thus understanding and thus acting, man would win all things to God, thus "hallowing His name" by this dedication just as he would help to bring about the "coming of the kingdom" by receiving. And in both functions man would open his being in all sincerity to the will of God, which would thus "be done on earth as it is in heaven." Living in God in all things, taking all from Him and returning all to Him, man imitates the inner divine life of the Trinity, of which he is an earthly image.

True, in Holy Scripture we read: "God rested on the seventh day," after having said to man: "Subdue the earth," that is, continue the work of creation and complete it, since in My image as Creator I called you into being. But what is meant by saying that God rested? It simply means that we no longer perceive His activity as such; it is now enfolded and deeply hidden in the activities of His creatures, especially in the creative powers of man who, as "the little god of the earth," mirrors God's eternal and unending creative power.

The subduing of the earth can be effected only by an intimate cooperation with God and His instruction, power and objective; indeed, only by a constant and vital union with God—by listening to God and giving our reply, by looking at Him and doing as He bids us, by conceiving God and bringing Him forth. To will what God wills is to love Him, and such loving discourse extends even to material things. They too are "eternal thoughts of God," divine conceptions. Although embedded in matter, they respond to that same rhythm of receiving from and dedicating to God, which animates the human soul. Thus could the universe come to participate in the inner divine discourse. God cannot—if we may say so—glorify Himself by adoration. But it is for the universe—inferior to God, immeasurably inferior by the very fact of being created—to adore Him and to turn to contrite expiation where, in the freedom of man's volition, it has disobeyed His holy will.

Man is the priest of creation. For we were ordained a "priestly caste" so that through us the universe might chant the praises of the Most High and become one single voice of jubilant response to His call of love. We are to pray, and in us all shall pray and find the way to God in and through us. And there shall be no end of giving and receiving, of loving reciprocity, widening and deepening forever.

When and wherever God's will is recognized and carried out in the freedom of devoted obedience, prayer, which is the discourse of love between God and His creatures, permeates all the orders of creation.

And still all this would not mean ultimate and perfect communion. There would always remain the infinite distance between Creator and created, the relationship of Master and servant rather than that of Father and son, even though it be the kindest, the most lovable and loving master and thus not unlike a father. Yet no equality of birthright like that between father and son would sustain their intercourse which, therefore, would not comprise *all* that God could say. Nor could it contain what creation might answer if it were endowed with sublime life, utterly true and real such as it is in God; or if man as its head were not only the image of his Creator, but equal to Him in divine origin and substance, so that God's very language would issue from his mouth.

Chapter 3

Christ the High Priest

ALTHOUGH in man the whole of creation raises its voice in an adoring response of prayer, it does not penetrate into the holiest depths of God. It merely picks up the "crumbs" falling from His table which it does not share. Hard of hearing and thus unaware of the soundless whispers within the heart of God, creation does not command the power of love that would answer them. Even before sin deafened its natural faculty of hearing and turned to incoherence its natural gift of speech, creation perceived but faintly and as from a great distance the word of eternal love.

But creation is to be equal and worthy to converse with God, able to hear all that He says, and so to answer Him that God will require of it no more. Raised and admitted into that ever blessed triune company, creation consumed in prayer is to share in the banquet of life eternal, receiving God forever into itself and losing itself eternally in Him.

That is why God became man. The "Word was made flesh" and thereby clasped unto Himself the human being in an inseparable and sublime embrace. In Him human nature is worthy of adoration, for in Him it is truly the body and soul of God, just as my hand is mine and not somebody else's. One may wish to kiss the hand of a benevolent person, not because the hand is kind in itself but because in some special way it is part of this person's goodness. Similarly, the human nature of the "Word made flesh," although not divine in itself, commands adoration because it is now the nature of the God-Man. In the Word humanity has been given both its true head,

7]

which reaches up to the very heights of heaven, and its most holy mouth, which offers perfect and worthy adoration in the name of all creation. The kingly priesthood now has its High Priest, in whom it is enabled fittingly to fulfill its office of exaltation.

In Christ Jesus creation has been brought close to God, has indeed become one with Him to the extent of "sharing His table." The nucleus, the innermost center of the created world, already stands in that same adoration which is eternally accomplished in the mind of the God-Man and in His Most Sacred Heart. Ever since the moment of the Incarnation there has been everlasting and perfect adoration, offered by the created world, but of divine rank and splendor. This adoration cannot be surpassed, it is ultimate. It is, once and for all, union between God and the whole of creation in an unreservedly flowing stream of life. God gives Himself to the adoring heart and it, in adoration, gives itself wholly to God.

In the Most Sacred Heart of Jesus, the "King and Center of all hearts," the entire universe exults, haltingly still, as though it would not quite trust itself, yet with the hymns of eternal love already intoned. But the blessed perennial discourse has begun, never to end again. The fountain of celestial joy springs up, the morning dawns, and the light rejoices toward the fullness of the day, when the "marriage feast of the Lamb and the bride is come."

Chapter 4

The Spirit of Christ

THE prayer of the God-Man Jesus Christ is His very existence in and for God, and this He performs in the Holy Ghost who is the love between the Father and the Son. There is such an impetus, such comprehensive force in this love, which is at once that which the Father bears the Son and that which emanates from the Son to the Father, that it becomes personified. Spirit of adoption, He is called, for it is in Him that the Word truly is the Son. Permeating the Son's obediently assumed humanity, the Spirit now draws it substantially into the inner divine conflux of love. And thus, by virtue of the union with the Word in the Spirit of adoption, the human nature of Christ, too, is wholly that of the Son of God.

In the love of the Holy Spirit, the Father's will is forever conveyed to the Son who, consubstantial with the Father, makes His response of loving acceptance in that same Spirit of love. Hence His most wonderful concord with the Father, with whom the Son wills and creates, sanctifies, saves and judges. The same Spirit of love carries the Father's will into the temporal human nature hypostatically united to the Eternal Son and allows His human faculties to comprehend it in a manner adequate to their essential character. From the Son's eternal divine essence the Holy Spirit pours forth, as it were, into the sacred humanity, imbuing and inspiring it with light and fervor. Thus the human spirit of Jesus perceives in the Holy Spirit the Father's will, which is already accomplished by the Eternal Son to whom this human nature now belongs. Similarly, the human will of Jesus is called upon to respond

9]

to the will of the Father which, as the Eternal Son now endowed with this human will, Jesus again already always fulfills. In a vision of light of the Spirit of truth and with an ardent will inflamed by the Spirit of love, the Man Christ gives His truly human but also divinely perfect answer in ever ready acceptance of all that the Father wills.

Very explicitly Jesus declares that "the Son cannot do anything of Himself but what He seeth the Father doing" and "what things soever He doth, these the Son also doth in like manner" (John 5:19). The Man Jesus perceives the will of the Father in utter clarity. In the bright light of the indwelling Spirit of God His human nature acknowledges it and, filled with the Spirit of love, accepts it in perfect compliance. Hence the Gospels abound in expressions with which our Lord affirms His absolute conformity with the will of His heavenly Father. It is in the fulfillment of the Father's will by the human nature of Jesus Christ in inseparable union with His divine nature that the harmony between God and creation is achieved. In the fusion of the two natures in Christ, made one in the Second Person of the deity by the loving mediation of the Holy Ghost, creation is affiliated to God, brought face to face with the loving and beloved Father, and is concerned only with that infinitely glorious and sacred will in which the Father's being is wholly portrayed and revealed. To carry out the Father's will is at once call and response, appeal and readiness, invitation and consent; it is all love and unity, discourse silenced in bliss and the purest prayer of self-surrender.

In the Holy Ghost, then, the Father's will and desire reaches the divine-human Heart which again in the same Holy Ghost abandons itself to the Father, unquestioningly willing to accomplish the errand of love. In the Spirit of love the perfect discourse between the Father and the God-Man is made permanent. Not for one moment is there any cessation of the flow of life and will and action between them. Not even when, seemingly, it can no longer operate, as, for instance, during sleep. For sleep, too, is part of "what the Father wills." It is part of man's nature, so planned and created, and therefore made manifest exemplarily and perfectly in the human nature which the Son assumed. Not as if, in His slumbers, Christ "prayed" by forming words and making acts of devotion, but sleep itself was a prayer because it was the acceptance of the Father's will.

The whole being of Jesus Christ is everlasting prayer, is receiving from and giving to the Father. Here it becomes quite clear how "praying" is not merely "speaking"; indeed, perhaps least of all. Rather, it is an interior act embracing the exterior action where this, for the time being, has to be suspended. It is a continuous manifestation of total alliance and communion of life, and as such it is finally the most sublime manifestation of being; and all this "in the Holy Ghost."

Chapter 5

Perfect Prayer for
the Children of God

CHRIST certainly did not intend to establish the sublime communion of life between God the Father and creation merely "in our name" and limited to His human nature. Nor did He come to conduct the holy discourse of love on behalf of us and in our place, so that we, merely looking on from afar, would never fully understand the meaning of this sacred dialogue.

Instead, Christ wanted to integrate us truly into the eternal discourse, and through us—and only through us—the whole of creation. His divine-human prayer was meant to be all-embracing, gathering into itself all the human speaking to and striving toward God, and thus lead it to the heart of the Father as in a majestic stream which would carry our voice to God on the level of Christ's own. There the Father's word would reach us not as mere bystanders, but as real friends, talking to Him face to face and intimately.

That is why Christ gained for us all not a symbolical, so-called sonship, but a true filiation as children of God. And Christ imparts this to every one of us, if and so far as we desire it. For, surely, something so unspeakably sublime as the "participation of the divine table," the communion with that life which God eternally enjoys in and with Himself, cannot reasonably be forced upon anyone. Supreme love is supreme freedom in purest and unquestioning allegiance. God is love. His life is the self-manifestation of love, and therefore nobody

[12

can be made to share this life of love unless he himself wills to do so, unless he, too, will love. By the gift of Christ which we call Redemption, we are also re-formed, in the sense that we are enabled to sink ourselves into the triune life of God and remain therein in spite of all that tries to separate us from it, and will, as we know from experience, always succeed to some extent. "He gave them power to be made the sons of God, to them that believe in His name" (John 1:12).

Faith is the beginning of hearing and obeying the Father's word which reaches us through the mouth of Christ. If we surrender ourselves to Christ in an inner readiness to be wholly one with Him, and through Him with the Father, we shall be engrafted in Christ by "water and the Holy Ghost," that is, by the symbol of earthly created life and the presence of the eternal life of love itself. In baptism we are made as new and raised to a higher level of being, to the highest possible plane of existence where God's own life is superabundant.

Baptized, we are truly, and not merely symbolically, one with Christ, "members of His body," "branches of the vine." Each one of us certainly retains his own natural life, even as the human nature which Christ assumed is and remains part of nature. And it is precisely this natural life which is elevated to the higher plane of reality where, in Christ, it partakes of supreme nobility and immeasurable strength. In the Holy Ghost the Father's life flows toward the Word and fills His human nature, and from that source it pours into all those who, by their rebirth in baptism, become members of this sacred humanity. "One Lord, one faith, one baptism; one God and Father of all" (Eph. 4:5–6).

This is perfect communion; not yet fully unfolded, but fundamentally established. The Father is no longer in "light inaccessible" (I Tim. 6:16). In Christ's face we have seen Him. We are before Him, we are in Him, and we share His life. That is why Jesus solemnly proclaims: "I will not now call you servants: for the servant knoweth not what his lord doth. But I have called you friends: because all things whatsoever I have heard of My Father, I have made known to you" (John 15:15). True, in the sight of the Father they are still "children"; they have not yet attained to the "measure of the age of the fullness of Christ" (Eph. 4:13), and they can, therefore, not yet follow and take part in everything: "I have yet many things to say to you: but you cannot bear them now" (John 16:12). But that is not essential; it is part of the unfolding and ripening, for "when He, the Spirit of truth, is come, whom I will send you from the Father, He will teach you all things and bring all things to your mind, whatsoever I shall have said to you" (John 15:26; 16:13). In the Holy Ghost love will become perfect; and perfect, too, will be the discourse between God and the soul, true conversation between Father and son, which will contain all that Christ, the Son, has "heard of the Father." This conversation will embrace all that is God's concern. And since nothing can exist outside this concern, it will be an all-embracing, a "catholic" conversation.

Moreover, it will be one within the innermost depth of the human heart and mind; not as if we were calling or reaching across to a far distant heaven somewhere high above. "He that hath My commandments, and keepeth them: he it is that loveth Me" (John 14:21). He who hears and obeys My words —and they are always first and foremost the words of the Father—responds by the loving answer of his heart. He who knows and fulfills the will of the Father, espouses Him with his whole being. And finally: "If anyone love Me, he will keep My word, and My Father will love him, and We will come to him and will make Our abode with him" (John 14:23). The triune God present in us, having made the gift of Himself to the beloved and loving soul, not in the general sense of His omnipresence, but as He really is in Himself, God now, within the soul, lives His own life, allowing the soul to share it just as He deigned to make the life of the soul His own. Now the soul listens, beholds and answers; apprehends God's will and fulfills it; receives the Father in Christ through the Holy Ghost

and abandons itself to the Father in Christ through that same
Holy Ghost.

Dulcis hospes animae. Sweet Host of the soul. As the Spirit
of Jesus Christ, the Holy Spirit is ours, too, and more specifically so when, in the sacrament of confirmation, He is given
to us to ripen us "to the fullness of Christ." "By Him, and
with Him, and in Him" we can now cooperate in the high-
priestly office which is our ultimate task in creation: speaking
with the Father, being messengers of His will to the universe,
and carrying all manner of being before the Father's throne.
Through the Holy Ghost our prayer is one with the prayer
of Christ. In Him it has divine-human character and meaning,
though it remains our prayer, determined in its individuality,
its special intention, and its inner rhythm by our own particular, created nature. Individuals that we are, we shall be dedicated, sanctified and integrated into the perennial prayer. God
gives Himself to us as a gift worthy of Him, and in a manner
worthy of God we return the gift to Him. Our entire self
speaks with God; our fundamental being has become prayer.

Chapter 6

The Scope of Prayer

WHAT, then, is prayer? Is it the same as talking? Forming words? Is that all? Or, indeed, do words constitute an essential part of it at all? The catechism teaches us that praying means lifting up the heart and mind devoutly to God. The heart and mind, that is, the innermost depth within us, the ultimate source, as it were, from which our personal life originates and where we are entirely and exclusively ourselves in all our merits and shortcomings. It is that which impresses itself upon all our thoughts, words and deeds, giving them color, fragrance and exquisite beauty, but also obscenity, iniquity and repellent baseness. Our heart is in and behind everything that we are or do. It is the essence of our being, as its roots and as its deepest, most hidden core, hidden in some measure and, indeed, almost entirely hidden from ourselves. Hence it is by our heart that God measures and appraises all our achievements, and therefore there can, strictly speaking, never be anything indifferent in or about us which is merely there, colorless and undefined. If the root of a plant contains healing properties, they will rise up and fill, though in varying degrees of strength, the different parts of the plant. If the root be poisonous, the venom will spread into the rest of the plant, though in hardly measurable quantities. In like manner, everything in and about us is conditioned by the heart and mind within.

To lift up this heart to God means to focus it upon Him. It must neither remain within itself nor give itself, or worse still, spend itself indiscriminately. Instead, it must direct itself

[16

ultimately toward God, thus acknowledging Him as its first origin and final goal, as the one in whom alone it can be good. This, then, is the meaning of "lifting up . . . devoutly." The heart can turn to God also in bitterness and anger, in open and secret rebellion, in blasphemy and obstinacy. Devout it is, when it lifts itself up in the love of God, in a beginning of love at least, even though this may yet seem to be enveloped in the fear of Him. A timorous approach, perhaps; one as yet uncertain of itself, but urged on by incipient desire. Only when our whole being seeks to approach God do we properly pray. Hence the Psalmist's reproach: "This people honoreth Me with their lips, but their heart is far from Me" (Isa. 29:13; Matt. 15:8). The lips, the mouth, the word—thought or spoken —can be a valid and genuine expression of the loving inclination of the heart. Expression, yes; but no more. Mere words would mean insult rather than homage, dissembling appearance, a beautiful mask to cloak our emptiness and indigence.

Prayer is the "breath of the soul," as St. Augustine tells us. Breathing is a basic function of life and so inseparable from it that its cessation indicates the extinction of life itself. Prayer is the corresponding process for the soul, and by that we mean in this connection the supernatural life of the children of God. As his spiritual breath, prayer belongs even to man's natural life; but this does not now concern us. It is only by taking God into ourselves and by giving ourselves "away" to Him, that we sustain our supernatural life. And this applies to all the different ways in which we receive something from God and respond to it: each simple wordless doing of God's will as and when we understand it, each humble daily duty done for the love of God, all this is prayer as long as the heart is given up to God without repeal. From God comes the task; from us, the act of loving obedience. Thus, in deep silence, hidden perhaps even from ourselves, the heart holds intimate converse with God.

This is the only way in which Christ's explicit command, that we ought always to pray, and not to faint (Luke 18:1), can be obeyed. "Always" does not mean again and again, regularly; it means without interruption, incessantly. Our prayer must not be like the milestones on the road, but like the road itself. Whatever we do "in God" is genuine and valid prayer. Words or actions, recreation or suffering, if it happens "in God" it has the character of prayer. For our heart, although it is in all these things, is with God.

That is why Jesus says: "The true adorers shall adore the Father in spirit and in truth. For the Father also seeketh such to adore Him" (John 4:23). Not those of many and beautiful words, but such as adore Him in the pure and true dedication of their hearts to the heavenly Father. There is one only— we know it well—who of Himself can achieve such dedication: the Eternal Son, Jesus Christ. He who is the truth in its essence, and in whom the Spirit lives in absolute entity, the Holy Ghost who proceeds from Him. As members of Christ we *are* "in spirit and in truth." Truth itself and the Spirit are within us, and they are our supernatural life. The mysterious breath— *spiritus* means both breath and spirit—the Breath of Love imparts itself to us, moves through us and, passing between the Father and the Son, carries us on. As long as we are in Christ and deeply remain in Him, the holy "Breath of the Soul" is in us. And there happens within us prayer—God's prayer, and now our own.

All this, however, is not to occur merely in the abstract, somewhere beyond our perception, as it were, and beyond our conscious exertion, like a stream passing below the desert sands. Just because we are to pray "in spirit and in truth" as the "true adorers" whom the Father seeketh, all our life and being must increasingly and ever more consciously become a life in and with God. That threefold divine discourse which occurs in the depth of our soul must absorb us into its light and splendor, its wisdom and exultation.

This could never be achieved without an effort on our part, and never, indeed, without our "word." The gift of the word is the most wonderful means of intellectual expression between man and man, indispensable vessel of all the profundity of which human thought and intellect are capable. That is why, of necessity, it must take part in the glorification of God. If everything is to become instrumental in the sacred office of divine praise and of the discourse with God, then certainly, the word, too, must be thus consecrated.

But let us beware; the most beautiful word and the cleverest word is nothing, is "as sounding brass or a tinkling cymbal" (I Cor. 13:1) if it does not rise up from the heart or is not quickened by the very heart wherein the Triune God has made His abode in all His unrestrained self-manifestation. In the "Word that was made flesh" the Father speaks to us. But this Word would leave us cold, would not deeply concern us, and might even mean something painful and cruel to us, were it not that the Word made flesh, animated by the Holy Ghost, abounds with love and is therefore our salvation, our life, our blessing forever. To this Word coming from the Heart of God naught but our heart can make fitting response. The Word of God finds our heart, because it proceeds from His love. Our answer reaches the heart of God if, and because, it is carried by our love. This, and this only, deserves the name of prayer.

Words are a means and a form of prayer, not its essence. Therefore they will, at one time or another, be superseded; they will become redundant, at least so far as they represent our everyday language. But they are part of the way which leads to God and are therefore important in any doctrine of prayer. Yet they are like crutches, or like steps: useful and necessary; you cannot "get there" without them. Once "there," however, they lose their importance and something else takes their place, something which does not exclude the words but includes them so that they become superfluous. Now, we know all prayer to be a matter of grace. And the higher its ascent, the more it is grace. Nobody can confer that upon himself. It comes from the love of God, as He wills it. Thereafter we must sustain grace and cooperate with it. Nor shall we fail if, in single-minded sincerity, our heart is forever God's own.

Chapter 7

The Way of Prayer

THE prayer of words is like a thin vein of water; narrow as yet and seemingly insignificant in the spacious landscape of life, it is already mysteriously part of that infinity into which it will issue and for which it is destined, unless, on its way, it were to spend itself and thus fail its original purpose.

Prayer begins with words imperfectly grasped and echoed by the child and soon known by heart. The child says the words and loves saying them as it becomes aware of speaking to one who is invisible and yet so near and so surely Someone. Though unconsciously, the young soul is already fully alive in those poor words; they are its breath and its food. Gradually such short-lived prayer, sparse and slender, widens and deepens with the soul's growing consciousness and increasingly free resolve, until the little brook has grown into a swiftly moving river which moulds the surrounding landscape. Cities and towns spring up on its banks and innumerable trades owe to it the greater and most important part of their existence. Finally, the stream loses itself in the boundless sea, whose infinity is its predestined goal. Perhaps you can trace it yet far into the bay as, carried along by its waters, a yellowish sand reveals its flow in the embracing ocean. Then this trace, too, disappears; the little vein of water has become what, in a sense, it had always been: unmeasured strength, superabundance.

The prayer of words becomes more and more one of the heart alone, although we should never disregard the value of the words. Even when, at last, the soul will have lost itself entirely in God, words will still at times serve the purpose of prayer. They will, as it were, reveal the swell of the soul within the ocean of God. But they will no longer have an ultimate or decisive significance; indeed, a new understanding of their true significance shows that they were but a means to an end, a help on the way, indispensable for a long time and once again be it said—never completely unnecessary. But prayer itself had always been at a much deeper level, as the very life of the soul safely anchored in God. Verbal prayer had helped the soul to become profoundly aware of and consciously permeated by the presence of God, until the inner discourse of the Trinity had drawn the soul wholly into its orbit and made its prayer perfect. Henceforth the words of prayer will be not so much a means for the soul to reach its goal, but a manifestation, in one of so many ways, that the soul has at last attained the desired end.

Again, the life of prayer is like a long journey, rich with astonishing experiences, with joy and ecstasy. But the way also leads through desert land and ice-covered wastes, where there is not a sound, where fear abides, and where the demons lurk; where sudden depths and dangers trap the unsuspecting wanderer's hesitant foot.

Progress in prayer, however, is not automatic. Many remain forever at the starting point or come to a standstill at an early stage. Perhaps they were unfortunate, because there was no one to point the way ahead. More likely, however, it was their own fault, for they did not heed the guiding voice of the Holy Ghost or they lacked the stamina to persevere when everything seemed lost, and to trust the divine light to illumine the dense darkness.

Everything in prayer depends on grace, though we should not think of grace as something falling into our lap and making us suddenly perfect at prayer. Our very first prayer we owe to grace, which is sure to increase with every prayer faithfully said. With each good prayer the soul is widened to receive yet further graces which will always lead on, even though for long spells the soul may not be aware of any progress. Think of a mountain brook; long before any water comes to the surface, its hidden source is secretly alive, seeping, struggling, pulsating, until one day the waters flow and you can draw water from its stream.

In and through prayer the grace of prayer is at work. Imperceptibly at first, until from stage to stage new perceptions quicken the soul. If we could always fully exploit the specific grace which both begets and springs from every prayer, nothing could check our inner progress, let alone bring it to a standstill, which in this sphere is always equivalent to a particularly perilous decline. Hence we must ever in our prayer ask for the spirit of prayer itself, the right spirit, like the disciples who so earnestly begged: "Lord, teach us to pray!"

It is one of the spiritual works of mercy to counsel others. The marvel of the communion of saints, that is, of the union of those who are one in God, must prove itself with particular efficacy in the double exercise of this work of mercy: to pray for others that they may learn to pray, and to assist their life of prayer with practical advice, where it is needed or asked for. In the mind of the Church, education in prayer is one of the first essentials of Christian existence; it is, indeed, the great concern of the Church. For he who prays well, will lead a godly life, will love God, and win for himself the kingdom of heaven.

This book endeavors to serve this end. It would give a few hints for the inner way with God and toward Him, for private personal use as well as for the instruction of others. It owes itself to the experience of the saints—those so accomplished in prayer, those whom God inspired so that they might be beacons to us on the intricate, strange, and seemingly unlikely way of the inner life. No more than a suggestion itself, this book hopes to encourage the study of the saints' own writings which will amply fill each individual need.

Before we begin carefully to trace the way of prayer, let us approach it by the analogy of the gradual unfolding of a human relationship into friendship. Meeting a stranger is, at first, a matter of some formality. Not much is said—only what is necessary to establish contact, such as a customary salutation or a question regarding the other person's well-being, a few non-committal words on generalities such as the weather, politics, or some current event, all of which could equally well be discussed with any other person without the slightest difference in manner or circumstance. Nevertheless, such talk need not be a "set formula" only. If conducted by sincere persons it will surely, though inconspicuously, manifest true human concern. The question about the other's well-being and even the first "Good morning" will, no doubt, mean something. Somehow the heart will be in those words expressed by the mouth, for here is true "expression," not just "chatter."

The more it is "expression" the more likely the contact will deepen. Soon, especially if meetings occur not too infrequently, more personal matters will become part of the conversation. There is talk of one's problems and the sharing of those of the other person. Vital questions are discussed, touching perhaps on religion and ethics. The conversational formulas become less rigid, livelier, more earnest; they come from greater depth and therefore reach the partner on a deeper level.

"Understanding" constantly improves. Already there is less need for quite so many explanations, paraphrases, elucidations. One begins to understand the other soul and its peculiarities, and how to "handle" them in the best sense of the word. The two find themselves on common ground in certain basic matters, and a gratifying harmony has been established.

By now, gestures such as raising one's hat or shaking hands have long ceased to be needed in support of words. A faint smile, swiftly passing across the face; a slight movement of the hand, hardly noticeable to anyone else; an almost imperceptible emotion in the voice; a glance directed exclusively to the other person; any of these now suffices and expresses more than previous lengthy conversations. The two understand one another fully, and are united in judgment, criticism, or resolve.

Others cannot keep pace with them because matters have become too personal by now. They have already met in those deep reaches of the soul which others cannot share.

Eventually words become almost a nuisance. The friends go for walks together, but they scarcely speak. There is no need. They have found one another, and the life of the one has become the life of the other. If some topic is brought up, both are surprised to find that they had simultaneously arrived at the same thought, and sometimes both will start a sentence with the same word. The word rises up spontaneously, not to join threads of vital contact, but to prove that it already exists. Words now carry a vitality which has become a shared experience, which fills and animates them, reaching far beyond the literal meaning of the words expressed. The consciousness of each person has, as it were, been widened by the measure of the other's horizon. Each one knows how the other feels, "sensing" it, as if told by an "inner voice." Here is a manner of perception and participation which no outside person shares. Here two people have achieved a vision of each other's interior image. Now the great silence ensues between the two minds, no longer empty as in the beginning, when one had at times looked feverishly for a "topic," but filled with deep vibrations. They seem now to resent words, as too harsh is their power of expression, too crude, and more of a hindrance than a help.

On this way of love (what else could it be but that?) there are some crucial turning points. The first is reached when "formal" conversation becomes easy, uninhibited, spontaneous. The second marks the beginning of a genuine effort to comprehend and share the other person's life; an earnest wish and a persistent will to penetrate with reverence into the other's being, because one feels that the other person equally desires it. The ultimate and, indeed, decisive stage is gained in the first flash of wordless comprehension—that knowledge of having "spanned the distance"; the knowledge of acceptance and of an innermost response. Then, finally, comes silence, in which mutual sympathy perfects itself in unison of life, beyond words, beyond all conscious effort.

Each one of these stages has its joy and its pain, because finding always means abandoning. And each period between two stages has many degrees of intense mutual experience. Nor will transition always be abrupt and unexpected; a first gentle intimation may be a gradual preparation for the new stage which is to come.

Similar to this unfolding of a relationship between two human beings is the growth of love between God and the soul. To pray, as we noted, means communion with God in awe, intimacy, love; it means a long "way" full of events, strains, discoveries, suffering, and deepest joy. Such is God's nearness to man and such His will to embrace our rhythm of development that there is effected a real union of life which is but faintly mirrored by human friendship, however deeply penetrating and transforming.

At first, love between God and the soul resorts to the simple formula, the prayer learned by heart. It can certainly come from the heart, and one should strive for it to do so and to be always sincere, but it will hardly reach beyond general notions, faintly touching on personal aspects. Some people never reach further; their life of prayer stiffens in conventionality, and sometimes suffocates. We are here talking about vocal prayer, for which set formulas of definite wording are used. If the formula is used earnestly and sincerely, the heart will express and reveal itself by it and soon will speak more freely, finding its own words. The manner of self-expression becomes easier, less constrained, more natural. The words as such lose some of their importance; they are more like a delicate veil, enveloping the stirrings of the heart. While there is a certain deliberation about the formulas, these short and fervent words just "happen"; they well up, and here they are, on the lips. This has been called the prayer of affection, the prayer of the heart. The so-called ejaculations belong to this type of prayer.

The soul now perceives clearly that it must penetrate further into the Beloved who draws and ties it to Himself, and therefore it proceeds to think about the Beloved, to enlighten itself about His ways and His attributes. It has known Him really for a long time; a little from experience, but mainly from the Scriptures. Into both the soul will sink itself again, and just as psychology is often called upon to promote a better understanding of the human partner, so the soul now employs certain methods to achieve with greater success its penetration into and innermost recognition of the Beloved. The soul now has arrived at the stage of meditation.

Then, however, comes the time when all methodical meditation becomes stable and even agonizing to the soul. It senses clearly that virtually nothing more can be gained in this type of prayer. Instead, method tends to be an obstructing wall between the soul and the object of its yearning. God is too close now to allow the attention to be focused on any single feature of His being. The whole God, that is what the soul now desires to have for its own, to sink itself into, and there to live. Therefore God leads the soul into that silence where its own activity, its words and careful meditations recede more and more. An entirely new manner of conversing develops. God and the soul understand each other without many words; they know each other and are profoundly united in a pure and intense love. Words still play an occasional part, just as silence is not constantly kept between even the most closely united friends, but words are no longer a means of spanning the distance between them but are the natural expression of having arrived safely. Even at the stage of being quite close to God, the soul will still "speak"—at the appropriate time, under duty or inner impulse, or for whatever other reason there may be. But the characteristics of this state of the soul will be quietness and a simple and unreflected union with God and interior possession of God. Now prayer has become contemplation, which is the threshold of the beatific vision.

It is one of the most insidious and frequently repeated errors to maintain that only a few souls are called to this stage of prayer. We are—all of us—called to it! Moreover, if we fail in this life, our souls will have to master every stage of the way after death before we may behold the divine countenance. These stages are the normal way for the Christian soul, as normal, indeed, as is the analogous advance of a true and deep human love, as we have just traced it. As certain as it is our ultimate calling to share the divine life, to possess God, and to be wholly and forever His, so our soul must make this pilgrimage of prayer. The distressing fact, mentioned earlier, that it is all too often not accomplished in this life, merely proves once more the consequences of original sin and the certainty of purgatory. There we must bring to completion all that we left undone in this earthly existence, though no personal merit will then attach to our endeavors. But the way will be shown; and they will be led who have the firm will to follow it faithfully. To a truly desirous heart God will always give both guidance and means in the measure of its needs, though it is for Him always to decide the manner, the moment, and the span of time in which He will train the heart that He loves, for Himself.

Chapter 8

The Earnest Duty to Pray

Christ teaches it

CHRISTIAN existence in its every aspect has its measure in Him who is its founder and its substance: Jesus Christ "in whom alone we come to the Father." From His teachings about prayer, scattered throughout the Gospel, let us select some that He uttered with special emphasis. Quite generally—as we quoted before—Christ demands: "You ought always to pray and not faint" (Luke 18:1). Thus not only occasional but continual prayer is required. There is in this a gentle hint, too, that prayer is by no means always joy and bliss, or else nobody would be tempted "to faint." In spite of difficulties, then, and independent of one's mood and disposition, prayer is a *must*, and indeed one so imperative as to recall the strictness of the Old Law, which Jesus quoted in repelling the devil: "Thou shalt adore the Lord thy God, and Him only shalt thou serve" (Luke 4:8). *Thou shalt!*

Prayer as a natural part of Christian conduct follows clearly from the introductory words to the Our Father: "When you pray, say . . ." (Luke 11:1), because this "when" means as much as "every time when," though this, by the way, does not imply that we should always and exclusively turn to the actual wording of the Lord's Prayer. It does imply, however, that all our prayer should be determined by its inner content. How often, then, should we say the Our Father, either in its actual wording or in a metaphorical version of our own? As often as we need the "daily"—or more precisely translated, "tomorrow's"—bread; and that is *every day*.

[28

Not for the bread of weeks and months ahead are we to pray, but for that needed tomorrow. That means that prayer pertains to us "like the daily bread," and how true, since prayer is the mysterious bread for the soul, from which the soul receives its supernatural strength and the power to continue on the way to God without flinching or fainting.

Occasionally Jesus adds specific reasons why people must pray. On the Mount of Olives He warns the sleeping disciples: "Watch ye and pray that ye enter not into temptation" (Matt. 26:41). Not enter into it, nor fall and perish in it. "To fall" means to lose Christ, or at least to withdraw from Him to some extent. That, however, spells extreme danger, the possibilities of denial and betrayal, and therewith the danger of certain perdition. Only the soul that by its prayer has learned to focus and rivet itself upon God and His holiness, upon His love and upon the help therefrom, is armed against being taken by surprise from within or without. The soul clutches His hand, as it were, so God cannot allow it to fall. For His is the hand of the "Strong One." Moreover, the heart accustomed to frequent association with God is thereby diverted from a great many unimportant, superfluous and doubtful things which would otherwise fill and disturb the imagination. A prayerful heart will find in God such infinitely precious aspects for its inner preoccupation that other matters begin to be a nuisance and therefore they lose their fascination and seductive power. What took place a few hours later in the courtyard of Caiphas—the denial of St. Peter—is unequivocal proof of the absolute validity of the warning which Jesus addressed to Peter and to the other two. If Peter had prayed instead of sleeping, he would not have fallen into temptation.

When in the Lord's absence the twelve had tried in vain to heal a boy possessed by a devil, they complained to Him afterwards. He enlightened them: "This kind (of devil) is not cast out but by prayer and fasting" (Matt. 17:20). The devil's power and man's addiction to evil cannot be broken by human strength; not even by the simple reference to the authority of

Christ. The soul desiring to effect such deliverance must be more deeply embedded in God's being and majesty. To achieve this, the soul must disengage itself from the encumbrances of the world, by fasting and by ardent abandon to God, that is, by prayer. Since, however, creation is everywhere trapped in the snares of diabolical malice and is groaning for its liberation (Rom. 8:21–23), is not prayer the necessary task and sacred duty of the children of grace who will lead creation back to God?

In the opposite direction lies the motivation for prayer, which Christ gives in His last discourse: "Ask, that your joy may be full" (John 16:24). God, who is love, is therefore also purest joy. The Indian proverb puts this with unsurpassed intuition: "Out of joy all beings are born, and into joy they return." Out of God, who is joy, we come, and we are called to return to Him once we have passed through the darkness of suffering, sin's natural consequence. But even as we make our way, joy will blossom within us as an exquisite possession of spirit and grace, as one of the fruits of the Holy Ghost, and that as a result of prayer. The soul who in prayer wholly attains to God arrives at the source of eternal joy, rising above to all things terrestrial, so that ultimately they can trouble it no more. The vocation to God is the vocation to joy, and also to prayer.

Jesus shows how we must pray

The words, "I have given you an example" (John 13:15) and "Follow Me" (John 21:19), do not refer only to this or that individual moment in the life of our Lord. If He, "the Way, the Truth, and the Life" (John 14:6), imperatively binding in every respect, standard indeed and measure of all, if He so strongly insists that He reads everything in the Father's countenance and that "He cannot do anything but what He seeth the Father doing" (John 5:19) and if He wills us to be "perfect, as also your heavenly Father is perfect" (Matt. 5:48), then surely He exhorts us unequivocally to pray—to pray with Him and like Him. Now of Him we are told that He—alone, and who knows how often—"went up to the mountain to pray" (Mark 6:46) and "passed the whole night in the prayer of God" (Luke 6:12). It had been just such a night of prayer with its unspeakable sublime converse between the Father and His Beloved Son, when the disciples, all seized and shaken by the radiance of His face, begged Jesus: "Lord, do teach us how to pray" (Luke 11:1). No doubt they, too, prayed; but how soon they finished, knew nothing more to say, and truly suffered from this dumbness of their immature souls! What did *He* have to say, all through the night? Their longing to do —if only by remote comparison—as He had done, makes them express that heartfelt request, which then is rewarded by the Our Father. Here we can trace the descent of *His* prayer to that of the apostles and of the whole Church, who ever since has been keeping and handing on the Our Father as its most precious treasure of prayer. Here the "imitation of Christ in prayer" reveals itself as an imperative necessity.

A few of our Lord's invocations to the Father, mostly short but infinitely tender, have been handed down to us, testifying both to the duty of prayer and its specified content on certain occasions. This is not the place to examine them closely, though we would stress the significance of Christ's last prayer for His disciples, with which He terminates His last discourse and public life. This sublime prayer majestically transcends all merely human converse with God, and invites us irresistibly to unite ourselves with it. As we contemplate it, we perceive that praying means existence in its most exalted sense, and is thus a supreme duty and right.

Prayer, witness for itself

If "lost to the eyes, lost to the heart" holds good even among human beings who have, in the power of their imagination, no small bond to unite them, it must be truer still when applied to the soul's relation to God, according to St. John: "If any man loveth not his brother, whom he seeth, how can he love God, whom he seeth not?" (I John 4:20.) As soon as we cease to regard God, we are bound to forget Him. To start with, He is gradually pushed back to the periphery of our consciousness, becomes steadily less a measure and spur for us, and only occasionally and without much consequence determines our thoughts, judgments and actions. Finally He has no longer any part in our conduct of life. Inevitably this means separation, loss and desolation. For he who does not love God, cannot come to Him. Hence the following words of a saint: "All those who are saved, have found salvation because they have prayed much and prayed well; all those who are damned, met with perdition because they have not prayed or have prayed badly."

On a higher level, the necessity of prayer is founded on the absolute claim of the Lord our God to be acknowledged and adored by His creatures in the measure of their respective capacity. The nature of man appropriately demands understanding and abandoning of the will in prayer; these two become one in the inner consent. If we do not pray, we are either spiritually blind to the dominion of our Creator or in revolt against Him.

What has previously been said regarding the inner divine discourse of the Trinity and God's bounty to draw us into it is the final and purest proof. Can any child live with its father in heedless unconcern? Without eager give-and-take? Without loving him with all its heart? Such a child would be a freak, and more so if the Father in question is love in person! Responding in love, yet refusing to pray, that would be a contradiction, a sheer impossibility. Prayer and love correspond meticulously. He who loves much, will pray much; and whoever is fervent in prayer, loves fervently, too. Similarly, our salvation, God's greater honor, and the marvel of the union of life of love between God and the soul, all prove that prayer is necessary, imperatively so, like life itself, if it is to go on.

Chapter 9

Basic Intentions of Prayer

THERE is nothing which could not, and in one way or another does not, become the subject of converse between God and the soul. Is there anything about the beloved which is not love's concern? Now everything is God's, and therefore also the soul's regard, whose interests He makes His own. Nevertheless, we can condense the immense possibilities of topics into a few basic ones. Depending on whether we proceed from the human situation or from the majesty of God, we can enumerate them in opposite directions. We shall not start with our human experience, which ought to begin with reparation, but we shall follow the ontological order in its basic origin and first claim upon us.

Adoration and praise

The essentially appropriate attitude of the created being before God is that of adoration. Hence this is the essential prayer, embracing all other forms and subjects of devotion. To adore means to acknowledge God as the one who is All and before whom the creature is nothing. Not an absolute nothing, for then it could not adore, but nothing of itself, owing all that it is and has to God. God alone has being of Himself, in absolute independence and complete self-sufficiency. Not only in existence as such, but also in every manifestation of it, however trifling, the creature is entirely dependent on God, and without Him is nothing and can do nothing. Before His majesty all consciousness of personal dignity comes to naught, unless it be recognized as His free gift. Measured against God's holiness,

33]

all our own goodness becomes pitiful and a pretense. His wisdom stamps all our own cleverness as folly. And so it is in everything.

The recognition of this truth finds expression in adoration. It would be wrong, however, to think of adoration as synonymous with a feeling of self-destruction, of self-effacement. Rather, it is a blessed self-oblivion and an immersion into this glorious God; a deep union with Him in sheltered tranquillity. It is a clear knowledge that now all is well, that now God *and* the soul will both be given their due and their joy. Adoration is profound bliss, supreme freedom from one's tiny self, and immersion in the fullness of God, who is loved above all.

As a natural consequence, praise is born from such adoring rapture, the jubilant acknowledgment that God *is!* That there is such beauty, abundance and light; such majesty and holiness! Also that this God is, and wishes to be, mine! But above all, that He is who He is in Himself! In pure self-effacement and singleminded regard for God the soul comes to know that sacred joy which of necessity springs from unselfish receptiveness for truth, goodness and beauty. Praise, like adoration, will feed on many an "accidental" experience or encounter which will reverberate in the soul as they happen. Thus, when considering how judiciously God guides another soul, one cannot but rejoice at His being so wise, so just, so full of mercy. To behold nature can arouse spontaneous jubilation, as the magnificent *Benedicite* and many other psalms testify.

Unfortunately, in our life of prayer, adoration and praise usually receive far too little attention. This but proves how ungenerous and narrow we are, how little detached from ourselves, how little absorbed in God and in His love. We should make deep and frequent adoration and praise of God our special duty of honor, at once sacred and infinitely rewarding. None of our prayers should ever begin or ever end in any other way, and many should have this for their sole object. Let us make better use of the countless occasions that are offered, such as the beauty of the world without and the baseness within ourselves. The former points straight to *the* Beauty and *the* Goodness; the latter directs our minds to the unique praiseworthiness of God, in whom we take refuge, sickened by the futility around and within us.

Thanksgiving

To contemplate the majesty of God, His beauty and the abundance of His attributes, induces the soul to give thanks to Him spontaneously, not so much because God gave or gives us something, but because in Himself He is such that He must radiate goodness. What *we* feel of it must not make us tarry over the gift nor over the inner gratification, but should direct us to His goodness as such, fastening our vision totally upon Him in reverence, joy and love. That is the task at hand. The countless occasions for gratitude to God must have a much bigger place in our prayers. Let us consciously remind ourselves that He has done this or that for us, and then we shall learn to give thanks even when incomprehensible adversity comes our way. Then we shall not turn inwards upon ourselves, but shall turn to Him and thank Him for being—even in the darkness and affliction of our heart—all to us, our life and our love, and for being who He is. Hardly anywhere is such giving of thanks in its detached purity more beautifully expressed than in the *Gloria* of the Mass: "We give thanks to Thee for Thy great glory," not for showing it to us nor for desiring us to participate in it, but because it is Thine, because Thou art perfect and cannot be other than holy above all. Here the soul really is "beside itself." It is no longer self-important, no longer thinking of merit, help or salvation. It has forgotten itself and sees only Him, the Beloved. That He is as He is, that is now the object of amazed gratitude, and for this the soul would acknowledge and glorify God through all eternity. Whoever faithfully cultivates this form of prayer will attain to a great purity of heart and will be gladdened by spiritual experiences hitherto unknown.

It is self-evident that our thanksgiving should include God's gifts. The Gospel account of the healing of the ten lepers shows us distinctly that God *expects* gratitude for His benefits, not because He needs it or feels "done out of something" without it, but merely on our account, because were we to neglect gratitude, we would reveal a base soul which He would not be able further to reward and guide to greater heights. Also because not to give thanks is contrary to the right order. It means withholding a response which, of its nature, should have been forthcoming. Yet, when thanking God for an individual gift, we should eagerly look beyond it to Him who gave it, to thank Him "for Himself," for His being so good.

It is of utmost importance for our self-education that we should also often and gladly thank God for what others have received from Him. The Church here guides us in many prayers on the feasts of saints, when we especially thank God for the favors which He granted them. We ought to carry this further into our daily life. It would vanquish envy, one of the most evil vices, so dangerous for interior progress, especially in its worst form, the envy of others on account of divine favors. This belongs to the sins against the Holy Ghost, which are classified as unforgivable.

Petition

A child will always ask for things, not just wait for them to be given. Much, no doubt, will be given to it without the asking, probably even the most important things, because the child's vision is not yet clear enough to realize fully what is necessary and essential. But that is irrelevant. In the very act of asking, limited as yet in scope and purpose, the child's outlook broadens. Let us not argue that it is an obligation of the parents to give the child whatever it needs; it certainly is. But it is equally proper for the child to ask. Either attitude is a duty, an essential mode of behavior among social beings. To ask for something is a manner of opening oneself for the gift to be received worthily, that is, not just factually, like a flower receiving the sunshine, but in a manner worthy of man

as the image of God, seeing love in the gift. Any gift deserving
of the name is always something infinitely beyond itself; it is
a giving of self on the part of the donor, who in and with it
gives his heart. Hence we can never repay in kind, never return
the favor, except by opening and giving ourselves in turn,
which happens when we give thanks.

We would not need to philosophize at length about the asking of things from God were not its manner and attitude so
often fundamentally wrong. For the children of men take their
needs naturally to God and just beg. The majority of prayers
which have come to us from pagan rites, that is, outside of
revelation, contain only requests. There is rarely a thought
that soars beyond the purely material and natural needs. To the
child of God these, too, are objects of prayer, but obviously
in a very different perspective, shown clearly by the place
allotted to the request for our daily bread in the Lord's Prayer.
In petitioning God, His children touch exalted spheres, praying first for the glorification of God, then for the strength to
will as He wills, and finally for supernatural needs—their own
and those of others. All this our Lord teaches us in His own
perfect prayer, which is composed of seven *requests*. To beg
in prayer comes of a sincere evaluation of oneself before God,
of true humility. Therefore it is foolish to reject such prayer
as undignified. Sincerity is the very opposite of unworthy demeanor!

Much could be said about asking favors from God. Let it
suffice here to touch upon an objection which is often raised:
that there is not much point in praying for anything, since
everything is already foreseen by God and in that sense is determined beforehand. Why pray for fine harvesting weather, if
the law of nature will take its predestined course and nothing
can change the inescapable sequence of cause and effect? After
all, one may not presume on God to answer every prayer by
a miracle. Moreover, in certain chemical processes a so-called
catalytic substance is necessarily required for the cause and
effect reaction to be effected. Here is a kind of causality which

can in no way be measured, is hardly definable, and yet it exists. If such things happen in the material sphere, why should not God at any time be able to use the laws of nature in their appointed course just as He pleases, even though our intelligence is unable to grasp His efficacious presence other than by faith and through the veil of nature's seemingly inviolable laws?

St. Thomas Aquinas has an even simpler explanation: God has certainly foreseen and ordained everything; therefore He also knows all our prayers in advance and He integrates them as a cause or motive of His laws and ordinances. Things work out as they do, events are connected in the way which experience shows us, because God foresees our prayers and has already incorporated His answer into the pattern of life. This becomes still more evident when we remember that in God there is no "prior to" or "once upon a time," and therefore no "reflection prior to creation" either. God is absolute presence and nothing else. He lives in His eternal day, and before Him everything is *now*, in the full depth and plenitude of harmony, interaction and consequences.

Reparation

Being what we are, and have been ever since original sin, the prayer of reparation has become our very special mark—the prayer for forgiveness, the prayer of a penitent heart. It restores the relationship, so deeply disturbed by sin, between Creator and created, between Father and child, so far as this can be achieved or at least attempted by us. In actual fact, *we* do not succeed. If it is possible to consider all previous forms of prayer as purely human efforts, capable of true significance even without first being received within Jesus Christ and sanctified by Him, the prayer of reparation without Christ can never be anything but a helpless stammer. It does not "reach across"; it cannot bridge the chasm created by the suppliant himself. A child can well put fire to a house, but he can never build it up again. A knave is able to deface a guiltless soul, but never will he succeed in re-instating its nobility. What we have wrested from God by sin, no reparation, however fervent, can restore, unless the reparation be made acceptable in Jesus Christ, the Savior.

What then is the prayer of reparation? It is atonement for adoration withheld. If we idolize a created being with a love beyond due measure, and therefore offensive to God, we deprive God of what is rightfully His. Repenting, we desire to adore as we ought and to make amends for the failure of the past. The glorification refused to God and squandered on a created being, shall be recovered for God. Now we want to do more than our strictest duty, though it is impossible clearly to see the limit of obligation. We wish to make up for thanks not given to God, but foolishly rendered to His creatures. Finally, we desire to make the requests for which hitherto we have been too indolent, too proud, too stubborn. Or if our petitions had previously been wrong and worthless in manner and purpose, we now endeavor rightfully to pray for rightful things. Thus the prayer of reparation is complementary to the other three types of prayer. It is made necessary by sin which, after all, consists in their neglect. Reparation strives to restore the rightful balance.

This form of prayer is often disregarded, and yet the terrible frequency and callousness of sin is such that there should be much voluntary reparation and penance as a kind of compensation. It is the child's strict duty jealously to safeguard the father's honor. If there were more people deliberately devoting more time and strength to prayer in order to replace those who hold both God and prayer in contempt, the face of the earth could be indeed renewed. For great love is creative; nothing else is. All devotion to the Sacred Heart should recognize in this its most essential purpose.

Chapter 10

Proper Dispositions in Prayer

TRUE prayer consists of several essential parts which constitute one indivisible whole, but they must be studied in their individual characteristics. If we understand them clearly, we can direct the training of our heart toward them, emphasizing in our prayer now this, now the other property. Such emphasis, however, need not always be applied; the good prayer will contain all the qualities in question, even though we, while at prayer, are not aware of them.

Reverence is the principal foundation in the structure of prayer and is so decisive that without it, the other properties could not exist. But when it is present they are a certainty, for reverence contains them all. Reverence and adoration stand most closely related, but while adoration is directed only to God, reverence is an attitude demanded of us, though in varying degrees, toward all manner of being.

Reverence is more than mere respect which holds a person in such esteem as is his due. Reverence is awe, not in any sense of dread, but in the sense of a devout shyness which would not take liberties with persons or objects of high honor. The Latin *reverentia* expresses just this: to draw back. Reverence has its roots deep in the soul, where it springs forth. It is the internal, and where necessary and appropriate, the external acknowledgment of such perception. A reverent person sees and respects the given boundaries. He does not push himself where he has not been asked; he "stays put," as it were, and waits for the other to decide whether and how far he will open any doors

[40

and grant a sharing of his life and person. The fullest dignity of a deep human bond can rest only upon such reverence.

But its rule applies, as Goethe wisely holds, both in the lower and still more in the higher sphere. Why is that? Because in every being there is something of the infinity who created it. Because, watched over and preserved by God, each has from Him and in Him an essential life of its own. With persons this is more especially so, for to be a person means to possess oneself and to decide the giving or refusing of oneself. This becomes final and absolute in God, before whom reverence attains its total depth and utmost seriousness.

Reverence in the sense of shy respect and awesome self-restraint before God is first of all an inner disposition. But it embraces the material world as well, since our physical being is, or at least can and often must be, an adequate expression of our inner self. Certain bodily attitudes are consistent with a reverent mind; others are incompatible. Joined hands are quite appropriate; crossed legs and unrestrained staring are discordant. True, as we perform such physical movements, our soul could be with God, even in deepest reverence. Moreover, we may thus deliberately conceal from others what for valid reasons we prefer not to reveal. But in general we feel that it is unnatural and impossible to combine inner reverence and outward disrespect.

Reverence by no means excludes love; rather, it contains it, or better, love comprises reverence. True love is not greedy for itself, nor demanding; it seeks the other person's greater good; it is solicitous, protective and devoted. No harm, no loss must come to the beloved; so far as love can do so, it will let him be a master of himself and have full freedom in all the spheres of life due and assigned to him. To that end love serves as best it can. Love without reverence would be an absurd lie, but deeper love means greater reverence, and the more reverence, the deeper the love.

Next, *devotion* is allied with reverence before God. How could anyone pray with genuine reverence and at the same time deliberately think of something else? Deliberately, we say, for in the midst of greatest reverence *involuntary* distractions are liable to torment the heart and carry off the mind into spheres where it would not dwell. It is important once and for all emphatically to stress the fact that devotion is entirely and exclusively determined by the will, and that our prayer suffers no loss whatever in merit or efficacy if, *against* our explicit intention, it is plunged into distractions and consists of practically nothing else. The reverence of the heart, and quite likely that of demeanor, guarantees the value of our prayer and the sincerity of the will to be anchored in God.

For what, after all, is devotion? It is the recollection of one's thoughts on a given subject. In prayer this may mean a concentration of the mind directly upon God, as happens in contemplation, or that the mind reaches God through some vehicle such as reflections and meditations or vocal prayer. Then devotion simply means that the mind concentrates upon the contents of the words which it either forms or finds, as when reflecting on the inner sense of "Father," "Our Father," "in heaven." But here, as with most other conversations, as one explains a complex subject the mind carefully proceeds from one word to the next, bent on the right choice of words, the proper combination and the correct deduction. In this way the mind circumscribes the subject it is trying to expound. The more familiar the subject, the more handy the words and phrases. More than that, they hover, as it were, about the theme in question, like a delicate, almost transparent veil. The mind now possesses the subject, lives with it, has appropriated it, and no longer needs to grope for words. It simply seizes on the right expression for what it clearly sees within.

The same thing occurs in recollected, devout prayer. The more difficult it is for us to grasp God's presence within us and be calm before it and the more we must exercise the mind to comprehend a little about God, the more our mind is bent on actual words and phrases pertaining to God and signifying

Him. But the more familiar God becomes in and by prayer, the more closely the mind "holds" and knows Him and the more the actual words of prayer lose their weight. Transparent in regard to God, the word now comprehends Him vividly, and in it He Himself is, as it were, embraced. Devotion then no longer consists in concentration on the particular word and its specific content, but in a conscious nearness to God. The words of prayer gradually fade and diminish. The mediating function of prayer becomes more and more redundant as the goal is approached. Simultaneously, devotion increases in scope, depth and vitality, and the soul clearly understands that it is not so much a matter for the brain, for study, but rather for the heart. Devotion is simply union with God in love and joy and harmony of mind.

This kind of devotion—the "recollected heart"—must essentially be part of our prayer, while we cannot—or certainly not always—command at will the recollection of the "head" and of our thoughts. Devotion of the heart can be destroyed only by deliberate distractions, but never by involuntary absent-mindedness, however much this may at times appear to disarrange all our prayer. But of this we shall have to treat again later on.

Once our very heart looks upon God, it cannot do so but with an abundant trust. It would, in any case, be a strange contradiction if doubt of fulfillment always accompanied our supplications. Even when making a request to a human person, the confident hope to see it granted should—to some extent—outweigh our doubt. And if the other person were to notice the doubt, we might as well immediately abandon any hope. However furtively sustained in the petitioner's heart, the doubt would prejudice the urgency of the request and therewith any chances to be heard. Imagine a child saying to his mother: "Please, let me have some bread," and adding: "but you are probably not going to." That child could hardly count on having his request fulfilled. All lack of trust signifies disbelief in either the power or, worse still, the benevolence of him whom we petition. And how can we ask a gift of kindness and in the same breath hurl an insult at kindness?

One might object that things are different with God, that He is, after all, superabundant in benevolence and not dependent on our pettiness and prejudice in the good that He does. But simply on the strength of His munificence we may not ignore the immanent "self-respect" of God and His sacred title to the recognition of His dignity. It is inherent in God's essence that He should be honored and that He should be known for who He is. He cannot tolerate the doubting of His might or kindness, apparent in a prayer without trust, though we may certainly assume that He will always graciously uphold a weak and struggling confidence and fortify it gently until it has grown according to His will. From God, whose penetrating knowledge of us is absolute, we cannot hide even the smallest doubt against His power or desire to assist us.

There is this also: if our supplications are not wholly free of doubts and hesitations, they do not open our soul enough and it will remain unable fully to receive God's gifts, even though God is willing to grant them in spite of this deficiency in trust. The trusting soul is open both for the giver and the gift. The soul that does not trust, or only feebly—deliberately feebly—is more or less excluded from the giver and his gift. These are internal laws of existence itself and no one can circumvent them. Nor will God, who made them, grant dispensation.

But what if we must struggle for this trust because, perhaps, our heart is naturally suspicious and unyielding, or because God has seemingly been unresponsive, to our bitter disappointment? If so, let us recall a certain man who took his epileptic boy to Christ. And Jesus asked him: "Dost thou, then, believe?" And he, replying and entreating in one breath: "I do believe, Lord; help mine unbelief" (Mark 9:22–23).

Perfect trust must and will prove itself in *perseverance*, because it is based entirely on the certainty of our belief in the power, wisdom and love of our Father in heaven. He can help, and nothing can get in the way of His solicitous will. He surveys and discerns whatever can happen in the past or future, and so can order and direct it perfectly. And God loves me; no one more than He; and no one is as intent as He on what, in this world and the next, is best for me. Such is His love for me that He preferred to suffer death rather than let me perish. And withal He has promised: "Ask, and it shall be given you; seek, and you will find; knock, and it shall be opened to you" (Luke 11:9). Whence, then, while talking to Him and begging God, my Father, could I be filled with any mistrust?

Perhaps from what so often seems a long wait for an answer. This is where our perseverance has its place. We must be steadfast, and our heart must learn to go on waiting and believing. If God inspired us to any one request, He will surely fulfill it in the sense in which it was inspired. But it is only in the very process of asking God that our supplication reaches its proper height. God is never in a hurry. All eternity waits at His command. Why should the progress of His works be hastened? Everything around and within us has its own law and rhythm; often its own "endless" time. The whole of history is but one thought of God! Incidents which seem to break suddenly, have in reality been long prepared. The lightning flash, suddenly striking across a placid sky, presupposes a vast number of individual events which imperceptibly led to the moment when the burst was due.

In like manner our prayer of petition develops gradually to such a point that it becomes both capable and worthy of its answer. This is not arbitrary on the part of God. It certainly is "trying," but in the sense that our comprehension and sincerity are being tried, until they are ready to receive and receive rightly. That is in no way a lesser skill than to give rightly.

Often we realize the full weight and significance of our request—or its doubtfulness—only when we have been imploring God for a long time. Then, when it has been granted, we treat the gift quite differently than if it had given us at once. Only now, since we have had to try for it with all our heart, do we appraise its value. "Here today, gone tomorrow." What we gain without much effort will soon be wasted. But he who had to fight hard for his treasure will fully value and possess it in prudence and in gratitude. He will avoid the danger of offending the giver by either not evaluating or not using a precious gift well, having requested it "in vain." He will also avoid ingratitude, which takes all things for granted and leads to serious damage of the soul.

Persevering prayer makes the soul patient and strong, impervious to its own softness and irritability, its hastiness and innate arrogance. It is made purer, more unselfish and more humble. That in itself is so valuable, that having had to wait is a grace rather than a trial, unless we wish to see in every trial—because it is a trial—the highest grace of all. Sometimes in the course of patiently sustained prayer its content and the supplicant are both transformed. As he waits, the supplicant regards the object of his prayer differently; he takes away from it; he adds to it. Perhaps his heart will reach a point where it has far outdistanced the original request; he abandons it and recognizes in its non-fulfillment the deepest answer and the one most worthy of God.

And so we come to the last and all-embracing property of good prayer: *submission to the will of God and unconditional agreement with it.* This follows naturally from all we said before. What a strange sort of reverence, for instance, that would try to extort something from God against His will and His all-holy resolution. How could we truly glorify Him if our heart were not of one accord with Him whom we thus praise? Again, how could we sincerely thank Him if we are not at all in accord with Him whom we thank? And trust, too, is an offering of ourselves. We look to Him in whom our trust is placed and not to any strength within ourselves by which to "force His hand."

The will of God, which as we know is essence of His being,

is His reality, His holiness, His justice and His love, all this in one. His will is ultimate, the absolute measure in and for everything. He alone is perfect and holy; He alone is truly good, the final sum of all imaginable values. Anything has part in His will so far as it is good; and so far only. The degree of our consent with His will is the measure of our holiness and perfection. All holiness consists in this consent. Therefore I can never be more holy than God's love and wisdom has decreed for me. And were I to desire more, I would detach myself from His will and prefer my own; and then I would fall into unholiness. We simply cannot be sufficiently alive to this.

Like the whole of our life, and more so, our prayer must be permeated and prompted by this devotion to the will of God. Was not our prayer supposed to be love? Love in and with God? And love is conformity of will, the concord of two wills which lovingly incline toward each other. Prayer which seeks not self, but God, is love, and consequently it means the offering of the will. Hence, in the Our Father, when we have first requested the hallowing of His name, which means the reverent and adoring recognition of God's being, and that His kingdom come, we ardently implore: "Thy will be done on earth as it is in heaven." Both are effected by the doing of His holy will by all that He created, especially by the human heart, from which renewal of the earth shall spring. Only from and by our hearts turned good, redeemed, can the world also be made good again. Redemption culminates in the delivery, by grace, of our perverted will; in its renewed and voluntary captivity in the love of the Father in heaven, which hastens to meet and embrace it; and in our being able and prepared to follow God's love wherever it may lead. Thus and thus only can we do justice to God; within us first, and through us in creation. "In heaven" His will is done eternally, within Himself, within that triune love of the divine Persons, and within every being finally brought into that primeval harmony. All that, we call "heaven." And that it may be like that, too, "on earth"; within ourselves, within the universe, and within everything as yet imperfect but still tending toward that blessed life of love in God. That this may "come" we are, according to God's teaching and His will, "daily" to pray.

All prayer aims at this merging of the will with God. Our nature finds this hard to understand and to act in accordance with it. Our love of self is plainly monstrous, and the most monstrous thing about it is that we hardly notice it. Only as we struggle for its conquest, for the unspoiled, unstinting acclamation of God's will, do we learn who and what we are: self-centered and rebellious, always ready to impose our will upon God, though this may well disguise itself in a humble, persevering, heartfelt supplication. Most of our prayers are perhaps secretly the opposite of "Thy will be done on earth," that is, within myself, as far as I am master of myself, "as it is in heaven," which is, in Thyself. We want to make God do what we think fit, to "talk Him round," as it were, and change His mind for Him. All that is indescribable folly, and were we to do it consciously, it would be unequalled audacity and revolt, a reversal of realities, at least in our wish and will; a deposition of God for the sake of putting ourselves in His place; an attempt to enlist God for our personal aims, to use Him and so to debase Him to a means. Such "prayer" basically is a kind of magic, a trick to possess God's power according to our will and whim. That means the end of all religion, most certainly of all Christianity.

We have tried to show that the ultimate meaning of our existence is the participation, in purest concord, in the life of the Most Holy Trinity. This means a harmony of our will with God to the remotest and most delicate ramifications of our being. In all our prayer this must be the aim, more or less clear to our inner vision. It will then steadily grow clearer, will order, guide, transform. Slowly, all our thoughts, judgments and desires, and with them our nature, will be changed. Slowly, for this transition of ourselves nearer to God is the task of our life and is therefore as long and deep and hard as life itself. But what of that? We were created to fulfill our task, and this is it. Everything else that we may call our task is but another area in which that other essential task claims our efforts. That is why those of deeper understanding will always tell us firmly that "what," "where" and "when" do not matter in our life; only the "how" is important! Whether we do what must be done and do it as God's will, that is all that matters. St. Thérèse of Lisieux used to pray not that she might accomplish extraordinary things, but that she might do ordinary things in an extraordinary manner. That means to do them out of a pure and devoted love for the Father's will, which comes to us in the ordinary, trivial things of life. They are often concealed in beggar's clothes, as the Son of God was cloaked in the frail nature of man and in the nakedness and folly of the Cross.

To know how to embrace the will of God is what we pray for. Prayer is the offering of oneself to the divine will, a single "yes," an oft-repeated wish for the strength to say this "yes" without reservation. God's will comes to us in everything, but we must, through prayer, become "single-eyed" to see it and accept it lovingly. He gives as well as takes away; He grants and He refuses; He makes us happy and He sends us pain. For it is not His gift that is important, it is He *in* that gift. Are we so miserably self-concerned that we do not look at His face, but only at the gift, without regard for Him who gives? Indeed, the gift may seem a poor and bitter thing, not at all like the one we longingly expected, but that is the fundamental error: to wait for "something" rather than for Him. As long as we live on earth, God comes to us in some disguise. Even in the deepest and most enthused state of prayer we do not reach Him in the vision which is reserved for heaven, but in a darkness which at once shows and conceals Him, but gives Him to us all the same. And that will happen in and through all the things sent to us by His will; in them *He* always comes. And prayer searches for Him in everything in and around us, reaches out for Him, wants Him; the immediate object of prayer is subordinate. "Seek ye first the kingdom of God, and all these things shall be added unto you" (Matt. 6:33). Seek Me, your God; seek Me with a single heart, and Me alone. I shall give you the rest, that which you consider so important and which, compared to Me, is nothing; no more than a faint glimmer compared to the sun, the smallest crumb compared to the rich man's banquet, indeed, infinitely less than that.

Pure love sees in a simple flower as much a gift from the lover as in precious stones, and often even more. And love trusts the beloved and receives him no less in a refusal or a seeming harshness than in a loving word or deepest tenderness. And sometimes in this way the love of the beloved stirs the soul even more deeply and convincingly, as long as it can be sure that this is love treating it thus. Then we forget the pain, the humiliation, the disappointment, and are one with Him who came in disguise to free us from all self-love and to lead our heart into that freedom in which uncreated Love can be espoused to the created.

How beautiful God is! Beautiful things often conceal Him more than they reveal Him, and therefore His most acceptable and desired gifts can be an obstacle for us; a shadow darkening His presence; a force diverting us from Him. If, poor and barren, He comes in the refusal of what we asked, then it may happen that only in this "nakedness" we recognize Him fully and we blissfully adore Him for leaving everything else behind and coming alone. An unanswered petition can be a priceless grace, love's highest favor, because now it can only give itself. What are the clothes, the precious stones, the flowers in the hands of the beloved when compared to him who loves her? So with the soul awakening to supernatural love; it does not care to see or hear much else but God, and all her prayer now seeks Him directly and not something *from* Him.

We shall not dwell unnecessarily on the well-known comparisons that God deals with us like a wise mother, who does not give the child a knife, matches, scissors, and such like, however much it begs and cries, because she knows the child would come to harm. God does the same, no doubt, and our submission to His will always allows for the proviso, "if this be good for me." But this is hardly adequate. Better to say: "If this be Thy will. Even if what I am asking for were the most excellent thing (though nothing can ever be more excellent than what God has planned for me already), even then, only if and because Thou dost will it so." Not with an eye on self—"If this will profit me"—but quite immersed in God: "If this is as Thou wilt."

Love alone should decide. Love sets the pace. Love governs and directs, builds and decrees. And what it does is always the good pleasure of the loving soul. That is why there are no unanswered prayers. Good prayers will be answered, always. They have, in fact, been answered while in progress, for in and through them God already comes and fills the soul with His most precious presence. That is the answer. In the ultimate and deepest sense all prayer means: "I ask for Thee; I want Thee; Thee, Lord, in and above all!" And that, precisely, will be given us. "What do I seek in heaven, what on earth, but Thee, O Lord?"

We may seek many a thing and never find it; and if we do, it does not gladden our heart. As before, we are dissatisfied and hungry. But if we seek for God, we shall certainly find Him; and He is all to us. He answers our prayers in giving us what we most truly need: Himself. If He denies us something, we accept and welcome *Him* in this refusal. If we train our heart faithfully, over and over again to say: "Thee, Lord, I want, only Thee," when things happen differently than we had hoped and prayed for, we conquer ourselves and say unhesitatingly: "In this Thy 'No,' Thou, who hast said it, comest. In this void I receive Thee, who dost not give me this or that, but Thine own self." If we pray thus, we are truly blessed. Amid the torment of distractions we should say: "In these natural weaknesses, in my fatigue, in the crowding in upon me of odd images, and in whatever else disturbs my recollection, I can find Thee. As I accept them, face them, will them, I have Thee; and with Thee ultimately I conquer the distraction." Though it may still persist on the periphery of the soul, the soul itself is one with Him whom it adores and loves.

And so in everything and always, God alone matters. That is why unconditional submission is a part of prayer and in itself an anticipation of the goal of every prayer: loving union with the loving God.

If, in affectionate reverence, we examine the life of our Lord, we find the same: the Father's will is all. It is the same with the saints, nor could it be otherwise, because this union with the will of God is in itself the very essence of their saintliness.

That is also why even our praying for virtue, for progress on the way to God, for sanctity, must never leave this out: as Thou wilt, Lord, and no more. There is unspeakable delight in pondering deeply over God's having planned my path from all eternity, and lovingly—how lovingly—foreseen how He will go with me and to what heights of love He will escort me. And then to say our *"Fiat"* to this singularly glorious, loving will of God. To pray for individual things becomes almost impossible; the soul will find it almost strange to make proposals to God. We simply offer our heart and being. "Take me, O Lord, into Thy hands; take me entirely, now and forever." And we are certain of the Lord's response, of His abiding presence and embrace.

Once we have understood that we are to pray only for God Himself, our heart knows all. It will continue to pray for this and that, as God inspires it. However, such prayer no longer comes from our narrow little soul, but from His Holy Spirit, who has become its life. Our *"Fiat"* once again. The Beloved directs the soul gently to other objects, and because of Him the soul can but obey and follow, only to find itself more closely knit in His embrace. That God may grant such a grace to every one of us, should be our mutual prayer. Then in His blessed love the true communion of the saints will blossom forth.

Chapter 11

Preparation for Prayer

Asceticism as negation

Prayer is the core of Christian existence, its soul, the breath by which it lives and subsists. Even now in the depth of our being it is constantly in progress, Christ operating within us through the Holy Ghost, uniting to Himself our innermost being and offering it to the Father. In prayer, as it is commonly understood, this secret union with God becomes articulate: a conscious resolution of the will, an explicit effort. Gradually it develops into an inner process which accompanies everything in and about us more or less distinctly, though frequently interrupted, no doubt, since we are normally capable of devoting our full strength and undivided concentration only to one thing at a time. Any serious duty, for instance, would claim all our conscious attention for the time being, leaving no surplus energy for the additional effort of prayer. But then we pick up the threads again and pursue them and find that all those intervals during which no particular output is expected of us are being used for and even governed by prayer. In fact, the inner association with God, the perpetual prayer in the depth of our being, eventually becomes like a mighty river-bed which carries all the life of the waters. Even without allowing our attention to be deflected from the task at hand, God is in it, and our handling the matter is done with Him and in Him. It is like being busy with some task and yet sensing another person's presence in the room, and that person being someone we like and for whose sake we are doing the task. Living and praying thus merge into one another. And while at first our

53]

everyday life seemed to run parallel to our life of prayer, we gradually realize that it had always been embedded in it and had taken its origin there. When one day all things will have been made perfect, our actions, permeated and transformed by divine efficacy, will have adopted the character of pure prayer. But the transformation of our life into one thoroughly inspired and sanctified by God demands not only that we pray every now and then by directing our thoughts explicitly to God and leaving the rest to Him, whether and when He will make us all His own, but it demands also that we strive to conduct our lives in every way according to God's purpose. Only if our life has thus been made capable of being sanctified and transfigured by God, will it one day be capable also of participating in the unending glory of being and acting with God eternally.

Now all that we do, in spite of our redemption from original sin, is subject to its consequences, steeped in them, like the soil which, even after the poisonous plant has been plucked out, retains a meshwork of delicate fibers. They remain active and can only gradually be destroyed by digging up the soil, by insects that feed on them, or by slow decomposition. The presence within us of these tendrils of sin, known under the term of concupiscence and experienced mainly as covetousness of the eyes, carnal desire, and pride—greed, lust and presumption—is forever brought home to us in a manner as confusing as it is painful. And our awareness of this persistent presence, far from diminishing, steadily increases. People who do not bother much with their interior life are almost inevitably satisfied with themselves; they see nothing. In the obscurity of their soul things cannot be distinguished; it is like a dark room, where you do not notice dust and dirt filling its nooks and crannies and covering everything. But with the first glimmer of spiritual comprehension a miracle happens; they are suddenly full of faults, just when they fancied that everything inside them was glorious and blissfully good. Just as if into that dark and dusty room a gleam of light were falling, conditions inside can only now be noticed. And the brighter the light, the more the dirt, accumulated but never really seen, will show inexorably, mercilessly, unbearably. Hence the feeling that their wretchedness increases by the same degree that their love of God is growing, and with it their inner clarity. To be thus given the vision of oneself as one really is, belongs to the greatest interior sufferings that have to be endured. And unless God granted this knowledge slowly or even withheld some of it, the mental agony might well annihilate them and destroy their will to live. For this reason, when giving such insight, God likewise gives great trust in Him and a deeply penetrating understanding of His love for that very soul that has just recognized its hopeless inferiority. Here, too, everything is wonderfully balanced by purest loving-kindness, wisdom and grace.

May they now simply leave it to God, whether He will deliver them from all this hideousness that pervades all and everything in them? This secret complacency, this nagging at everything that others do, this disguised indemnification by spiritual enjoyments (since they do, after all, deny themselves other pleasures), this presumption over others, the incessant revolving around self, and all this as if by right! Ultimately, of course, there will be no alternative but to leave it all to God. But not before they have struggled so earnestly and sincerely that He will take pity on them and cleanse them Himself. When God does this, they are given to know it. But more of this later on.

For the moment we have to realize that we must fight. The whole area of self-discipline, where grace must always be presupposed and prayed for, has been called asceticism, which is tantamount to practice. It means that one may not confine himself to occasional and somewhat haphazard efforts if any good is to come of it. As in every achievement that is to last and have some prospect for the future, practice is required, and more especially in the matter of our sanctification. Practice means frequent repetition until a habit has been mastered; it means doing it systematically, consistently, according to methods which have been tested and proved and adapted to one's need and ability.

Such practice must definitely have a place in the life of a Christian; first as a negation, the rejection of evil, the fight against sin, the avoidance of danger and sources of temptation. Knowledge of oneself through frequent examination of conscience and the education of conscience resulting therefrom, vigilance, heedful concern for what happens within and without, faithfully kept resolutions, and the correction of failure by sincere remorse: all this belongs to asceticism. It is the alphabet of the Christian life. Without it, there can never be spiritual progress, greater nearness to God, and an inner life in Him. Not as if by such efforts we could extort or forcibly acquire something from God and then on our own authority determine and direct our spiritual progress. Rather, it happens that we have been working hard at some particular interior point, without noticing any success, but meanwhile God is accomplishing His work in the soul at a different point, of much greater importance for our whole interior life. At times this is an almost insufferable burden for the soul, to fight for years against one clearly discerned fault, without being allowed to see the shadow of success, and still to have to maintain patience and an undiminished confidence in ultimate victory. But God never allows such things to happen without simultaneously doing what He knows is good for us and what, in fact, we need much more urgently than what we ourselves had visualized and striven for. It can then happen that, once God has completed His decisive work in us, the problem that tortured us will be dispelled as if by a gentle breeze.

Asceticism as cooperation

We have considered the practice of asceticism in the first instance as a negation because it is a question of tearing oneself free. We are redeemed, delivered, but we are not wholly freed from our fetters. We are like a man tied with ropes in such a way that he could not possibly free himself. Someone now cuts that part of his fetters which the man just could not have loosened by himself. But in order to give the man himself the honor and happiness of his own delivery or because now with help in sight he longs to be rid quickly of all his bonds, he is allowed to cooperate or he does so spontaneously, twisting and turning, straining every muscle, pulling at the knotted ropes. Gradually he gains his freedom, thanks primarily to his helper and then to his own efforts. Prevenient grace, efficacious grace and cooperating graces are all here combined in an effort of negation, that is, of destroying those fetters, and of trying again and again, until the efforts are crowned with success.

In actual fact, however, our struggle will be more successful and more rewarding if we make it one of cooperation by practicing the virtues opposed to the faults which we have recognized and must fight. If a man wants his garden free of weeds, he will pull them out and burn them, and untiringly pursue any new ones. But after that has been done, will the soil ever of itself become rich in grain or vegetables? No; they must be sown, planted, and nursed. And when something good is sown and carefully cultivated, the spot in which it grows can no longer be dominated by weeds. In like manner, it will be much more efficacious for the struggling soul to sow the good seed rather than merely uproot the bad weed. For instance, instead of saying: "I will no longer be uncharitable to this or that person," one should resolve: "I will always speak with kindness, appreciation, indulgence, and if this is not possible, I will hold my peace and quietly say a prayer for that person." Again, "Instead of warding off temptations against purity, I will turn at once to our Lord and to His Blessed Mother, take refuge in their purity and ask that they hold me fast and let me share their virtue." Instead of "no more distractions at prayer" better to say: "I will try the following means: to be recollected and devout, and so on." What about pride? The very struggle against this most sly, most devilish of all vices can become a means of self-satisfaction and secret complacency. But the humbling of ourselves before God, the quiet acceptance of little crosses, that is the right way to conquer pride. Who would stop in the middle of the road to stare at a heap of refuse and start screaming at it: "I hate you, I don't want you, I despise you"? Only a fool would do such a thing. Normal people would see the refuse, perhaps feel a slight nausea, and quickly walk on, trying to forget the ugly sight as soon as possible. And it is easy enough, for there is beauty everywhere. Why, then, should the soul stare at its temptations and deformities, crying: "No, no; go away, I don't want you"? Much better quietly to proceed and to make as little fuss as possible. This, by the way, applies especially to the examination of conscience, when we should by no means recall dangerous occasions, temptations or the manner in which we previously sinned. To establish the fact is all that is required, followed promptly by remorse or gratitude, as the case may be.

If we succeed in engaging in this positive fashion our efforts for the practice of virtue, for establishing the kingdom of God in our hearts, then the way has been wonderfully cleared. Countless anxieties, repressions and distractions, which otherwise can seriously prejudice our life of prayer and sometimes cause it to dry up, no longer worry us. We do not continually look into the abyss of our nothingness, but at the infinite expanse of latent goodness, at a full and wonderfully rich life which can belong to God and be offered to Him. For in its essence *everything* is related to God, and we can therefore refer it all back to Him. Everything can and shall become His kingdom; that is the truly catholic attitude which is basically anchored in the incarnation of the Son of God and exemplified by His life. If we proceed accordingly, we shall go straight to God; more and more our whole life will turn into prayer, in that triumphant and all-embracing sense which we have tried to explain.

Asceticism as renunciation

But we cannot help allowing a place to negation. The practice of the Christian life, the life with God, can never really prosper unless voluntary sacrifice, that is, self-denial beyond the strictly commanded avoidance of sin, be part of it.

Such mortification has been more than grossly misunderstood. It has nothing whatever to do with disregard or contempt of the created world. To the Christian neither creation itself nor any part of it can ever be evil. Only the ill use of it is evil; or rather, only the human will can be evil, so far as it directs itself away from God by preferring a created good. For how could the child of God decry anything created, when the Father in heaven "saw that it was good" and "very good"? Mortification is never directed against anything good in itself. Its object is the unruliness of desire, the excess of certain "goods" which have to be restricted to their proper place by mortification. A gardener, when pruning trees, does not intend to destroy the life of the trees; on the contrary, he wants to develop it fully, to help it attain the plenitude for which it was intended. For the tree is not meant to produce as many branches and leaves as possible and so to squander all its vitality. Rather, it should blossom abundantly and bear fruit, for this expresses its essence to perfection, guarantees its future life, and enables man to carry out God's ordinance: "Of these thou shalt eat." Merely by removing, by mortifying the unrestrained life which was digressing in a useless direction, the tree is made fit to achieve what, left to itself, it could not attain. For its own good these things had to be done to it. This is precisely what is meant by asceticism in the sense of voluntary mortification. It intends to clear the way for genuine life. Our powers must not be vainly squandered or used in a way that could be improved upon. We are concerned with the ennoblement, the raising, the transfiguration of ourselves, or at least with laying the foundations for it. If mortification has the power to dispense us from the deep misery of our insufficiency, then, indeed, it is indispensable.

It is that in yet another sense of even greater urgency. Is it possible to brake your car and stop it unimperilled right at the edge of an abyss after having driven to the brink at a frenzied speed? You would brake in good time, knowing that the extreme "just possible" is usually too late. Theoretically, maybe, there is still time, but as things really are, there is not. If we insist upon enjoying what is "allowed," to the very last boundary line, where the "thou-shalt-not" begins, we are almost certain to fall. Not the first time, perhaps, and not every time, but in the long run and in most cases. To live a life with God is possible only if innocent things, too, are cut out and forbidden by our own volition. Our secretive heart—often hidden even from ourselves—is too easily enamored of God's creatures. Their powerful charm casts its spell on us. They ensnare us more firmly each time we yield, unless the balance is restored by voluntary renunciation.

This renunciation can be applied to vital needs, for example, by fasting, and shortening one's hours of sleep. Such mortifications have their own grave risks and sometimes do greater harm than good. They should never be arbitrarily self-inflicted; another person's counsel should be sought, who as an outside party is in a better position to judge. This applies, though in a lesser degree, even to those smaller mortifications of the so-called "little" sacrifices. Anybody who performs them habitually, knows that they are hard enough, though the difficulty becomes less and less noticeable as the soul habituates itself to this self-discipline and self-restraint in which it finds a happiness of very special worth. We need not here go into the subject of the custody of the eyes, the ears, the palate, and the tongue. Suffice to say that there are great and important things to be done in this field by all of us. But the real mortification touches us on a more profound level: that of the mind. To try to replace unnecessary and self-indulgent fancies by something better, occasionally to waive one's own opinionated judgment, to comply with other people's wishes instead of imposing upon them one's own—that is the sort of thing that touches our real ego and does hurt us. Exterior severities are in some cases merely a question of sound skin and healthy bones. They can even become a sport. To gain control of the inner person is much more arduous, and consequently much more creative. To persist in faithful patience toward a child of many faults is a greater mortification than to restrict oneself for several weeks to a diet of bread and water.

Now the three forms of asceticism all create the framework and atmosphere for prayer, i.e., for the surrender of the heart to God. Conversely, only through prayer are they wholly purged from any harmful or dangerous elements that still remain. Now they become genuine love of God, and as forms and expressions of love they, in turn, impregnate the life of prayer. As soon as any asceticism—and not least that of voluntary renunciation—feeds upon love, it loses the stigma of mere negation and becomes pure consent. The accent shifts from the "away-from things" to the "nearer-to-God," from repudiation to longing desire. A child absorbed in play and suddenly seeing its father come home, runs flying into the father's open arms, having "torn itself away" from its play. But can that still be called "tearing oneself away" if love caused the game to be wholly forgotten, utterly lost to one's vision? The deeper the soul's love for God, the purer and more perfect its union with God in prayer and the easier for it to "let go." It does not even hurt very much. And again the reversal: such love seeks to express itself, and so everything is turned into welcome fuel; it burns, fades and withers, and love alone remains. God alone is enough.

The connection between asceticism and prayer is even closer. The most important and most effective part of ascetical training takes place in prayer, which becomes the source to feed the remainder of the Christian way of life. For here we learn what later we must practice and apply. Prayer thus stretches across the whole of life and pervades it, making it part of itself, its own sphere of action. It becomes the soul of all the rest. Prayer that ties itself to certain times of day will often enough have to fight against moods, inconstancy and spiritual disloyalty. Involuntary distractions will sometimes force it to prove itself immensely patient. Turning away from images, detaching oneself from happy feelings and agreeable sensations that come or seem to come from prayer itself, the self-discipline of spiritual sobriety and moderation—all these are aspects which we shall have to elucidate later on. Asceticism everywhere: the brave and persistent practice of negation of evil and the practice of virtue. Also the abandonment of impressions and experiences, not evil in themselves, but a hindrance and a brake to the soaring flight of prayer. Thus prayer itself becomes the soul's foremost "drill-ground," where all its practice engenders love, because the soul does it in and for the love of God, with its glance firmly fixed upon Him in conscious and solemn resolve.

Christ our model

It is impossible for us to implement a Christian life from our own resources. True, it already exists by virtue of our baptism, but that, at first, means hardly more than a seed, as yet imperfectly developed. If a child were left to itself, it would scarcely flourish, even if its vital forces and propensities were all in good order. It needs guidance and instruction, not so much by words as by an example capable of exercising a strong influence. Neither can a truly godly life do without a model. We must be shown what causes a life to be truly rooted in God, quickened by God, intent on uniting itself to God. We need a life that can be, in the different ways of different individuals, a model for us. This we may find in the writings by or about such a model, as an instruction from life itself which will exert a creative, formative influence on those who try to follow. Here the great religious founders serve as evidence. Usually the first circle of disciples, who lived entirely by the sharing of the master's life, was the most congenial community and gave the most unspoiled and unmistakable expression of the nature of their saintly model.

But all the saints, however important as models, themselves point always to the one supreme model: the God-Man Jesus Christ. In Him human existence is demonstrated in totally inviolate, faultless union with the life of God, in such perfect harmony that we could never discover the slightest variance. It is as if here the divine and the human were mutually absorbent. *His* human nature is open in all directions to the manifestations of God, to His eternal coming.

Therefore each gesture of our Lord, each silent step is as exemplary as His carrying the Cross or His kindness to the disciples when He wants them to enjoy a few days' rest. Allowing, of course, for the actual miracles which by that very fact cannot be an object for our imitation and to try to imitate them would be presumption, everything in Christ is "human." Yet everything is also wholly divine, worthy of adoration. There is therefore not one line in the Gospels—which, after all, we owe to the Holy Ghost, His Love—which did not authoritatively place before us our Lord's example in one respect or another. Here is the school for holiness and therefore the school for prayer.

Prayer always means association with Christ our Lord, Jesus of Nazareth, the God-Man. It means becoming through Him and in Him, what—again in Him—we have been called to be. Whether it be His fight against evil, always conducted as constructively as His "thou shalt adore the Lord thy God and Him alone shalt thou serve" (Matt. 4:9), His practice of virtue, or His disdain for something to which He is certainly entitled, such as honor, power, prosperity, we always find it in the Gospels, clear-cut, final and imperative.

So we can never do without the Gospels, if we want to lead a life of prayer. Not that we should read them while praying, but we must *know* them; they must be our conscious property, so that we can refer to them at any time. And since Christ *lives* in us because the mystical Christ is actually present within us, His image, as received from outside from the Gospels, is vitalized in us by the light and love of the Holy Ghost and through prayer we come into contact with this *living* Christ. We learn not only to address Him present within us, but even to *behold* Him spiritually.

Yes, the praying soul looks at the living Lord, present within it and ready to lead it; looks at Him through the medium of those Gospel accounts which it knows and contemplates together with the Lord Himself. Thus Christ exerts an increasing influence on the soul. Imperceptibly at first, as in a human relationship, when people gradually become more alike in thought, judgment and demeanor, the holy image penetrates more and more deeply into the praying, adoring soul. Think of that cherished tradition which states that our Lord imprinted His sacred countenance upon Veronica's veil. So now He leaves the impression of His being in the soul which, adoring Him, opens itself to Him and, free of all reserve, gives itself up to Him. The first likeness, as we remember, already exists through baptismal regeneration, which "fashioned us in the likeness of the First-born." Now the divine-human model asserts itself gradually, conquers the whole man as he prays and offers himself, takes possession of him in an ownership of sanctification and mercy, and so carries him into the depth of the Father's mystical life of triune unity. Prayer in which God Incarnate is not given a primary place, even though it present itself as highly spiritual mysticism, can only be a grave error, a way to lead one away from God rather than toward Him, for "no man cometh to the Father but by Me" (John 14:6). He is "the way" (John 14:6) and "the door" (John 10:9).

For that reason the Church, as our teacher in the ways of holy living and praying, while praying with us and "opening our mouth" for us, shows our Lord to us over and over again. He is not only the hidden mystical reality of her liturgy, but the living model for the faithful; alive in the Gospel accounts and there accessible, as it were, to all our powers of comprehension. The loving encounter of that inner vision turns into

a union, replaces our ego by His sacred presence, and transforms us in a "consecration" which leaves unchanged our
created nature but allows it to be so deeply absorbed into God
that we may well speak of it as being transformed.

To pray is to hold the hand of Christ, to turn our eyes upon
Him again and again, to let Him become the transforming
power within us, and with Him and in Him to make our way
to the Father.

Recollection

If we strive to have the vision of our Lord frequently before
us, we shall gradually find our innermost self. We shall rescue
it from the multiplicity of our distractions and the scattered
confusion in which it is usually caught up. When we think
of the thoughts that cross our mind, the images that float
through our brain, the countless impressions crowding in
upon us—dislikes, hopes, worries—there is no end to it all. Most
of the time we are, in the undesirable sense of the word, beside
ourselves. We let ourselves be dragged and pulled and driven,
and rarely keep ourselves under control, except perhaps in
exterior activity, but our external control is deceiving; it is a
cloak thrown over the confusion inside.

By nature we seek this distractedness. It prevents us from
being forced to bear with our own company. We shy away
from this solitude. There really is such a thing as escapism. To
look at oneself squarely is not very edifying. We are afraid
of the ugliness of our spiritual appearance; we do not want to
know that there is something, or almost everything, wrong
with it; and we certainly do not enjoy the warning coming
from that quarter and admonishing us to do penance. So we
always find excuses to wander about somewhere else, any-
place except "at home." We are, to ourselves, undesirable
company.

But that is not living at all. True life must have a center, an
origin and a goal. It needs a center from which the life forces
radiate, but which is also influenced by the right manner of

contact with the surrounding world. But we can never be that center wholly and exclusively by ourselves; we always are somehow beholden, bonded even, in a good or bad sense. Distractedness means being in bondage to the trifling; after that, to the imaginary, the deceptive; and finally to the diabolical. The Christian knows that his life belongs to Christ. He is the ultimate center, the head and the heart. Only in Him can we collect ourselves; when and so far as we are with Him, we are within ourselves; we possess ourselves so far as we possess Him. For our true, our higher self rests wholly in Him, the primordial Word, and from Him comes into our concrete human reality. The space in which our shadowy being strays, His presence fills. And now, only now, we "are." In a sense we cease to be, when He comes; as St. Paul said: "I live; now not I, but Christ liveth in me" (Gal. 2:20). Our puffed-up ego, noisy and playing at running the world, reveals itself to Him in all its shallowness, vanity and make-believe. He enters our being and establishes it in the way in which it had always been in His mind. He becomes our innermost self, its depth and its absolute response; He is so much one with us that He becomes our actual and higher self. Now we act in Him, He acts in us, and something is brought about which is foreshadowed and made possible in the union of the two natures in Christ. Now His thoughts govern ours; His desires kindle ours; His love ignites ours; His acting is embodied within ours. Surely we are right now to talk of the "living Christ" within us, of Him who supersedes and embraces all that gathers round and collects itself in Him.

A recollected life is the sublime purpose for which we should strive passionately. It does not consist in our going into the desert and never again attending to anything except Christ. This would be possible and permissible only for very few. God calls every individual to his particular work, and *there* He wants to work with him. Our life is recollected when we shed more and more of the superfluous, the diverting; when we turn our eyes and keep them more and more on our Lord's presence within us; when, in fact, we pray. If we are recollected, we can pray well. And, as often happens, the reverse is also true: good prayer will make us recollected; will make us be with Christ and, through Him, with the Father; will make us do everything with Him. True, that is an ideal, but one that we can approach, step by step. It was a reality in Christ and in His Blessed Mother and in the saints. It is also a reality, more or less, in many hearts that love God and are one with Him.

We must be prepared to work hard for this recollection. It is one of the most important results of those "practices" mentioned before, and of our frequent and loving gaze upon our Lord. Why do we read so many books which only carry off our imagination, goodness knows where, fill it with more fantasies, and rouse our desires? Must we really peruse every paragraph in the newspaper? Is each piece of news on the broadcast of vital importance? It is terribly and fundamentally sad, how much we deceive ourselves. If we were to imagine Mary absorbed for hours in the sounds of the radio as she does her housework or devotes herself to her Child, we would sense something of the folly of the mental and spiritual conditions which we create for ourselves by those interests which are hardly worthy of the Christian way of life. And so much of our social life with its chatter, even when this is not detrimental to our neighbor, so much of our active interest in matters which hardly concern us or which we have no right or power to change—all these things pass away the time which is so very precious and which, according to St. Paul, we should "buy up" instead of selling it wholesale, pretending to ourselves that we are doing it all for earnest and noble reasons. This should not become a prejudice, for the Christian more than others receives from the Holy Ghost the gift of discretion, the ability to distinguish between the essential and the unimportant, between the God-given and the self-selected tasks. And if he turns to this divine instinct, he will experience the divine guidance becoming stronger and clearer. For that very reason we must investigate that which only empties us and disturbs our recollection, even matters which at first seem quite guileless. A delicate enchanting flower, who would not enjoy it? I meet it as the herald of God who is beauty itself, like the distant, infinitely soft tone of a violin conjuring up a whole symphony with its glorious wealth and scope of sound. Seeing the flower in its delicious beauty, I look beyond it to the ultimate beauty. If I were to stop at the flower, though that would certainly not be sinful, it would not become for me what it was ultimately meant to be: a symbol of something beyond itself. If I follow the quiet suggestion of its beauty, its lucid order and ingeniousness, I can in one flight of the spirit behold the Creator and Father in all His power, wisdom and glory, and I stand in adoration. The flower has helped me to be recollected in God.

There is room here perhaps for two observations. No recollection is possible without the practice of keeping silence. From time immemorial all the different schools of spiritual self-discipline have known this, and whoever strives to follow the inner way will soon enough come up against the necessity of keeping silence. We ought to practice it every day. The dawn of the day belongs to God; if we can help it, we ought not to speak before having said our morning prayers. The same thing is true after night prayers. And again on the way to church, especially when we are to receive Holy Communion. We should at least confine our conversation to spiritual subjects. Wherever possible, one or another hour of the day should be fixed for keeping our own company and avoiding unnecessary talk. Unnecessary, let that be remembered. If we were to growl at anyone who asks us a question because we are thus prevented from keeping to our "practice," we would turn the whole exercise into a wicked folly. Charity must have priority, always and everywhere. Charity is and ever shall be the measure of all that is good. To answer politely, even to ask a necessary question or show a sympathetic interest does not cancel our silence. Anything that we make our practice must always remain flexible and must never be allowed to harden into rigidity and violence.

Above all, we must carry the outward silence into our inner person. Though it often does not work at all, we must try our best to avoid all unnecessary wandering of our thoughts, all curiosity, the plans and resolutions of many kinds with which we often fill our time, knowing quite well that nothing will come of them.

In controversial conversation two topics should be avoided as far as possible: the religious and the political dispute. On both of these topics unenlightened passions usually become very heated and cause agitated minds which take a long time to become calm, having meanwhile lost a great deal of strength, much charity and all recollection. And to what end? Religion is no subject for a quarrel; it is too precious, it is invested with too much love. And one can love one's country deeply, even when one is not given to political discussions which only cause hot tempers and sharp differences. If we want to be wise, we avoid such issues and do not allow ourselves to be drawn into them. Renunciation here will only benefit the soul.

The second observation is the wonderful rule of Father Surin, S.J.: "*Pas trop d'empressement*": never devote oneself to anything of this world so that one is totally absorbed by it; never entirely lose one's heart, one's soul to anything. Even when surrendering itself to genuine passion, the heart must keep an innermost reserve, an ultimate distance, and in the space between "myself" and "it"—be it person or thing, delight or pain—God must dwell.

Haste, too, is wrong. Not only because in practical human issues not much good can be expected of it, but even more because it is a real danger for the soul, which under the domination of haste cannot become inwardly still, recollected and open to the voice of God.

Spiritual direction

We need guidance for everything, if it is to be mastered and appropriated. Only a curious misapprehension could make us consider this unnecessary on our way to God. What do I know about it, if no one has preceded me on my particular way and if I cannot perceive the path ahead because of the darkness? In the Apocalypse we read that God will "give to him that overcometh . . . a white counter (stone)" with "a new name written which no man knoweth" (Apoc. 2:17). That shows the relationship between God and each individual soul to be absolutely unique. Having created and formed the soul, God alone knows it down to its innermost recesses. And each soul's perception of God is necessarily unique, because there is no other soul like it. Now God, who alone knows the soul's being and destiny, gives it that "name." As yet the soul does not own it; nor can it, of itself, ever come to possess it; only at the end of its long journey will the soul be impregnated by it, and even then not by virtue of its own powers.

Who, then, will guide the soul? The Father, through the Son, in the Holy Ghost. Our way is to the Father; He is the beginning and the end. Christ is—and points—the way. And the Spirit of Love, emitting fire and light, makes the soul ardent and eager with love, and as Spirit of Truth makes it see. The Holy Ghost is the actual guide of the soul, the "friend of the bridegroom," who adorns the bridal soul, transfigures its whole being with love, and leads it to the marriage feast. The soul, ardent with prayer and longing to be wholly steeped in it and so to become one with the life of God, will therefore gladly associate with the Holy Ghost, invoke Him, keep itself open to Him, follow His gently stimulating hints; and if the soul fails, it will fervently ask His forgiveness. The Holy Ghost initiates the soul to prayer and helps it along its intricate, bewildering paths. We must deeply understand that through prayer each soul has its own relationship with the Holy Ghost. And if the worship of His Person were to increase, there would certainly be a wonderful new tide in the life of prayer of the children of God, and in their sanctification as well.

The Divine Spirit guides us by His seven gifts, which have the highest importance for our interior progress. To consider them here would lead us too far from our present subject, but we must certainly make them the subject of frequent prayer.

Now the Spirit of God was not promised to the individual person as such, but to the whole mystical body of Christ, to the Church. He is the bridal Spirit as love toward and love within the heart of the bride. Only as the Spirit of our collective unity and within it can He bring about the constant exchange of forces between individual members and groups, exactly as it happens in any other living organism: all its parts depend upon each other, the same life-stream operating through the various members and organs. It is no different in the Church. Not as single individuals are we being led to sanctity, but as members of the one Christ, and hence through mutual mediation, help and stimulation. A person is no judge—or he is a bad one—in his own case. One is too close to oneself; he is not sufficiently detached to be objective. We love ourselves too well and are forever inclined to decide in our own favor. Pride and complacency are much too deeply rooted not to play tricks on us when something all-important is at stake on our way to God. Anticipating our goal, we are forever trying to credit ourselves with virtues, abilities, dispositions which really have not even begun to exist in us. This results as much from our vain self-love, which will accept no defectiveness of ourselves, as from our indolence, which shirks the lifelong struggle and hopes to escape it by a kind of anticipation.

Consequently we are much too prone to falsify the Holy Ghost's voice within us. Perhaps we mistake our own thoughts for His inspiration. This is the very opportunity for Satan to intrude, of whom St. Paul says that he likes to disguise himself as an angel of light to deceive us. Satan knows how to flatter our self-love—and we, like our first parents, believe him only too delightedly. On the other hand, we perhaps

misinterpret genuine inspirations of the Holy Ghost, and arrive at premature conclusions. For all these reasons we require
human guidance, too. It can rest with our confessor, provided
he understands the life of our soul and knows the ways by
which God usually leads a soul. Or it can rest with anybody
who knows our soul and in whom we can confide because he
has genuine authority, whether because of a vocational calling
or because he possesses virtue strong and mature enough for
any reasonable person to acknowledge. For example, the
"starietcy" of the Russian Church, those great directors of
souls, often are not priests, but they are known as "saints,"
that is to say, persons completely abandoned to God and
consequently possessing an empirical knowledge of Him. But
again, this subject cannot now be pursued beyond stressing
the point that we must pray for the right spiritual director
and, having found him, we must faithfully obey his counsel.

The specific distinction of a spiritual director lies in his
guiding the soul *under* the Holy Ghost. It will be given to him
to understand the soul's condition. Often he does not know
beforehand what he will have to say, but when the time comes
he will say it, and the soul feeds on his words, conscious of
having been understood, encouraged, or rightly warned and
even censured. But the actual guidance, far from turning into
a procedure of merely human instruction, remains with the
Holy Ghost. No doubt experience in the pedagogical and psychological field may play a more or less important part, but in
complete submission to the light from above. It is not as if
director or directed must necessarily receive revelations from
on high, sudden infusions or enlightenments of a miraculous
character; though that, too, is possible, on the whole, everything happens entirely "naturally." But by faith we know that
this is the normal channel for supernatural efficacy. The more
trustingly the soul relies on and sincerely looks for the Holy
Ghost working in the spiritual director, and the better the
director recognizes himself as an instrument and a vehicle of
divine love, the better everything will work. The soul will

then not find it too difficult to disclose itself without reservation, especially with regard to its life of prayer as the center of its communion with God; and it will all the more readily accept guidance and follow it. The purer our obedience and our listening to the voice and instruction of God reaching us through the human vessel, the safer our soul's progress, even when at times the wrong advice has been given. Even through the medium of a not so "spiritual" director, the soul can receive all that it needs, since God can use any—even the most contradictory means—to lead the soul in His own way.

Any ties too human in character will be avoided in this relationship, especially that of an awkward spiritual servility which, instead of attaining to inner maturity and assurance, keeps looking furtively for the apron-strings and feels lost as soon as guidance is not forthcoming. All genuine education aims at making people independent, capable of judging and acting in a rightfully found inner self-sufficiency. And although our spiritual task will never be finally accomplished and we shall, in all likelihood, continue to need assistance, basic inner freedom and independence must be achieved. So much so that one must be able, if necessary, to leave one's spiritual director on the inner conviction that he cannot lead the soul any further; that its paths remain concealed to him; that he gives the wrong directives. We refer here to the distinct knowledge of having received the wrong counsel. Even if the spiritual director were to try to detain one in such a case, one would have to go. Thus, St. Frances de Chantal changed from her ungenerous and narrow-minded confessor, who completely tyrannized her, to St. Francis de Sales. But all this will turn out well if accompanied by intense prayer.

It is also possible that for a time the soul finds no one to understand it; no one whose counsel gives any help or new perception, but the contrary. Indeed, to some, in spite of their intense desire, no spiritual guidance is ever granted; they must find their way alone. And others, though knowing the right person to turn to, do not find it possible to formulate and express what happens in their soul. Even as they speak, such persons know that they do not say what they wish to say; and the response, of course, will be a disappointment. These are hard trials indeed.

But it is not as if God has left the soul all to itself; on the contrary, He Himself truly leads it then. That, too, can happen in many different ways. Sometimes it is a casual word caught somewhere; an insignificant event, suddenly become transparent to the inner eye; a surprised look, noticed in time, perplexing to the soul and the beginning of an entirely new understanding. At other times it happens in a most unlikely situation, without a warning; even without one's having been aware of that particular problem now offering itself together with its solution. The writings of the saints—and also other books—can open the door for the light to break in. Often a person is led to important works on the spiritual life without ever having been told about them; and at just the right moment they show the soul exactly what it needs. Then the soul knows with wonderful and blessed certainty that it is God Himself carrying it and providing the food it needs, even though He seemed to have forgotten it for a long, lonely time.

Out of the early calamity—sometimes lasting for years—of a person's incapacity to speak and the consequent privation of human guidance for the life of prayer, a glorious clarity then arises and an assurance that comprises both purest trust in God and the irrefutable knowledge of one's own helplessness.

One more remark: to leave one's spiritual director out of caprice, inconstancy or through a failing sense of obedience is as unworthy and dangerous as to be faithful to him out of excessive human respect. Neither attitude has anything to do with listening to the voice of God within. In either case the decision must be one of great sincerity, prayed for persistently; it must be carried out in peace and a deep confidence that God so wills and orders it, and that He will take care of the future. For our inner life, if anything, must be protected by our sacred trust in God's perpetual nearness and His love.

Spiritual reading

As we have said, a religious book can sometimes replace or complement the spiritual director. In addition to this, spiritual reading ought always to accompany our daily life. From it we draw new inspiration for our prayer, both with regard to contents and to method. It is impossible for us to find it all within ourselves. We forget too quickly, and modern life, with its countless fleeting impressions, makes it almost impossible to retain anything. But when our eye rests on the printed word—really rests—the word sinks slowly into our mind and becomes a vital influence on our life as Christians. We have too many things to think about and religious thoughts find little place among them unless we consciously and deliberately gather the material through our spiritual reading. Without this it is safe to say that there cannot be much progress. A good choice of spiritual reading matter should be made, preferably with one's spiritual director, who should at least be informed. People without a director will find that faithful prayer will be rewarded by the right guidance by divine providence.

We should never say that we have too little time. Only the devil has no time. People who never have time prove that there is something fundamentally wrong with the way their lives are ordered. Life cannot be considered to be properly arranged if it does not allow time for the essential. There may be exceptions every now and then, but we are here concerned with the general rule. We can all dispense with a few things hitherto considered indispensable: a newspaper article, some of the time spent at the television, a bit of window-shopping, an idle chat, etc. In this way, if we are serious, we can snatch the ten or fifteen minutes required for our spiritual reading, preferably in the morning or evening, when our mind is more relaxed, less preoccupied, and more receptive than at other times of the day. The morning has the advantage of enabling us to carry the good thoughts into the day; the evening allows them

75]

more quietly to sink into our soul and even perdure while we sleep. One need not exceed fifteen minutes, but once the resolve is made, it should be kept firmly, irrespective of one's "being in the mood." Spiritual reading thus becomes our daily bread quite naturally, and soon also quite indispensably. When more time is available, as in the holidays or on a journey, one may confidently devote an hour or more to such a book of inner guidance. It will be more rewarding than any other book that is avidly consumed.

Spiritual reading is very different in method from our general reading. There should be a short preparation: a lifting up of the mind to God; a keen prayer for our reading to be fruitful. No set purpose should be aimed at; it is for the Holy Ghost to decide how He will make our reading spiritually effective. The point of it is just to be with God for awhile, rather than engage in any particular study. Hence two aspects become imperative. First, spiritual reading must not be done critically, but "faith-fully"; not from curiosity or desire of knowledge, but from yearning love. If, for instance, having chosen the Scriptures for your spiritual reading, you wracked your brain over a seeming "contradiction," you would hardly benefit. This is not a critical study; this is "listening"—and listening truly "like a child"—in order to "enter into the kingdom of heaven." Let us not lay down the law, not judge, and certainly not censure those books which the saints have left us and the Church recommends to us. Let us be "simple as doves," for true wisdom is wise through hearing, believing in and totally assimilating the heavenly gift.

Secondly, this is not a matter of finishing or getting through any given number of pages. The more slowly and thoughtfully we read, the more we gain. Haste, indeed, spells harm; far from increasing the love of spiritual reading, it soon has us bored and disinclined to continue, because much of what we read we seem to know already, to have heard before or, perhaps, even thought ourselves. But the purpose here is something totally different: to be with God through the medium of that book. There is in this a strong similarity with prayer, and a bridge to prayer. When we have progressed far enough to fill our fifteen minutes with only one sentence or one half of it, then we have read well. It will not happen at once, but gradually. We must first learn to pay attention to the gentle stimulations which, as we read, the Spirit of God will give us. Usually they do not consist of beautiful thoughts or pious sentiments. No need to bring our beautiful thoughts to God; His are better. And our sentiments usually weigh precious little. We know the divine stimulation by a gentle feeling that seems to arrest us very tenderly. Our soul senses it and, if heedful of it, will understand it ever more clearly. We must not then continue to read—not one line, not another word—but pause immediately and allow what we have just read to have its effect upon us. That means dwelling on it. It will become increasingly clear to us that we are with God through the words just read; they are pointers, if you will. Now they recede, having been but an aid, now superfluous once we have reached the goal. For a few seconds—and longer later on—the heart "tastes" God. No more thinking to be done; just quietly resting with Him, until the stimulation fades and we are ready again to continue our reading. As we return to the book and the words just read, we may feel the same stimulation once more. Let us submit to it immediately. Never, though this may be repeated several times, should we be dismayed at our slow progress. To "get on" with the reading now would in reality thwart our efforts.

This method of reading slowly helps to create the preliminary conditions for contemplative prayer, when we no longer ponder about God but have come to rest within Him, simply; when the heart is with God, adoring, thanking, loving Him with no further desire, since this was its goal. Everything else is far removed. And the heart, already enjoying a foretaste of eternity, knows that this, and this only, is the true fulfillment of its whole being.

Spiritual conversation

Reading is in a way a converse of the mind with the author or with him who is the subject of the book. But you cannot ask questions, except to the Holy Ghost. His response, however, is very different in our experience from that of a human person. Here spiritual conversation comes into its own. As a rule it will take place with our spiritual director, in the confessional, which is certainly right for that purpose, too, or at specially appointed times. Also by correspondence, although there is the disadvantage that a letter cannot always capture the vivid reality of the moment and no immediate answer is possible. Moreover, a distorted picture may result because an inadequately formulated question cannot at once be rectified. On the other hand, a letter has the possible advantage of greater maturity and precision of thought. In practice the choice of method will be determined by circumstances, but some people can only express themselves aptly in writing, while others can only speak their thoughts.

Spiritual conversation can, however, engage any two people sincerely searching for God. And what a blessing it would be if it happened more often. There is so much exchange of thought, experience, planning; why should it be restricted to housekeeping and holiday events? Apart from the recreational value, is not the purpose of any conversation the give and take between the speakers? Are we so niggardly that we part but reluctantly and with very little of our interior treasures from God? Or are we so miserably poor that we have nothing to give? Or so indifferent that we do not feel the desire to share the riches of others?

With people who are at all spiritually alive, it is mostly because of awkwardness and timidity that they do not touch upon these very personal matters. And there is a right place for such shyness as a barrier against that loose chatter which, like a splashing waterfall, enlarges happily on spiritual matters, self-satisfied to reveal itself and advertise its wisdom. This pseudo-religious volubility is repugnant and often destructive. Though it may mouth pious maxims and Scriptural quotations, raise pious eyes to heaven, measure all against its yardstick of virtue, and allow a halo visibly to brighten its appearance, one notices all too soon the emptiness of it. But even without belonging to that "pious lot," we are, through frequent religious talk, in danger of a gradually increasing passion to perform, a veritable insatiability to exhibit ourselves. We once again exchange the means for the end. We should not engage in spiritual conversation merely for the sake of talking but to advance more closely to God. We find Him and hold Him in our silence; within the quietness of our heart, and that is where all spiritual conversation, as well as our spiritual reading, must lead us; otherwise it spells corruption. Moderation, here as in everything, is of the essence. Again, it is best to start the talk by praying—together or each by himself—for God's blessing. Thus the danger of falling into complacency will be modified.

All this should happen simply, plainly, single-heartedly. No big words, no chasing of particularly mystical notions, which are easy traps for spiritual vanity or even pride. Nor is the purpose to lecture. Who is to know whether the other soul is not, perhaps, incomparably richer in grace, though just now it finds itself greatly confused and in need of counsel or incapable of an exact description of its inner state? It is always well to remember the parable of the first and the lowest seats, especially in spiritual matters. And let there be no laying down the law; spiritual conversation is essentially different from a discussion, which has its place in scientific theology, but never in the common effort to approach nearer to God. It was not God's pleasure to redeem us through dialectics. Argument, which often brings out differences and hot tempers and leaves empty hearts, is an enemy of interior recollection as well as of love of God and neighbor. While controversy separates, true spiritual conversation will unite the partners with God and hence with one another. If too strong an inclination should develop for talking to one special person, ascetic self-control must counteract the danger of a humanized relationship. What began in the spirit must not end in the flesh.

Chapter 12

Organization of Prayer

Proper time

Our life of prayer should aim at our being with God constantly, listening to Him, acting with Him, "and not to faint." We shall not reach this goal unless we fix certain times for prayer and observe them as faithfully as we can. If then we pray well, the spirit of prayer will penetrate everything that fills our day. Think of a number of burning candles spaced out in a room. Each one is surrounded by its own circle of light which, though fading toward its circumference, overlaps into that of the nearest candle, so that there is light everywhere. From one moment of prayer the sacred flame of the love of God is handed on to the next, and thus all our time is "in God." Experience shows that frequent and culpable neglect of well-ordered prayer will lead to a harmful interior slovenliness: always some degree of indifference toward God and the supernatural, a gradual indifference to grave moral offenses which lack the necessary counter-check, and ultimately a total loss of faith. Therefore let us be severe with ourselves. There will be exceptions, naturally, but it is part of true Christian freedom and agility even then properly to adjust our resolutions.

The early morning belongs to our Lord and Creator, who gives us this day in which to serve Him and win eternal bliss. It belongs also to our Father! Fancy a child meeting his parents in the morning and hurrying past them wordlessly to play or work. A greeting, an embrace, a few affectionate words, born of the knowledge of mutual love and the desire to devote the day to it, will surely be the natural expectation of any human parent.

Our heavenly Father expects the same of us, His children. With our morning prayer the day's true order starts; now all is orientated toward God. As yet the soul is not involved in the day's multifarious tasks. No need, therefore, as yet to free itself from that persistent absent-mindedness in order to unite itself to God. Coming out of the depth of slumber that carries us away from everything and causes our inner being to become supple, light, agile, willing and alert, the soul can now pray well. In this connection let us remember that the example of adults is of extreme importance to young children.

In the evening also, the last thought of the day, the last emotion belongs to God. Morning and evening are symbols of our birth and death; of our rebirth, too, and our homecoming to God; of our beginning and our end in Him. The mystery of prayer thus enfolds us like the embrace of our Father's arms. The evening, of its nature, is an ending, a tuning down, in spite of modern manners which make it the beginning of a "night life." While no argument against the evening's significance and sacred right, it is an argument against humanity's good sense. As the autumn bears the fruit of spring and summer, so does the evening gather up the morning and midday. The work is done; results must now be judged—and harvested. All is committed now into the hands of Him who gave it. We rest, as on the sabbath, in our Father's love.

Between the two limits which confine the day are the times of our repasts. If our morning prayer asked for the daily bread —today's bread—should we forget to thank God for it, now that it is granted? Are not both our Father and His gift worth our gratitude? All human usage has surrounded the meal with many customs and formalities which rescue it from being a purely carnal procedure: we wait for everybody to assemble, we do not pounce upon the meal at once, we do not use our fingers but proper tools, we sit upright, not stooping down greedily to the plates and dishes. Thus we gain distance, and with it the mental freedom which, here as in the sexual life, is particularly exposed to crude sensuality. The Christian is above the merely human level, even above his own civilization; he is a child of God, and only as such, as one existing entirely within God, as one "whose walk is in heaven" though his duty is to "plough the earth," is he enabled to fulfill the worldly task committed to his care. Through prayer, even thoroughly material acts such as eating and its complementary acts are lifted into God's presence and grace, sublimated through right moderation out of love for Him and reverence for the innate laws of creation and the body that is a member of the mystical body of Christ and a temple of the Holy Ghost. Not to pray before and after meals represents either an astounding forgetfulness or a miserable cowardice, unworthy of a man who "knows Him whom he believed" (II Tim. 1:12). And there is no valid reason for grace to be confined to lunch and dinner; breakfast is God's gift, too, and a cause for gratitude.

There is a special demand for prayer in times of need, especially interior need, such as the strain and torment of strong temptations which, by their violence or their persistent recurrence, are apt to undermine our resistance. That is when we must pray more and better than ever. We must! Our soul needs it. It is like the desperate shouts of a drowning man or the additional food for a heavy worker, whose greater output demands more strength and consequently better food. That applies to spiritual condition as much as, if not more than, our physical life. And here, by the way, temptation is seen as a special offer of grace, permitted for that very reason, for it induces us to turn to God much more often. Many a heart has learned the secret of living with God and before His eyes in this painful way. Temptations are like bad roads that help to sharpen the eye and improve the skill of the driver.

Urgent intentions, our own and others, also prompt us to pray: material worry, anxiety about the family, the sorrowing care of souls, the sufferings of our Holy Mother the Church, the love of our country. Whatever moves the heart should always drive it to God in supplication and reparation.

Where the *Angelus* is sounded, one should gladly join the beautiful custom. If tiring of too many Hail Mary's, we can always say instead the seasonal Marian Antiphon as found in the Office of the Church.

Finally, passing a Catholic church should not only remind us of our Lord's bodily presence there but should prompt an act of adoration. If two to three minutes can be spared, let us go in and join the mystery of His eternal adoration. That quiet moment will be like a bath for the soul, restoring and relieving it and clarifying the meaning of its being and acting. The soul becomes united with the rhythm of the Sacred Heart, the center of the universe. Those scanty moments are infinitely precious, a worthy replacement for our customary waste of time.

We need not speak of the times for prayer that are especially prescribed and binding in obedience, such as attendance at Mass on Sundays and holy days of obligation. The Church's precept urges us to "assist at Mass devoutly." What is demanded is that our will truly be united with God in a genuine submission of the heart.

Proper place

Here, too, what is strictly binding, will not be discussed. To assist at Mass is, of course, only possible where it is being celebrated, but the law requires our physical presence. For there is to be a congregation both spiritually and bodily gathered around our Lord's sacred act, and to be sanctified by it.

Three places are especially suited to good prayer. First of all, a church, which is dedicated to God and thus singled out from profane life, blessed and consecrated perhaps by the prayer and devotion of centuries. Christ is here present in His sacred humanity, and to know this by faith is, no doubt, a most powerful help toward recollection. Then there is the influence of so many symbols, especially the tabernacle lamp, the altar, the candles, the tall pillars arched like entreating hands, the images of the saints. Also the quiet and solitude, although in many particularly beautiful churches visited by hosts of lovers of art, these advantages may be looked for in vain. People react differently to various architectural styles. To one person a mighty basilica means amplitude, freedom, propelling rhythm; another one feels there as if rent asunder or stunned. One person feels stifled in a small chapel while another feels safely enclosed. We are certainly entitled to our own choice in the matter, though we would do better to free ourselves of its restricting influence and all preference as to place. Prayer is mental association with God and is therefore possible and desirable everywhere. Servility to the merely expedient at the cost of the essential would be unworthy. One must also learn to rise above the various disturbances which are never wholly avoidable in any public place. People coming and going, rustling the pages of their prayerbooks, clearing their throats, none of it concerns us, and it would be ridiculous to allow our devotion to depend on such things. They may prejudice our feelings considerably, in which case these are hardly worth having. The spirit must find its own way, soaring beyond these disturbances, unless a person suffers from some nervous affliction, and then special rules would apply.

The other privileged place for prayer is the privacy of the Christian home, dedicated to be, as it were, a supplement to the temple of God, and as such also a copy of the universal Church. It is animated by the religious life of its inhabitants, themselves temples of the Holy Ghost, who readily adorn it with the symbols of their faith: holy pictures, statues, the crucifix and a holy water font—all testifying to the desire to sanctify the world.

The home is the appropriate place for one's daily prayers. These prayers sanctify our daily life, the greater part of which is spent within its walls. They train the children to form the vitally important habit of such prayer. They sometimes remind the guests of something long forgotten. At home one can also more easily make time for special prayer, since he can organize himself and be left in peace. Mothers sometimes have in their bedrooms a large crucifix with a prie-dieu in front; there they take refuge with their joys and worries, and they know how much of their fortitude, their kindness and their supernatural attitude they owe to this source of strength.

And finally the realm of nature, vast and sublime, is an admirable guide to higher spheres. The grandeur of the mountains, the majestic seas, the glory of the constellations, and the beautiful flowers—all will spur the sensitive eye and heart to love and adoration. It certainly is true that love of nature can induce us to greater love of God. By the clear tenets of his faith the Christian is protected from false mystical enthusiasm which would mistake nature for its Creator and serve idols in the place of God. In all creation and its attributes he sees God and His glory, and thus his heart and lips spontaneously form words to "praise the Lord and all His works." But he must train himself, because created beauty could beguile him, too. Though not confounding it with God, he might yet for a time find his contentment here, thus delaying the progress of his interior life.

A few remarks on "technique" may be timely here. If out of doors we really want to be very close to God, it is important that we walk alone, or that at least the company of others does not prevent the observance of silence. Moreover, we should not then aim at special feats of distance to be covered or heights to be attained. Such secondary objects would claim far too much of our inner attention for our heart to share the harmony of nature's rhythm and thus be carried to God. Above all, we must not stop too long anywhere. Our perceptive powers must not engage too deeply in the world around us, but should leave the mind scope for the essentially "other" world. So, walking slowly, our eyes turned inward, we summon to thanksgiving, praise and love the inarticulate creatures, uniting them within us to the *Magnificat* of the Mother of God, to whom we dedicate alike the beauty of the spring and the autumn's fruit-fulness.

Now there is scope for prayer always, everywhere. Practice will make it easier: on the way to the office, though there must be no haste; when waiting our turn in shops or at the bus stop; or riding on a street car or subway. All are opportunities once we know how to use them. The rosary in the pocket of your coat; perhaps more people than we think say it that way. A litany can easily be learned by heart to be at our disposal any time, so that, unknown to others, we may ponder the beautiful, rich and profound invocations. The interior life has its own ways and rules, which run across all else to take all things to God's throne.

Expression and posture

Under this heading we propose to consider the outward attitude of prayer. That this should play a part at all in our worship of God as Christians follows from two facts. First, being created to form a unit, we must adore as such, our physical exterior nature lending expression, support and intensification to our inner being. Secondly, our membership in the mystical body of Christ embraces, through His transfigured divine-human body, our physical nature, too, and bestows upon it divine-human dignity in God's eyes.

In a certain sense we may say that the body is the manifestation of the soul. Not that definite psychological facts can be known with certainty from certain gestures or movements, but the soul's presence in the body is such that its vital functions are to some degree manifested through the body. True, there are "two" here, but they are so deeply one that they exist more within one another, than side by side. And this one whole is man, called into being for the glorification of his Maker. Deliberately to disregard the body's part in our relation with God, as some pseudo-mystical teaching tries to do, runs contrary to the inner meaning of Christianity and, indeed, of human nature itself. It is a heresy. True, as the life of prayer advances interiorly, the part played by the physical element will change noticeably, but it will always be present. Even when in the flight of the spirit referred to by certain saints, the soul has lost all memory of its body, that body remains present, transfigured by the beauty of the soul and by the rapture of the Beauty it beheld.

The change which we just mentioned is noticed primarily in the fact that bodily manifestations of interior prayer gradually become more and more frequent. Ultimately they reach a great stillness which corresponds exactly to our interior tranquillity in God. It may appear as if no physical movement were possible at all. This is usually not the case, but there is the impression of immobility because the soul is so completely absorbed in God that it does not exercise its will upon the body to move it. Any form of rigidity beyond this should, according to the teachers of mystical prayer, be considered as mere weakness of the body which has not yet learned to keep pace with the soul's rhythm. All mystical theologians maintain that external manifestations recede and finally disappear as the soul's powers of interior prayer increase. Deepest ecstasies can occur without producing any abnormal physical reaction. Indeed, it is a rule for interior progress that anyone noticing such strange physical manifestations when at prayer should strive with all his strength to ward them off. That is required for a healthy spiritual life. To look for perceptible peculiarities is very foolish and highly dangerous. In this way one can undo everything and fall a prey to the worst influences. Our ego will only too readily use the conspicuous to deceive itself and others and claim a superiority in the spiritual life, when such things prove nothing.

The second change of bodily manifestation occurs when deliberate and conscious movements are replaced by those which proceed gently and spontaneously from within. As if of their own accord the hands rest on the chest, the head inclines slightly or the arms become extended. The less the attention given to the body and what happens to it, the greater the harmony between the inner experience and its exterior expression. Here, too, we find an exact correspondence. The soul is no longer as active as formerly but is much more under the guidance of the Holy Ghost and cooperates with what He does within. The body, like a second rainbow appearing as the shadow of the first, mirrors the soul's response to the inspirations of the Spirit of God. One should not resist this gentle exertion; it is perfectly balanced in its effects. But any singularity must always be avoided. Extending the arms in church, for instance, while others can see it, is certainly open to doubt as long as the movement remains a conscious act, even when resulting from inner inspiration.

The general rule is that the body should assist the soul. It does that perfectly when it is no more than pure expression, as we tried to illustrate just now, but it must never molest the soul. For this reason St. Teresa of Avila teaches us to adopt whatever physical attitude proves most conducive to the best, easiest and most unhindered prayer. Kneeling, standing up, walking or sitting—even lying down—any one of these attitudes may serve the purpose, though none will be permanently chosen. One may kneel although great fatigue and an aching back may make it a painful effort, and this will serve as an ascetical practice, provided no harm is done to one's health, which would be wrong. But if neither mortification nor obedience determine our choice, we should adopt a position in which our body does not assert itself so strongly, so that the soul can better concentrate upon God. The point here, as always, is the end we have in view. If laziness or indolence make us lie down for prayer, we are lacking in the necessary reverence toward God. If we do it because it will prevent our usual headaches or fatigue, we should certainly profit from that position. The essential thing is always that our heart should not be diverted; that it should abide in God as quietly and recollectedly as possible. Any strain or stress, any will-power in the sense of a physical exertion is no good here; it obstructs the way, strains the nerves, makes us tired and refractory and, finally, weary of everything, all because of a wrong method which could never reach the right end. But let us discriminate; often enough we shall feel physical strain, even when praying, no matter what position we adopt. Such is God's will, a blessing to us if we submit to it, and a different thing altogether from self-selected or excessive bodily discomfort during prayer.

Many details could be added on the significance of the various bodily attitudes. Beautiful and memorable things have been written about them and a few remarks may here serve as reminders. Great inner joy in God is best expressed in a standing or at least in an upright position. Kneeling could scarcely express the mood of the *Gloria*. A sense of guilt inclines the head, but as we become deeply conscious of being safe in our Father's love and forgiveness, we raise the head spontaneously. Distinctly the soul senses what gesture of the hands the moment requires: folded hands, their fingers interlaced, denote something different than when the palms are joined and the fingers straight. Again, it is different whether our hands meet at some distance from the body or are drawn closely toward it. Laid crosswise on the breast, they speak of deep and peaceful recollection. In profound inner prayer concentration is often helped if the hands are placed separately on knees held parallel, the fingertips slightly stretching beyond them.

Breathing, in prayer as elsewhere, is generally given too little attention. Most people breathe disjointedly, unrhythmically, and it shows in their lives. It would be foolish, of course, to base a spiritual life on a breathing technique; let us not distort the right order of values. But some attention to quiet and regular breathing can certainly be of help especially to interior prayer. As a symbol of the Holy Ghost, the Breath of God which He breathed into man, it has a profound relation to the divine life and hence to prayer. When one is restless, distraught and agitated, it is useful, as the time for prayer approaches, to start breathing quietly and regularly. Soon this enforced tranquillity, which pervades the whole body, imparts itself to the heart, the mind, the soul, and our prayer runs its proper course. Again, when during prayer distractions as-

sail us or temptations confuse us, it is well to make these soothing, conscious, calming exercises of slow regular breathing.
When the soul is very still, it may sometimes feel as if all
breathing stopped, so gentle and light is it, so well adapted
to the soul's interior state. To make and keep our breathing
light and thus to try, when possible, to assume that disposition
can have a relaxing effect when our inner being is tense and
rigid. Some saints and teachers of the life of prayer also speak
of the practice of using short ejaculations to accompany one's
breathing. They bring the "breath of the soul" into wonderful
conformity with the body's breathing, conditioning a harmo-
nious unity of all the processes involved in the exercise of
prayer. Breathing in, the soul knows: "Thou lovest me"; exhaling, it responds: "I love Thee." This can be repeated for
some time. An inner distaste, due to lack of experience and
practice, may have to be conquered, but it will soon recede
and the soul will then gradually disengage itself from the actual
words which will no longer be explicitly noticed or stressed.
Thus, the "spiritual breath" will carry us quite close to God.

A prone position, too, sometimes helps the soul to be recollected. We ought to use waking periods at night to this end,
otherwise they often cause us only to be angry or to reach
for the pills. Much better to accept such waking as a gentle
reminder from God, always with us and wishing us to think
of Him lovingly, at a time, too, when probably many sins are
being committed against His sacred laws and His love. To try
to lie quite still, not actually saying any prayers but just seeking
to be with God, will benefit both the soul and the body.

God with us, we with Him; no more is needed than this loving knowledge of His being, His presence, His faithfulness.
Naturally, if we are caught up in the mad dance of our imagination, such recollection will not be easy, let alone a lasting
success. But a quiet glance toward God, when a moment's freedom from that whirling confusion is regained, will be sufficient.
We shall discuss this later.

One other exterior feature of prayer must not be overlooked:

the use of the crucifix, statue and picture. To reject these on principle would be quite wrong. Some people may never need them; others all the more. There is no fixed rule. At moments of inner dryness it is in any case much wiser to look at a crucifix, thus keeping one's eyes at least concentrated on the presence of God, than doggedly to struggle for thoughts and waste one's time. The artistic quality of the object does not matter; merely the devotion which it helps to arouse in the soul. Sometimes a fleeting glance up the image of our Crucified Lord or that of His Blessed Mother is sufficient to recover our recollection, and then we may safely dispense again with those objects.

Contents of prayer

This, too, shall here be considered under a few aspects only. While things can and, in a way, must become the object of our prayer, such a general statement is hardly ever helpful to anyone. Better to differentiate a little. To begin with, it is essential that we should have a definite purpose. No doubt, this can be contained in the desire just to be with God for a while; such closeness, such resting within Him is the "intention." Yet it is certainly good and for most of us simply necessary to have a definite object when devoting ourselves to prayer. Otherwise there is always the danger of nothing at all happening. In vocal prayer it is perhaps easiest to fall back on memorized prayers or on a prayer book. The particular choice will depend on one's actual disposition, intention and circumstance. In meditative prayer things are a bit more complex. Here the material must first be sorted, unless one prefers a book of meditations which offers well-developed and ordered thoughts. But even these, if they are not to serve merely as spiritual reading, have to be followed up inwardly, in our own mind. For example, when using the Gospels as our material, we would try to comprehend the context of a given paragraph, ponder the facts related, the words employed, and then draw specific applications. We will show later how the material thus generally prepared has to be further worked upon. Once the soul has been guided across the threshold of contemplation.

prayer will become more difficult in some ways, though easier in many others. Easier certainly as to its content, in that it is simply the divine presence, or rather the omnipresent God. No need here for the previous preparation and choice of subject matter. Conversant with the Scriptures and the books of the saints, the mind is well stored with phrases, images and examples which now come to it, more or less spontaneously, to assist its prayer. This means that the material is always now at hand, the fruit of long experience in the spiritual life or of profound insights in matters of the faith.

Two points must be especially observed: simplification of the substance of our prayer and readiness at any moment for new enlightenment from God. Both are closely connected, for God will guide us to simplicity, to ingenuousness in the exalted sense of filial love. Advancing in prayer, the soul needs less and less material. At first, more and more seems required; there is no end to the efforts made, which after a while burden the soul like a chain, clogging rather than stimulating it. There is too much to grapple with, so that none of it can receive its proper due. There is too little time for the necessary tasks because of all those self-imposed spiritual duties and practices. This can go so far as to make a person intolerable or to deprive him of all taste for prayer. A wrong way, obviously. Nothing depends on quantity; here less is truly more. Quantity is nearly always achieved at the expense of depth and true spirituality. What can God gain from all our busy chatter? Does He not know already? Does He need words? Once more, He wants our heart, and that has nothing to do with quantity; only with earnestness, devotion and concord of the will.

Thus the soul will do well to turn away again, to free itself from the excess that temporarily seemed necessary. And it will breathe again as if it had just escaped from prison. No longer will God seem so exacting that it is futile to hope ever to satisfy Him. He is the Father, looking propitiously upon the soul from which He wants nothing but itself. Now the soul is content with far less words; only a few perhaps, but those repeated often. Only now do they seem to reach down into the depths of God's unbounded love, whereas formerly several litanies seemed necessary every day. Now just an invocation, or a few at most, will suffice. Formerly meditation had to consist at least of three main points and many minor points—pages of them. Now just a sentence or a phrase will do.

To this end God, perfect simplicity in Himself, will guide the soul. But the soul must be obedient, not trying tooth and nail to stick to its self-chosen practices. When the soul senses clearly and repeatedly that God wishes to spoil this surfeit for it, that He wants gently, very gently, to teach it stillness and continuity, then it should never foolishly oppose Him, but readily follow His soft enticement and offer Him its stubborn will. Here the spiritual director's counsel should be sought and obeyed.

Finally, we would mention that prayer gains when several forms combine; for instance, vocal prayer of set formulas, quiet meditation and prayer of the heart as its results, unstudied recollection in the presence of God. It is well to leave oneself considerable scope. In the early stages, however, this may not always be feasible. At times, some forms of prayer seem impossible to use, though great efforts are made, nor should they then be employed. Later, when the various forms have been mastered, they will in a certain sense be at our ready disposal. But things will be arranged differently. While previously one form had to be linked with the next, they now seem to spring forth from one unifying center. What was an arduous ascent now ends in rich abundance. Jesus, whose vision penetrates the depths of God's being, uses a psalm, i.e., a set formula, for His prayer on the Cross, as well as individual words which He Himself fashions at that very moment. Such is the truly human way. The use of words, drawing as it does on our material existence, should not impede the totally spiritual act of the inner vision, nor should this in its turn suppress the physical aspect. We are not called to be spirits, but sanctified human beings, fashioned in the likeness of the God-Man, Jesus Christ.

Chapter 13

Final Preparation for Prayer

THE more important a thing, the more time and care are needed in its preparation. It would be irresponsible to make an off-handed effort in preparing for something of great consequence. Not that occasionally one might not succeed, but this would be a matter of chance or a special grace and not the general rule. The same is true as regards professional life, where genuine persistent achievement can hardly be expected unless preceded by serious training, thought and application. There is, of course, a difference in degree; to become a doctor demands a different training than to dig ditches or plant potatoes. But one thing is common to all: proper training will insure attainment of one's goal, when it will all become second nature. The head need not inform the hand how to manage; by this time it acts spontaneously. A rule book need no longer be studied in all its details, for now one thing will naturally follow from another. Words are no longer pondered carefully, because careful, prudent talk has become part of one. Gradually various activities and duties, at first so exacting in their prerequisites, become familiar, natural and even delightful. One would not want to be without them, would miss them if he had to give them up. Then the servant is almost like a son and heir because he moves about the house with such ease and freedom; but he knows his place and observes due respect and propriety.

"Before speaking with God prepare thy soul and be not as a man that tempteth God" (Eccl. 18:23). It is certain that yearning for God, praise, thanksgiving and remorse rise up from the heart's depths, and certain, too, that these are often the most blessed and propitious moments, but the general rule still holds true that converse with God requires preparation. It is more so in this matter than any other affair in life; more in the measure in which God is more. If He is everything, then everything must be directed toward Him, must somehow serve as a preparation. What we have considered in the preceding chapters is long-term preparation for that essential prayer which is accessory to communion between God and the soul, prayer in a strict sense. All of it is more or less indispensable. It is the formation of the whole Christian life, whence prayer rises like the bloom from the root, trunk, branch and bud. Conversely, as we have already seen, prayer continuously forms all else and molds it into something like itself. This wide and all-embracing preparation must be completed by a special effort to precede each individual act of prayer. The two are linked by a significant connection: anyone consciously cultivating the remote preparation will soon notice that the immediate preparation becomes progressively easy and simple. Conversely, people less concerned about the ordering of their whole life to God usually have much greater trouble in preparing for and persisting in actual prayer.

Again, long and faithful practice will produce ability, spontaneity, freedom and ease in our relationship with God as our Father. In prayer itself the soul experiences that He is our Father, always inclined toward us to care for, support and heal us; to forgive and encourage us. Gradually the barriers of scruples or clumsiness give way to the deeply reverent, yet infinitely natural and rewarding relationship of father and beloved child. More and more the individual acts of preparation decrease until they are condensed into one glance of faith, hope and charity; a single look that contains them all and far surpasses them. At first the various points which we shall presently consider will have to be assiduously observed. The better this is done, the sooner they will be outgrown. Later, one or another will be more strongly emphasized, following an inner impulse or some special need. Once our heart has learned to find God without prelude whenever it wishes, there would be little sense in using all the steps of preparation. The heart knows when its time has come.

Recollection

However much we may try for a recollected life, avoiding unnecessary distractions, guarding our eyes, ears and tongue, denying ourselves this and that, and above all bridling our imagination, we shall hardly ever succeed in attaining a measure of recollection sufficient for actual prayer. A special push is needed, a rejection of the distracting aspects of our daily duties, a detachment of self in order to be able fully to serve the moment, and in it God. Who would, after engaging in trifling chatter, continue to read a substantial book by just taking it up and starting where he left off several days ago? First he must recollect himself. Would anyone about to speak a word of serious warning to a friend, simply turn away from some light matter and begin? Very unlikely. Even in ordinary life a brief span separates one action from the next if what comes next is something special, something requiring a personal or professional endeavor.

One major point: in recollection as in everything concerning prayer, the will alone is the decisive factor. Sincerity and the true effort it begets determine the value or unworthiness of our performance. Though the result of our attempt to concentrate may be no more than a chain of distractions throughout the time of prayer, the value, dignity and force of our prayer will never suffer any loss if amid all this vexation we retain the firm intention to be united with God, and with Him only. Even if our praying consisted only in the struggle for recollection (and without any success at that), it would be good—indeed, very good. More of this later on. Here we would first of all forestall the error that prayer had better not begin at all if recollection seems a hopeless quest. The struggle for it is itself a prayer, and one most pleasing in the sight of God.

How shall we set about it? In the beginning it is well to call upon the imagination. First, it is a great power, and secondly, it will thus be usefully employed and prevented from being a disturbance. A wise little book on the subject suggests that we imagine ourselves standing in the center of a great expanse. Now the circumference of the expanse gently recedes until nothing is left but ourselves alone. All else is gone, forgotten, of no further interest. Entirely by oneself, one is no longer tossed about, routed, dispersed, but truly self-possessed.

Or we may dissolve the picture, following the example of the fathers of old who fled the city's din for the desert. In our mind we relinquish all—people and things, obligations, tasks—taking nothing along except ourselves, until we are safely within that immense solitude that is wholly God's and now, within Him, ours too.

Or we imagine ourselves climbing the silent slope of a mountain, on and on, leaving below all that is incapable of rising to such height, and sensing how free, how easily we breathe as things begin to fade away and only the essential stays.

Or else we may descend into the depth of our heart. More and more inward, where no one and nothing can pursue, not even our ego, that fickle, irridescent, pretentious and obtrusive reflected image that caricatures our genuine self and is the prime vexation of our life. In the desert, on the crest of the mountain, or in the hidden recess of the heart—there we find God.

Often a few brief thoughts will help. "I want nothing but Thee." "How trifling is everything else; may nothing call to me now that I long to be with Thee alone." "What is there now to captivate my heart, when it may rest in Thy beloved presence?"

Recollection becomes steadily easier and simpler. Later it is as if you gently turn the inner eye from whatever held your attention and, turning to Him, you have already reached your goal. No more distance, no effort, no struggle. We just look from one to the other, from nothingness to fullness of being, from creation to the Creator, and so we pray. Now recollection simply means recalling to the mind the presence of God ever within us, waiting.

Posture

Recollection will benefit considerably from our physical bearing. Indeed, this is, or can well be, part of it. We kneel down slowly and, with assiduous deliberation, make the Sign of the Cross. Or we begin by inclining the head as we say the Glory be to the Father, thus combining recollection, physical bearing and prayer. Or again, standing or kneeling before God, we remain quite still for some seconds. Such bearing is different from our ordinary deportment and for that very reason will promote detachment and separate us from everything around. We have stepped out of mundane profanity, of what lies "before the sanctuary," and are now within its sacred orbit.

Presence of God

To collect oneself in the first instance means disengaging oneself from and leaving behind all that is incongruous. At the same time it means an approach, seemingly one toward self, since one endeavors to gather one's self together. But this is not the goal. We must reach through and beyond self to its mysterious and transcendental roots, where our being continually originates. Our ego gathers itself beyond itself; rises, or is being carried, above itself. God is the goal. The disengagement from what is without, and nothingness, is disengagement also from self which, in a sense, is still without and certainly a nothing, and it includes the turning toward God. To this detachment and simultaneous movement toward the transcendental, we should adopt a fitting posture. Thus, recollection and bodily deportment have God as their object.

We need not search for Him. He is "not far from every one of us: in Him we live and move and are" (Acts 17:28). For the Christian this attains an even higher aspect: "I live, now not I, but Christ liveth in me" (Gal. 2:20). God, not as Creator only, but as the triune God, as Father, Son and Holy Ghost is in us. To make ourselves consciously aware of this immanence of God above us, close to us and within us, is what we call the presence of God. It does not need a distance to be covered, for God need not be urged to turn toward us. His countenance is always turned upon us. Never will He avert His eyes from us, not even when we sin. Indeed, even the damned in hell will be eternally under His gaze. It is for us to turn to Him. That is what happens in recollection, in our efforts consciously to know "Thou art in me." And let us make a habit of this "Thou." In our thoughts of God let it not be, "How good He is," but, "How good Thou art"; not, "Will He help me?" but, "Wilt Thou help me, please?" We must use every opportunity to talk directly to Him. God never is nor can be merely food for our thoughts and words about Him; He is forever and essentially the other Person through, from, and with whom thoughts and words arise that have Him for their content. Thus, inner consciousness of God is no more than a simple turning toward Him: "Thou art within me; I am with Thee now, adoring Thee." Our prayer has begun.

There has been much discussion about the usefulness of the practice of "representation," relating the presence of God to space. It would seem that in the beginning this cannot be entirely dispensed with, similar to the examples just considered with regard to recollection. Starting almost invariably in the material field, we only gradually shed sense images in order finally to reach a very pure manner of spiritual vision. The human mind gathers itself but slowly, stripping itself laboriously of the many cloaks which form the connecting link between the spiritual and the corporeal world. Nowhere perhaps do we notice this as distinctly as in our life of prayer. Hence we may certainly begin by thinking of God in terms of space and time and place. Before the tabernacle the Sacred Sacrament becomes the focus for our whole being, and experience proves that there, before "the King and center of all hearts," we find ourselves praying particularly easily and well.

In any case, a spatial association is always correct, for God is everywhere, and wherever I turn my eyes, they will meet Him, provided my faith penetrates the veil of the visible world. One thing, however, must be guarded against: to exert one's brain. This may easily happen at the start. One wishes to concentrate all his faculties on that one point where he imagines God to be, almost as if one had to bring and then hold Him there. But it is not like that. Everything must remain easy, unstudied, as one at times relaxes one's body so that it becomes supple, light, submissive, and the gentle motion of one's organic life is felt. As soon as one notices an element of tension, artificiality and tautness entering into any part or stage of one's prayer—when the head may even physically share this feeling of pressure and strain—one must immediately relax and refrain from willing anything. When beset by emotions the will is often no more than self-deceit and has only the name in common with the act of willing as a spiritual process. On these occasions, therefore, no exertions, just quiet presence before God.

Occasionally it may be helpful to create in one's mind an image of God, though usually this will be to little avail. Better to look at a real picture, as we suggested earlier. How, after all, is one to portray God to oneself? Jesus, yes, that is different and will be examined more closely under the heading of meditation. For the moment, treating generally of representing God to oneself, it seems difficult and basically futile to call up such an image; it would be fictitious anyway, as it is merely our own production.

Before long, the finding and turning toward God will become an ever more simplified and more spiritual process. We no longer look for Him outside, in front of, or next to ourselves; He is there already. One look, and we know that we have Him within us. "God is closer to each of us than we are to ourselves." He is the primeval ground from which we spring: from His creative will of love and together with His only-begotten Son, in whom God creates us and because of whom, as members of Christ, He lets us be His children through grace. "In His image and after His likeness" were we created, and it is in our most spiritual self that He is thus reflected, and where we may behold Him, though in a manner entirely different from ordinary physical vision. This is an act of our innermost spiritual self which perceives and possesses in a wholly spiritual fashion. On this level the spatial element utterly recedes and disappears, except for the one divine manifestation properly assigned to it: the Sacred Host, that substance in space chosen by the Son of Man precisely in order that He might be with us in that particular manner.

Whichever way we look, above or inside ourselves, we must remember that either one only appears to make our approach to God easier because our mind is so deeply involved with matter and space that its movements, actions and tendencies are constantly affected by its concepts. Under the appearance of movements and such like we are quite simply impressed with what is already a fact: that God is with us and we are with Him.

This representation of God in order to make Him present to us is the most essential element of our preparation. It embraces the rest and is itself the beginning of prayer, the desire for God, the invitation to Him, the welcoming of Him, the union with Him in love.

Preparatory acts

The heart's gaze on God is one of loving desire, of yearning love, an offering of self and a reaching out for God. Not originating in the head, in the judging intellect, but in the core of our being, this glance already embraces the whole of our person with all our abilities, intentions and acts. Nevertheless, one will, unfailingly in the beginning and frequently later on, even after long years of prayer, perform some of those individual acts already contained in this opening of the heart to God, in order to make the preparation and disposition for prayer particularly deliberate, alive and fruitful. Acts—the

word can only inadequately be replaced by actions or processes
—are operations and manifestations of the soul in which the
soul is fully present, its abilities, powers and faculties being
awakened from their slumber or their latency. They are, if
you will, the soul's mental arms, by which it reaches out and
seizes things or hands over itself. These acts can vary in their
substantial reality, in degrees of depth and completeness. They
can emanate from the surface or from the most hidden recess
of our being. Here too, practice is the condition for progress.
More and more is being hauled up, as it were, scooped up by
the soul which digs deeper and deeper into its own foundations.
Doing this before and in prayer, the soul carries itself to God,
stands before Him and looks upon Him. Once more, this is a
matter of the will, and only the will determines the value of
these acts and their continued efficacy. It may well be that
they simply do not come off, but in our will and by it they
nevertheless have reality. We can hardly impress sufficiently
upon ourselves the fact that in all our relationships with God,
and therefore also in our life of prayer in all its stages and
spheres, it is always and only the will, stimulated and carried
by grace, that decides the issue, and never any particular
result, any feeling, experience, or vision as such.

The fundamental act is faith. We are here concerned with
the theological virtue emanating from and relating to God
and bestowed upon us in baptism by the Holy Ghost as a seed,
an incomplete beginning. Here, at the initial moment of
prayer, it refers primarily to the fact revealed to us of God's
omnipresence and of His presence here and now. "My God,
Thou art truly here, I believe in Thy glorious and all-lovable
presence." This act reaches yet further toward the whole of
God's essence. In this act the soul in the state of grace or at
any rate impelled by grace does not now distinguish individual
divine qualities but, together with Christ in the power of the
Holy Ghost, it looks upon God's being. "I believe in Thee,
Thou art God, Thou art all, in and above everything."

Of itself this act of faith becomes an act of adoration, of

deep reverence before God in a more or less distinct consciousness of Him as all, and of myself, praying before Him,
as a mere nothing by comparison. The soul need not express
this explicitly. If it is able to remain for a moment before God
and to be deeply affected by His infinite presence and majesty,
all is well.

Adoration at once turns into an act of renunciation, of self-
abandonment to this immeasurable depth of divine life and
essence. Since of myself I am nothing, since all I am, I am
through and in God, how could I now not let go of myself
entirely, deliver myself to His will, throw myself into His
arms, my eyes turned wholly away from myself and centered
solely on Him? "Thou who art all, take me entirely. Thine I
am now and ever, as Thou art mine. Lord, take me away from
myself and make me all Thine, without reservation, and in
and with me do according to Thy pleasure, always, and especially now while I am praying."

This attitude already contains the second theological virtue,
hope, that supernatural trust which is in no way dependent on
our own vision, volition or ability, but quite exclusively upon
God, whose being is pure fidelity. There is hardly anything
more exquisite, more soothing and relaxing, than this perfectly
trusting abandonment of oneself to God. "Cast all your cares
on Him" (I Pet. 5:7), we read; all of them, not just this one
or that. Concern for myself, what of it? God is all that matters.
I have had enough of myself, more than enough. What a gift,
that I may now have Him instead. He will give Himself to
me in the measure in which there is room for Him within me.
In the measure, that is, of my abandoning and forgetting
myself. Thus introduced, our prayer is by this time well on
the way and has already reached a high level. This is the
ascent to the spheres of infinity, where the soul no longer
looks for a branch on which to perch but, spreading its wings,
it flies through ethereal regions, weightless, at peace, hardly
moving its wings as the celestial spheres bear it away.

So to relinquish oneself trustingly is the beginning of love, is itself love, the final and perfecting act of our preparation, the third and most noble of the theological virtues which, by baptismal regeneration, miraculously and mysteriously mirrors within the soul God's inner being. "God is Love" (I John 4:8), and the soul will be love in the measure of and through its approach to Divine Love. In love all things reach their summit, our relationship with God more than anything else. Love is the ultimate and essential content of prayer and consequently the completing act in its preparation. Now, love means total conformity; its other name, one might say, is "Thy will be done." Christ says: "Whoever does My Father's will, he it is that loves Me." Conformity in everything between ourselves and God, that is perfect love. As a preparatory act for prayer it might therefore express itself as follows: "I want Thee, my God, and Thee alone. I want Thee as the measure of my existence in everything, even in what is humblest and seemingly an utter trifle. For in Thy sight nothing is insignificant as long as it bears the mark of Thy holy will and consent. I will as Thou wilt, what Thou wilt; now in my prayer and later, and always, forever." Thus our heart, by an act of the will, completes its renunciation, its self-dedication, its unstinting surrender. "Thou art all, Thou and Thou alone my sufficiency. I want but Thee, Thy will in everything. Thy coming and Thy blessing and Thy loving, all is mine." If we allow our prayer to be heralded by such acts and by the attitude they presuppose and strengthen, we are sure to pray well. We shall not lose ourselves on our interior way. God will support us, for His love cannot deceive nor disappoint us ever. He wants our heart. What He will do with it, let that be His concern, He will take care of it better than we.

Chapter 14

Vocal Prayer

THE path which leads us to the love of God has been traced. Not that it is necessary to know all these things before beginning the journey; on the contrary, only as we make our way along this path do we gradually see its pattern, recognize its characteristics, and walk with growing assurance. It is like the slow ascent of a mountain; the road winds and turns, sometimes the view is obstructed, sometimes there are wide vistas of the landscape below. At certain points, sections of the scenery will reappear almost exactly as they looked before, yet somehow different, forming part of a wider background until eventually, from the summit, the eye encompasses the whole expanse and for the first time appreciates the distances, the various levels, and the relations between the different parts through which the wanderer had been led. A mountain range, previously almost hidden, is now spread before us in its full splendor and magnificence; a brook, crossed at many points yet hitherto seen only piecemeal, now clearly reveals its source, descent and destination. Much which previously appeared vague or inscrutable is now enlightened and one knows that not a few things would be done differently were he to come this way again.

The way of prayer offers a similar experience. Even apparently trivial hints, including those which are readily appreciated and promptly put into practice, are subsequently shown to possess much greater depth and wisdom, so that in retrospect we understand that if we had not acted upon these seemingly simple hints, we would never have reached the present level; or again, had we grasped their full importance right away, we would have observed them much more scrupulously.

So often in the life of prayer the real issue is one of confidence, of trust in God and His Church, and in the wisdom of those to whom the light of grace is given in greater measure for the instruction of others and whom the Church sets before us as counsellors and models. There is so much that cannot be proved as effective and whose effectiveness we can, in accordance with such proof, merely test and confirm by subsequent action. Instead, we must accept things on trust, believing in and acting upon the experience of others until similar experiences of our own prove the wisdom of their counsel.

If we now attempt to represent the life of prayer in its three most clearly distinguishable stages, we do not wish to imply that the first stage must be left behind for the sake of the second, and this in turn for the sake of the third. In a certain sense such a leaving behind does in fact take place, but the inferior phase will be met again on a higher plane, pushing new and deeper roots and only now fully unfolding itself. From good meditation will spring a more intimate and ardent, a more spiritual vocal prayer; and although contemplation, while actually being experienced, allows no room for any other form of prayer, it will afterwards lend to oral prayers an increased depth and serenity far beyond anything previously possible. And what has been given on one occasion in contemplation may, at another time, become the fruitful subject of an unusually rewarding meditation.

In particular it is grossly foolish to assume that vocal prayer will gradually become entirely superfluous and that essentially it is but a lesser and inferior form of prayer. As if Christ, in the Our Father, had meant to teach us something that was second-rate, not to mention His own formulated prayers. No doubt in the beginning, vocal prayer will for the most part be rather flat and uninspired, something as yet imperfect.

How could it be otherwise? It is precisely through the later forms that it attains to the fullness of its own development. And it is certain that some people—possibly quite a few—will, through the practice of vocal prayer, attain these later forms as well when, under the guidance of the Holy Ghost, the manner of their vocal prayer is imperceptibly changed so that in this one form they gradually acquire facility in the others, until eventually all merge in exquisite harmony. There is no need at this point to examine these questions more closely, except to discountenance certain mistaken ideas and, more especially, to warn against that false and precious spirituality which is one of the principal pitfalls of the higher forms of prayer, and one of the safest and most ingenious hiding-places of our pride and arrogance. Those who consider vocal prayer to be too "unspiritual" have reason to be ashamed of themselves, because they have obviously not even begun to understand what is meant by "spirit," the human spirit which, in the person of the God-Man, was sublimely consecrated and ennobled.

What, exactly, is the vocal prayer? It is a prayer present in the mind in such a manner that it may be formed with the lips and be pronounced. Not, therefore, something which is merely formed with the lips; that would be no prayer at all, but merely an exercise in elocution or an impertinence against the Almighty. "This people honoreth Me with their lips, but their heart is far from Me" (Isa. 29:13). And so it dishonors Him. Prayer is either a form of conversation with God in faith, hope and charity or it is simply nothing. Just as you cannot "talk at" a person heedlessly, without somehow meaning him, and without intending to maintain or enter into some form of relationship, in the same way, only more so, it is impossible merely to "talk at" God without thereby somehow being with Him.

The experiences gained by the spirit can only partly be transferred into the sphere of verbal expression and thus be made communicable. The more sublime the spiritual experience, the more difficult is this transfer, until it becomes posi-

tively impossible. St. Paul talks of mystical experiences in
prayer which he cannot—indeed, may not—put into words. At
some point the distance between God and created matter becomes unbridgeable. Although the range of what can be expressed, delineated, or somehow represented is astonishingly
wide, it is never all-embracing. The purely spiritual, the
absolute Word of God, the Son, is the perfect image of God,
so perfect that we confess it to be essentially the same; yet
when this Word translates Himself into human nature, the
spiritual part of His human nature is quite incapable of render-
ing the Word whole and undiminished, and even more so the
body can never fully reveal and represent the immanent divinity. True, it somehow expresses the divine nature, even to
being worthy of adoration, but never completely. A writer
will hardly ever be fully satisfied with the expression which he
has given to his thoughts. God, admittedly, is satisfied because
in the order of His being that which is, is equal to that which
ought to be, yet something always remains inexpressible, and
this something is infinity.

Never, therefore, can all that the mind experiences in and
through God be made to appear in words, neither in those
which are merely thought nor in those which are spoken. It
is in this sense that vocal prayer remains imperfect, but it is
the imperfection of the created being which, since it results
from the will of the Creator, is both its honor and its sacred
dignity, beloved by God.

In the correct use of vocal prayer there is a resilient unity, a
vital wholeness which the mind sees and understands, a living
unity such as exists, basically, between the soul and the body,
but here applied to something specific. By the word the mind
grasps, possesses, handles an idea. The word is the medium of
this possession, and in prayer it is the medium of possessing
God in love and reverence, just as in shaking hands with someone whom we love or respect, our soul somehow possesses this
other person. There is more here than the mere throwing of a
bridge as a means of "crossing over"; more also than merely

grasping the other's hand. In taking his hand into mine I do in fact somehow take possession of the whole of his being. Why, if it were not so, would one occasionally hesitate or even flatly refuse to shake hands or, conversely, look forward to doing so, as a special privilege? So, also, with the word; it is not something standing between the mind and its object, but is the manner in which this object becomes present in the mind, exists in it, focusing the mind's attention and interest. True vocal prayer, not the mere recitation of set formulas, means "being with God," and vitally so. The word of the soul, empowered by the love of the Holy Ghost, wings its way into the Word, and in that most holy Word ours, too, stands before the Father, is with Him, and partakes of His divine life.

Whether the word formed within will actually be formulated and spoken is frequently a matter of circumstance. Sometimes one simply cannot do it; it is as if the lips refuse to cooperate. Unless one is under a special obligation, one should not force oneself too much; no more than is needed to ascertain that it is not simply a question of moods or sloth. Such an inhibition is not a perfection, since we are, in principle, capable of expressing our thoughts in words and in so doing we attain self-realization. What can be formulated internally should be capable of external expression, and when it is a question of homage rendered to God by the whole of our human nature, expression through the spoken word cannot always be dispensed with. God certainly desires us to "honor Him with our lips," as long as they are the instrument of our heart.

Set formulas of vocal prayer

At first the set formula of prayer which we find ready for use will appear rigid, immovable, lifeless. One might compare it with a crust of lava, dead and hard and frozen, seemingly devoid of all fertility. Yet this same lava, once erupted from the earth as a molten stream of passionate mobility, possesses the power to set on fire, to change the face of the surrounding countryside by piling up mountains and leveling valleys;

creative certainly, yet sweeping away much that was dear to the people. All our formulas of prayer were once such eruptions of spiritual fire, of a holy agitation in the depth of the soul in which it was born. Breaking through to the surface, it took shape, became fixed in the word, was heard, recorded and passed on to others. At the root of any valid formula there has always been the vital encounter between God and the soul, and it is in proportion to the soul's degree of holiness and the depth and intensity of its encounter with God that the formula will be more valuable, more precious and tempered. No need for it to be extensive; on the contrary, the most beautiful ones are often the briefest and most concise. St. Francis' "My God and my All" says incomparably more than whole pages filled with the outpourings of a common garden piety. How ineffably precious are the prayerful ejaculations of Christ Himself, recorded in the Gospels. And the Lord's Prayer far transcends anything that mere man has ever been able to formulate; it is worth more than the profoundest visions of contemplation because it already contains and embraces them all.

Yet, while the set formula may perfectly express the thought of the soul in which it originated, it cannot fill the same function in all the souls that will use it later. It must gain new and individual vitality in each of us. Lava must first be broken up —deliberately or by the elements—before it develops that unusual degree of fertility which will make things grow and flower on it in rare profusion. In the same way we must transform and integrate the adopted formula so that it may become the vehicle of our personal communication with God. And here we mean not only that the formula merely reflects our present spiritual life, but that it adds a life of its own to which we should respond. When these two elements coalesce, our prayer is taking shape. There is a similarity here to the reading of a novel or of a poem. We must first read ourselves "into" it, must somehow "get inside," until gradually our mind begins to feel at ease, at home even, and reluctant to leave.

We have at our disposal innumerable set formulas of prayer; there is scarcely a disposition of soul or a desire of the heart that has not, at some time or other, been brought before God in terms both beautiful and telling. Consider the sacred texts offered to us by the Church. Here is a wealth so immeasurable that it can never be exhausted. The Missal, the Breviary and the Roman Ritual, their very mention suffices, as well as the psalms, hymns sequences, the prayers of the saints, litanies and the Rosary. No one need be lacking; indeed, one may more properly ask how we are to cope adequately with such super-abundance. In any case, we would do well to choose our prayers from this treasury and to dispense with many of the prayer books which contain little that is truly profound and much—too much—that is emotionally overcharged. Books of this kind tend to misguide the soul and certainly do not lead it upwards. That they are easy and comfortable is no recom-mendation; the Our Father is easy too, but comfortable? And if one prays it well, does it really remain easy? Does it not gradually change and indeed reform us altogether, if only we let ourselves be claimed by its holy power?

The set formula of prayer is useful for two main reasons. First, it is always there, waiting for us, even when we are wholly incapacitated before God, distracted, tired, helpless, or when we do not know how to express the things that move us. Then the formula comes to our rescue, placing itself on our lips and enabling us to express our sentiments. Rather than torment itself in a vain search for the fitting words, the heart can act immediately upon its primary urge: to talk to the Father and to unburden itself. And in the light reflected by the formula's own content, our poor heart at long last understands itself. "Yes, that's what I mean and what I wanted to say." With the formula serving as a stepping stone, the soul swiftly ascends and throws itself into the arms of its beloved Father and Friend. Dumb before, it now is able to talk. In using the splendid prayers of the liturgy and of the saints, the soul will also avoid a most dangerous misconception: that in talking to

God it is necessary to use high-sounding words. In fact, this will merely do serious harm to the warmth and naturalness of one's relations to God, and it may even freeze the soul in a stiffly formal attitude, in forced and solemn courtesy. Of such absurdities the prayers of the Church and of her saints are serenely free. They have a simple grandeur; they are clean and compact in form, unassuming and yet immensely pregnant and precise in expression. They avoid all artificiality, all exaltation, frills, and insincerities. Like a spiritual bath, they heal the soul that is prone to such diseased aberrations, make it sane, simple, and straight again, communicating to it their own sureness, ease and clarity, until its whole bearing and behavior is transformed. Through them Mother Church imperceptibly educates her children.

The other reason for the set formula's especial usefulness lies in its capacity to uplift us. How terribly narrow is the scope of our prayer, if left to itself. Granted, we do pray, but for what? There is almost nothing that is not centered on self, or on those nearest to self—a miserly concern for what touches *me*. And there is far too much begging, an excessive preoccupation with mundane things. The set formula frees us from this terrible provincialism of the heart, from the lack of purpose and aim, because it was born in a great and generous mind whose noble thoughts it still contains. Unless we repeat these prayers in a meaningless babble, we cannot but be absorbed and elevated by them. For example, consider the prayers of preparation in the Mass; whoever recites them attentively must feel how his heart is simply carried away into new depth and expansion, from self to "those who stand around us," to all the living, to all the faithful departed and, finally, when the chalice is offered, to "all the world," so that they, like ourselves, may receive salvation from Christ's sacrifice of love. Thus the soul, however self-centered it may have been before, is gently drawn, nay, forced to be catholic in the most beautiful sense of the word. And if it prays like this often, it will be completely changed. All its hidden and seemingly withered finest possibilities are awakened and brought to light, and the soul finds itself in and through these prayers by which it is cleansed and ennobled. They will lead to heights never scaled before, where views will open hitherto undreamed of. Now the soul knows with wondrous certainty that at last it has found its true life and purpose. Hastening toward God, it is aware of a growing maturity, and although in its very progress it realizes, more vividly than before, how great is the distance that still separates it from the Father's grandeur and nobility. Nonetheless it advances, joyously conscious of such heavenly grace. All this is owed to the depth and the power of the "formula," the key to an entirely new world. "Tell me who your friends are." That saying has the particular validity with regard to our choice of the appropriate forms of prayer, because they determine the manner of our intercourse with God. The prayers left to us by the saints, and those of the Church, never cease to educate us further; forever they reveal to the soul things that are new and hitherto unnoticed. As the saint towers above us, so his prayers transcend our own, and they may, in their depth and power, raise us to his side. Here again, and in profound reverence, the Our Father may be especially mentioned.

There are no absolutely infallible ways to sanctification, and no infallible method whose simple application would guarantee success. And there is no form of life which is not, in one way or another, endangered until it has become one with the perfection of the divine life itself. More even; inexorably what is most precious is most imperilled, most exposed to abuse and corruption. Consequently, the prayer of the set formula is not immune to misuse, unless it is nursed with care, unless it is properly looked after. It is possible for this type of prayer to degenerate into something which, to a deeply religious person, would be obnoxious and revolting, and would kill every desire for external religious observance. Not only when—as is sometimes the case—one's life, in spite of much verbal prayer, remains defective, but even the act of prayer itself can, in its use or rather misuse, become repugnant and an insult to God and man. It can be debased to a purely mechanical function, to which the Tibetan prayer-wheel might well be preferred since of a mere gadget none would expect a human effort. The soul remains hidden behind the empty rattle of prayers and one counts out the number of words and is well content with this. And if by such senseless repetition of mere words one should even attempt to force God's hand (*Deum fatigare*, to tire God out, the heathens called it), then such prayer resembles those magic practices which are the very caricature of the true relationship between God and His creatures. True, such depths of corruption may hardly ever be plumbed even by the most superficial Christians, yet the possibility of this ultimate perversion does exist. Here then lies the first danger of the prayer of the set formula: that it may be considered efficacious as a formula, by itself, and all the more so if it was originally coined by someone of great religious significance. The true meaning is lost and the accent is purely on the formal effort.

The other, much more common, danger consists in the inadequate assimilation of the formula. Our efforts inwardly to grasp its full meaning remain insufficient and we do but thoughtlessly scrape the surface. Hence it cannot come to life in us; it can communicate only a fraction of its riches. We fail to consummate the full union between our own aspirations and the formula's objective content, and so we likewise fail to attain, through its mediation, the source from which it sprang: the personal relationship between God and the inspired soul. This danger is all the more prevalent as the formula will soon be known by heart, so that it can be repeated almost mechanically while our thoughts roam elsewhere. And since distraction does not prevent the prayer of the set formula, but merely invalidates it, the will must strive again and again to focus the mind on the formula's inner essence.

Nothing comes right of itself, good prayer least of all. If the prayer of the set formula is not to do us harm, but lead us to God, we must observe a number of things. First, never to pray too fast. Speed has as much in common with holiness as has quantity, which is precisely nothing. Advancing too swiftly, we can never penetrate; we may scrape the surface, but we shall never penetrate the depths. We should accustom ourselves to proceed steadily and with deliberation, and if pressed for time we should rather leave something out than try to finish the prayer in a hasty babble. Here "less" is really "more." Even if we fret and fidget, whipped by the inexorable "faster, faster," we must force ourselves to formulate the words even more slowly than is our custom, and must say to ourselves: "I have plenty of time—more than enough—especially for Thee, dear Lord. I am happy to be with Thee, and nothing shall make me shorten the brief moments which are to be Thine."

And in between we should often pause. In the Our Father, for example, first we might say it with moderate speed, request following upon request; and then we might say it once more, but now with a pause after every two petitions. We can be fully "there" in the first method, yet each new request almost seems to jostle the previous one before it has had a chance to unfold itself and impregnate the soul. But when we pause, each petition gains full resonance, an arc of silence forms around it within which it reverberates, standing quite by itself with all its earnestness, depth and yearning. The opening words: "Our Father," now somewhat detached from those that follow, begin to radiate in all their mysterious beauty, tenderness and power, penetrating into the very depth of the soul to rouse it, to make it ready and receptive. So, too, with the succeeding petitions, each one now sounds its own note, not mingled with those of the others, and with amazement we perceive the true splendors hidden behind their apparent insignificance.

What we have tried to explain—using the Our Father as an example—may be practiced with all formulated prayers. Not always, of course, but once in a while, now with this prayer, now with another. Sometimes also with a litany—and how richly does it unfold before our mental eye, especially when we notice that frequent use is "blunting the edge" of a particular prayer, that it pales and loses its appeal. Then we should try this method, and all will be as new. Each day we should work through one of our prayers in this way. But let there be no misunderstanding; the point here is not that, having thus singled out the various pieces, we should then consider them individually, think them over, and deductively arrive at certain precepts. We are not here concerned with meditative prayer, but merely with the need to let each invocation stand a while before our inner eye, and we pause before it and let it gently permeate us.

This manner of praying is excellent training for the soul. It teaches it to be calm before God, to be less agitated, to learn to wait, and not to exaggerate the importance of its own endeavors. It may thus become a step toward the prayer of contemplation, so far as the soul is capable of making a positive contribution of its own. That St. Elizabeth took one hour to say the Our Father clearly shows the degree of recollectedness in God to which these few words may lead us, if only we give them time to do so.

All this is made much easier if one is careful not to say too many verbal prayers, and particularly not to repeat the same ones too often in succession. It does the soul no good if it goes on adding yet another Our Father, one for one's parents, one for the poor souls, one for this intention and one for that. An increase in numbers usually means an increase in speed; after all, we must "get through." Concentration is bound to flag; subconsciously one argues that if this one does not come off too well, one can always do better with the next. To stop this we need only content ourselves with one Our Father, and, indeed, one is powerful enough to bring before the Father everything that we have at heart.

Does not Christ tell us: "And when you are praying, speak not much, as the heathens, for your Father knoweth what is needful for you, before you ask Him" (Matt. 6:7)? As we have said before, what matters is not that we should expain things to God, but that we should arouse in ourselves a proper attitude receptive for His love. And to achieve this we must not pray much, but we must pray well.

But do we not have the Rosary? Most certainly, and we say it gladly. But the Rosary is not a mere formula; it is a prayer which, through meditation, would lead us to contemplation. By its ultimate purpose the Rosary is decidedly a contemplative prayer, and those whom it will not lead thus far, have probably never prayed it right, and well. When prayed properly, the mind does not dwell on the content of the formula-prayers, of each Our Father and Hail Mary—even though time and again the mental eye is caught by their beauty, and the holy words are in a singular manner woven into the pattern of our mental disposition, of our being-with-God. No; the true essence of the Rosary is the mysteries, those tremendous truths of the faith into which the soul is initiated in adoration.

In like manner we should approach the repetition of formulated prayers which the Church imposes as a condition for gaining plenary indulgences, usually six Our Fathers, Hail Marys, and Glory be's for the intention of the Holy Father. They can, of course, be prayed as such, but in that case it becomes a very great effort to remain fully recollected right to the end. It may be that this effort is to be our particular penance. If this is so, then the stress would here lie not on the manner of our praying, but on the penance implied in the labor of the prayer's performance. No doubt we may thus understand it, but why should we not detect here a hint from Mother Church, anxious always to guide us upwards into contemplation, as the highest form of prayer? There, as we have said, these repetitive prayers would shed their particular content, to serve merely as an impulse for the heart to turn itself entirely to God. Under His loving gaze the mouth obediently forms the words while the heart, transcending them, dwells upon their inexpressible content. True, such prayer would lose its character as an effort, but is not ultimate perfection effortless? The accomplishment of the champion is not mainly effort, it is mastery.

What we have just considered will help to give ever-increasing depth to the prayer of the set formula. But we may also aim at greater breadth; this, too, will guard against shallowness and boredom. Variety should, of course, not spring from mere whim, from that inner restlessness which forever frets to have and to test something new. This is a deadly enemy of all spiritual life. Instead, the change must be carefully thought out, and orderly, and to this order, though self-imposed, we must feel committed.

Variety will have its place, first of all, in our daily prayers since they, more than all others, are prone to degenerate into mere routine. Our attention is no longer properly engaged; everything has become too easy, too familiar. If then, suddenly, we must change course, leaving the smooth rail of habit; if we must actually read a prayer, because we do not yet know it by heart, then this will be like a warning signal. We pause, collect ourselves, and are again, in a new manner, alerted.

We may, for example, select prayers from the liturgy which fit the particular time of year as well as our own requirements. At Christmastime, at Easter, and on all Sundays the *Gloria* from the Mass serves as a splendid opening chord for the day, a magnificent act of dedication of our whole being to the triune God. On special feast days we may use the *Credo* from the Mass instead of the ordinary short one. And to express gratitude, joy, the wholeheartedness of our consent, the current Preface with the *Sanctus*. In the evening, as the conclusion of a brief examination of conscience, the *Confiteor* and the short prayers that follow. At Pentecost, the beautiful Sequence, *Veni Sancte Spiritus*, or the *Veni Creator*. During the Octave of Corpus Christi, the hymn composed by St. Thomas Aquinas, *Adoro te devote latens deitas*, or the sequence and hymns from the Missal or Breviary, all so easily accessible. In times of emergency and stress, inspiration may be drawn from the texts of the Votive Masses or from the prayers for special intentions: for peace, for protection against the enemies of the Church, for those in peril or travelling, for the reunification of Christendom in the one true Catholic faith. The intermediate prayers of the Mass—Introit, Gradual, Tract, Offertory—are often indescribably beautiful and readily evoke a rich variety of thought and emotion; the mind retains them easily and they accompany us throughout our day, the mark of good prayer.

A wealth of material is also offered by the litanies. No need to say them in their entirety; we may take just a section, pronouncing the invocations slowly, with pauses in between. The litanies, too, may be selected according to the calendar of the Church: the feasts of our Lady, the First Fridays, the month of the Holy Souls, etc.

As for the psalms, if we become familiar with them through a really good translation, we will find in them countless verses into which the heart may gather all that it thinks and feels, all its manifold aspirations, its hopes and fears, its gratitude and remorse, and carry it all to God.

Lastly we may mention the *Hymnal*, in which the Church has hymns which we may use profitably throughout the year, but especially during Advent.

In family prayers—and wherever possible these should be practiced and cultivated—variety may be developed by assigning certain prayers to each member of the family circle. Or let each select his or her prayers and there will be a most noble competition in which heaven will delight. The children, especially, will thus form a most precious habit. One could even try to keep a record of the prayers selected for each liturgical season so that the diligence of the present generation would be preserved for the use and edification of later ones. Such a record would make a real family prayer book, full of pure and valuable mementos.

For prayers at meal times one would do well to use one of the standard prayers. They should not be too long, but brisk and concise, a lifting of the eyes, and a warm "thank you" rather than a lengthy before or after dinner speech.

Variety also means—as we indicated earlier—that the different forms of prayer should all be given scope. Especially in group prayers it is necessary to allow time for silence, provided that everybody present knows what to do with it: to give thanks, to adore, to make an examination of conscience, and to repent. And just before the end there should be another pause, so that each may concentrate on a particular intention and may also learn, for brief moments, to be wordless before God.

In conclusion, let us revert once more to the Mass. It is certainly true that we should not pray during the Mass, but should *pray the Mass*. That does not mean, however, that we must always follow closely the words that are spoken at the altar. However much it is to be desired that the faithful should use missals, the constant close attention to all the changing texts of the Mass can lead to shallowness and a mechanical performance unless these texts are at the same time deeply pondered and unless we try to make them subjects for meditation. There is certainly no harm in leaving out a few of these texts, especially if the priest reads the Mass rapidly, in order to attend to the remainder with greater concentration. Thus, at the beginning one could concentrate on the *Confiteor* and the little prayers that follow, then the *Gloria* and the Collect, Gradual, Gospel and *Credo*. Of the Offertory only the first three prayers, followed by the Secret and the Preface, and so through the whole of the Mass. Such a selection would give us everything that is essential, without overtaxing us. Occasionally we may do without the missal, praying inwardly in close relation to the unfolding of the sacred ceremony, offering to God whatever is fitting from the things which we read in our own heart, but guided by the relevant unchanging liturgical texts with which we are sufficiently familiar. Indeed, though this will offend the ears of the liturgical purists, even the Rosary may be said during Mass, provided we see to it that the mysteries selected are intimately related to what happens at the altar, a discipline which one will learn without difficulty. Here, too, variety becomes a most valuable aid for "praying the Mass," liberating us at the same time from that servility to the letter which some are prone to recommend as the truly liturgical attitude. The freedom of the children of God, the heart's holy freedom in its relation to the Father in heaven, ranks higher than any text, however venerable.

Free vocal prayer

Vocal prayer need not be restricted to set formulas. It may well up quite freely, or it may borrow from the formulated prayers previously learned by heart, as was done by our Lady in the *Magnificat*. Originally the formulas themselves arose in this free and spontaneous manner, and it was some time before they were cast in their now familiar shape. And in using these inherited texts, each of us makes them his own by alterations and additions which mark the progress of this inner appropriation.

Most natural, and therefore most desirable, is the unhampered talking with God the Father, spontaneously rising from within. In greeting his father a son may, at times, use certain standard phrases; on occasion he may also recite to him something that others wrote down, or some well-pondered composition of his own. But mostly he will simply say what comes into his mind, will describe things spontaneously as they strike him. This natural relationship—informal and yet full of reverence—is what should be developed more and more between the children of heaven and God their Father. Were it not to exist at all, one would be bound to suspect that something was deeply wrong, for it is impossible for a child to be so awkward, dumb or reticent before such a Father.

There is an intermediate stage linking formulated prayer with the spontaneous prayer which we call ejaculatory prayers. A brief raising of the heart to God: "Most Sacred Heart of Jesus, have mercy on me"; "Lord, I believe in Thy love for me, make me love Thee ever more"; or just the simple: "Thanks be to God." An emotion or mood, a feeling of anxiety or relief, and the heart turns to God and gives expression to the things that move it. These prayers have the advantage of taking very little time, but more important, they serve as connecting links between the various regular daily prayers with their fixed times and forms. Not only in the morning, at noon, and at night ought the heart to be with God, but again and again, and always gladly. To illustrate; a busy craftsman may only in the morning, at table, or after working hours find time to talk to his wife—about the children, an important purchase, or some trouble bothering him—but they will hardly for that reason pass each other in silence for the rest of the day. No lengthy conversation, perhaps, but proof of companionship, of close intimacy which is cultivated and expressed by these short remarks. They are like the links of a chain, joining these two together in a bond of mutual understanding.

So, too, with our ejaculations; they establish and make manifest a relationship between the soul and God which is never wholly interrupted. And because of this important function— "prayer without fainting"—the Church has endowed many ejaculations with indulgences, to signify the esteem in which she holds them and to encourage their use. This does not mean that one should say them simply "on account" of the indulgences; that would completely reverse the proper order of things, though perhaps in the beginning this may be the prime reason, just as a child may at first willingly fetch something from the grocer for the sake of the reward which the mother has promised, but later it will realize that it is not the reward that matters but the pleasure which it gives its mother by this proof of its love and obedience, though it will like getting the reward all the same. The same is true for prayer and indulgences attached thereto. Those who have learned the frequent use of ejaculations will no longer be interested in adding up the total of indulgences obtained; they will, from love of God, pray anyhow, and the indulgences will be "thrown in."

Occasions for ejaculatory prayer are offered incessantly, and it is up to us to notice them. The enchantment of nature's beauties or a minor fault committed once again; an irritation to be mastered or a joy to thank God for; someone passing whose aspect roused feelings of distaste; each time we can so

123]

easily reach out to Him who holds us constantly in His regard, lives in us and waits for us. The magnificent *Gloria Patri*, why don't we repeat it more often, quietly to ourselves, addressing praise and adoration to Him who lives within us, and thus attain to that "walking in heaven" of which St. Paul has written? Soon, other prayers will rise spontaneously, personal ones no longer cast in any definite mold.

Ejaculatory prayer rises truly from the heart. Far less deliberate than the set formula which we use with purpose and resolve, the ejaculations simply come forth. From the abundance of the heart the mouth speaks. Formulated prayer may be likened to water flowing through a canal, useful indeed, but somehow hemmed in, controlled, artificial. Free prayer wells and surges like a mountain brook, sweeps and sparkles like a river, like a mighty stream, to end up as an ocean, all-embracing. It is sometimes called "prayer of affection," i.e., prayer which originates in the soul when it is somehow affected, when it is moved or touched inside. It is certainly performed as a free act, but performed less in self-determination than in being guided and lifted up by God.

Naturally, free prayer is not limited to those brief and occasional utterances just referred to. It tends to occupy more and more space. Slowly it will replace many formulas hitherto used happily and often. The soul finds it odd to read things to God and always to use thoughts formulated by others. Why should I not speak to the Father in my own way? Surely He wants to hear my own voice, too, in the mighty symphony of living adoration, the voice that He Himself gave and created, the tongue which, through the Holy Ghost, He loosened and "whereby we cry: Abba, Father" (Rom. 8:15). Any formula may then become positively irritating, and the soul now frees itself. It talks naturally, without restraint, conscious of a wonderful nearness to the Father, and of His utter comprehension, however silent He may be. Suddenly the heart is filled with a deeper understanding, and with things to say to God which seem to know no end. There is so much now that can be said, that must be said, and that the heart ardently wants to say.

To pray becomes a deepfelt joy and urge, a passionate longing. Not always, but often. The heart feels that God draws it closer to Himself and claims it for Himself, that it must practice denial of some of the things hitherto loved and exercised, that faults must be fought with more vigor and noble impulses nurtured with care. Increasingly, in talking to God the soul will find itself arrested, will discover itself reiterating certain words as if "caught" by them: "God alone is enough," "My God and my All," or "Lord, to whom shall we go?" (John 6:69), or simply "Father" or "Thou." The soul will not weary of repeating them softly, tenderly, over and over again.

Here, but faintly, the contours of a very different mode of prayer become discernible. Precisely because it is no longer bound in the strict external discipline of the pre-cast formula, this type of prayer demands an even greater fidelity and faithfulness. It is much more delicately poised, a winging to and fro between the soul and God, more tender and more intimate, and therefore also frailer and more endangered. There are deeper pitfalls, and much more is now demanded from our entire way of life. At this point the guidance which we mentioned earlier is needed more often, and just because everything appears to fall into place effortlessly and we are seemingly well set on the direct road to the Divine Heart, orientation through those who actually do know the way is all the more necessary. This is a stage in which our heart is exposed to gravest tribulations and disappointments which might block further progress either completely or at least for a long time.

Evidently, such prayer, rising so freely and naturally from our innermost depth and carrying the heart to God with such assurance, must be most precious. Already the influence of the Holy Spirit is more marked. The soul's individuality is awakened and the inner countenance, the eternal and mysterious thought of God, becomes more clearly outlined. The contact with God, our nearness to Him in life and in being, is more distinct and noticeable and governs our days and actions much more forcefully than the previous form of prayer. The heart becomes aware of its increasing love. With this kind of prayer distraction is virtually impossible because free prayer consists essentially in that perfect harmony in which the soul finds for itself the most adequate expression of its own spontaneous thought. A poem known by heart can easily be recited even while our thoughts are elsewhere, but when we wish to repeat something which we have only recently considered, thought and formulated, we must be wholly attentive to the words. Were our thoughts to become arrested elsewhere, we would talk nonsense, choose the wrong expression, and sound ridiculous. Talking to God by myself and in words of my own, I must collect myself before Him, must be recollected.

This mode of prayer has its danger, too. Because it is so subjective, we may be tempted to overemphasize the personal element, particularly by way of emotional excesses, and may thus imperceptibly be led back to the same self-centered love which, for the sake of God, we were trying to abandon. True, our emotional life, the strength and power of our senses and of their nobler objects—all this is now to be activated, to be focused on God and thus be given its proper place. This is God's moment to remove the soul from the many baser things which attracted the senses and aroused the emotions so that we were preoccupied unduly and led away from Him, not only into frequent and prolonged distraction, but also into fault and sin. Even in a purely mundane sense, the experience of a deep and abiding love may redeem a life of misdemeanor because it focuses desire on goals of a higher, nobler and truly worthy order. Similarly, in allowing His own incomparable attractiveness to play upon the soul, God wants to rouse it and make it turn to Him with a passion strong enough to make it forget, or at least gain a certain distance from, all other things.

Giving free rein to our emotions, the soul gains a measure of freedom, but at the same time it becomes emotionally bound again as strongly as before, but this time to God. "God is Spirit," but for our sake He became man and therefore wants to be loved with truly human tenderness and affection. Did not Christ gently restrain Mary Magdalen when, after His resurrection, she tried to touch Him? "Do not touch Me" (John 20:17). The emotions which manifest themselves in free prayer are not yet unalloyed, and thus not wholly acceptable to God. What is to become of them will be seen later. What must be stressed here is that it is right and necessary to allow some play to the emotions but in their unpurified state they also present a danger which we must clearly recognize.

But how? By ascetic discipline, a real and even painful exercise of self-denial. Like all such discipline, this one will be richly rewarding; it will strengthen the soul to scale even greater heights in its communion with God. We must learn moderation. The emotions are certainly not to be stifled altogether; that would lead to distortion, emotional congestion, strain and dangerous inner tensions. It is for the Holy Ghost to determine when the emotions must recede and make way for other things. But that we should learn to keep the emotional element of our prayer in proper proportions is a task which we may leave unaccomplished only at our peril. Thus, when we notice the emotions surging too violently, we must deliberately restrain them, must neither passively yield to their appeal nor actively try to stimulate them. The temptation to do so will assail us whenever emotion produces a positive feeling of joy, a kind of "swoon" of the heart, a sensation of bliss and overwhelming happiness; or when, quite spontaneously at first, tears well up and we are strangely and rapturously moved. By trying to stimulate those sensations we shall promptly distort their purpose, because they are but secondary symptoms, serving as a "bait" for the soul's closer union with God. To seek such happiness or joy for its own sake is to degrade God to a means for the sensation of well-being, and would mark the beginning of one of those evil aberrations on which the whole life of prayer may founder.

Here it is imperative to be adamant with oneself, and to tell God quite explicitly: "I do not want this; I accept it only so far as Thou wilt give or permit it; I accept it gratefully as a spur and a stimulus, a help and an easement for my prayers. But when Thou seest me clinging to it instead of Thee, then please take it away, because Thou art what I seek, Thou art my God, and to Thee I aspire, no matter at what cost." Such entreaties are most pleasing to God, and He will answer them in the manner best suited to His honor and our welfare.

Secondly we must, as best we can, restrain the impulse to hold on to these emotions, to relish and intensify them. Thus it is foolish to make oneself shed tears, and the result will inevitably be a fake, even though tears as such must not be despised because the Church has a special prayer "for the gift of tears" and they can be a powerful aid. We repeat: the emotional life as such must not be condemned; it, too, stems from the creative will of God. Due to original sin it has many aspects that may lead us astray, but these defects it shares with reason and will, which (although they like to appear superior) are ultimately responsible for the perversion of human nature, including the emotional life. God does not desire the destruction of powers which He has Himself created, vested in us, and blessed; He wants them to assume their proper place. The emotions, too, shall be made to glorify Him, although they are so often exploited shamefully, greedily, unworthily. Infused into the right kind of prayer, they will be cleansed more and more so that, together with reason and will, both similarly purified, they may stand before God as the triune manifestation of the life of the human soul to praise His divine glory. Those who on principle disdain the emotions are only too often people who, for the sake of reason, have suppressed their emotions; not an advantage, this, but a decided defect in the composite structure of human existence. Yet once again, "blackmail" from our emotional powers is contrary to the proper order, and against this we ourselves must firmly draw the line.

Thus, if we know that certain thoughts or aspects will arouse our emotions excessively, we must carefully leave them aside and refrain from meditating upon them. This will mean sacrifice, no doubt, but almost always the heart will experience, upon such inner re-orientation, a strange freedom, clarity and purity spreading within, a mysterious peace, as if a special blessing were laid upon this act of self-denial. This new experience is no longer an emotion in the normal sense; it is something much more spiritual, a nearness to God far more immediate and distinct than could hitherto be felt by means of our impure emotions. And here again we discern, delicately traced, the path that leads to greater heights.

Chapter 15

The Suffering of Prayer

IF the fellowship of Christ means, inescapably, to carry His cross until we have reached the fullness of life in God, it cannot cause surprise that the inmost core of Christian existence, the converse with God in prayer, is both blessed and overshadowed by the sign of the Cross. Overshadowed because there is real and often indescribably deep suffering; blessed because here, if anywhere, grace issues directly from suffering, changing it to a participation in the bounty of divine love. Here, too, and particularly, "the path is steep, and few are those that walk it"; rather, many shy away as soon as suffering must be faced in earnest. They withdraw from prayer altogether, or cut it down to the merest essentials, thus depriving themselves of the greatest gift held out to them by the Almighty. There is no form of spiritual purification which does not hurt. Too deep are the roots of perversion, and it is too much a part of us to allow of easy elimination. This has long become clear in all we said of the necessity for asceticism generally, and just now with particular reference to curing our emotional excesses. By the law of inertia everything wants to remain as it is, ourselves included. The adventure of leaving our present state, of stepping out of ourselves and, blindfold, to follow the lead of another to do with us as He pleases, seems well-nigh impossible. With all our strength we resist this challenge and try to escape it. One can get used to a splinter in one's finger, provided there is no inflammation; just a little more care is taken, but otherwise the trifling inconvenience is ignored. To remove the splinter will cause a single stab of pain sharper than what we have

[130

felt before, and from this we shy away—if we are foolish. In the spiritual life such folly seems part of our very nature. We would rather retain our wretchedness and imperfection than undergo the painful "operation" necessary to set us free. True, to endure it needs real constancy, all the more because it may well take a long time. That we should be afraid of it is only natural; but if we refuse ourselves altogether we may as well bury all desire for improvement, for special nearness to God in prayer, and with it also the hope of reaching on this earth that stage of development which God's providential love has placed within our grasp and which we would certainly attain if we surmounted that fear and, in prayer, delivered ourselves unconditionally to God and His mercy.

Our own efforts will be of small avail. Ascetical practices are necessary and good, but although performed under God's grace, they are less a real and decisive achievement than a suppliant glance, a cry for assistance. It is impossible for us to reach down to the very roots of our being; only He can do so by whom we are created, quickened and sustained. And it is He who sends the sufferings of prayer to cleanse us, and they are incomparably more effective and beneficial than anything designed by ourselves for the same purpose, even though at times the former sufferings seem insignificant and trifling by comparison. But then, the delicately pointed needle removes the splinter better than the knife. God knows exactly what I need to shed my particular faults and to resemble Him more closely And so He does not use the same purifying agents for everybody, but different ones, and in varied strength. Those who are weak, He will console, as once He comforted the presbyter of the synagogue who showed such small faith in the saving of his child. Others He will try more severely, leaving them uncomforted for a long time, as the woman of Tyre whose request for the healing of her daughter was treated with such incomprehensible harshness. In this there is for the faithful soul only one answer: to follow God's lead with unquestioning confidence, looking neither to the right nor the left but only upwards into His eyes and into the radiance of His love. Whatever suffering God permits, it is precisely what the soul requires, because He guides us not into exhaustion and collapse, but that eventually we may reach our goal.

To purify us, God will preferably choose those moments when His influence is strongest and most immediate because we are "open" to Him, the moments of prayer. The way of prayer is therefore inevitably a way of pain, though equally a way of joys most unexpected, for the sake of which one suffers gladly, if one does not already do so for the love of God. The agents serving the divine purpose will be manifold. Mostly He uses some peculiarity or bent of our own nature, a certain weakness or defect in the condition of our body or our soul. Even when, as in distraction, things from "outside" preoccupy us, they would not do so but for something within ourselves which permits them to gain a foothold. So far as the world causes suffering, it has power over us only because our flesh, i.e., our human, terrestrial nature, is so deeply beholden to it and subject to its sway. Yet without doubt the life of prayer knows other forms of suffering which are of diabolical origin. They are presumably far less frequent than was supposed in earlier times; perhaps one may say that just as our guardian angel fosters our good moods and impulses, so the demon lurks behind the bad ones which he guides and exploits, though rarely by direct intervention. It is pointless now to go into further details, since the suffering in prayer requires, more than anything else, the guiding hand of the spiritual director and it is for him to draw distinctions here. In the last resort, to know the origin of such suffering is certainly less important than to know how it should be dealt with and turned to one's benefit. At the same time there certainly exist border-line cases of genuine illness which can never be treated by exclusively spiritual means, but require medical attention. Here, too, the sufferer should leave the diagnosis in the first instance to his spiritual adviser.

Temptations

Among the most painful trials of the soul which desires close
union with God are a number of temptations which might well
cause it to lose all taste for prayer if it were to give way, not
to the temptations as such, but to the urge to avoid them by
shirking prayer. Strangely enough, they always present themselves just when prayer is about to begin or when a certain
degree of recollection has been attained, and the more the soul
dreads their coming, the more unbearable they will be.

Sometimes temptations are penalties. We have been too curious or have allowed our eyes to stray without restraint; now
all these pictures re-appear and torment us. We may have been
brooding unnecessarily about the faith, and now the thought
continues where it has no place. God permits this because our
attitude displeases Him; He will protect us only if we do not
recklessly court dangers. From their harmful effects on its
prayer the soul learns not to go astray in future. Once this lesson has been learned, temptations of that type will cease directly.

At other times temptations are allowed so that we shall be
thoroughly humbled. Without humility, i.e., without the practical and profound awareness that, but for God's grace, we
would be utterly evil and that from Him and through Him
alone do we attain to goodness, there is no life with God. The
further God wishes to lead us, the more He must first break
our arrogance. Temptations achieve this to perfection. They
teach us who we really are, what there is in us, and what our
capabilities are. The notion that of ourselves we were already
agreeably virtuous and had progressed far on the interior way
will be effectively dispelled, and the sooner we are ready to accept the lesson, the sooner can this particularly tormenting
form of instruction be dispensed with. To this is closely joined
another aspect: temptations are permitted so that we should
at last stop thinking of ourselves and instead give ourselves

up to God's grace and love without reserve. If we are what our temptations clearly show us to be, we can be safe only in God and nowhere else. The soul must learn more and more to lean on Him and to get away from itself, to trust Him more and more and to mistrust itself. Only when the soul has become quite small in its own estimation can it grow to full stature in God without courting new and even graver dangers.

In all this the soul exercises various valuable powers which will gradually become stronger. First, resistance against the encroaching evil; next, those specific acts of virtue which check the evil's approach; lastly, that patience which will be needed more and more on the journey—a patience which is all faith and trust, all devotion, the renunciation of self-will and bias in matters of salvation. In the fire of these temptations the soul will be doubly purged, by cleansing and by consolidation.

The temptations may be of various kinds. Mostly they are of a spiritual kind, affecting either faith or our senses, or both simultaneously, or one after the other, always where purification is mostly needed. The temptations of the senses are sometimes connected with an excess of affection in prayer itself; another reason why one should curb any exuberance. Our nervous structure is such that vibrations are readily echoed; an affection at first wholly centered upon God suddenly spreads throughout our whole being without the slightest deliberate encouragement. This may reach a degree that is almost unbearable for the soul. It may suffer like St. Catherine of Siena, who felt as if consumed by fires of lust and was helpless while her heart continued to seek God. Later she asked our Lord: "Where were you during those abominations?" He answered: "Deep within you, otherwise you would have fallen." This above all the soul must cling to; He is present, within, and nothing can happen unless we consent freely. St. Francis de Sales advises that when the pressure becomes severe, one should murmur softly: "May Jesus live, may Jesus live," and repeat this often. As long as the soul can voice this invocation, it has certainly not given way. In many cases the temptations of the senses may be controlled by a slight change in bodily attitude.

Other grave temptations assail one's faith. They can go so far as to make it appear that everything hitherto firmly believed was folly, illusion and fraud. It sees clearly that nothing is real, neither God nor grace. Sometimes this temptation is strongest in connection with the Eucharist. One wants to receive Holy Communion, but an inner voice seems to whisper: "Stay away, it is only bread; you do not believe in it." It is as if one's former interior life had been swept clean away. Here the rule of action is simple: now more than ever I will go to Communion and by my action I will give testimony to my faith, for faith is born of grace and of free will. Grace is granted always, certainly to Christians, and it is up to us to give consent, with a freedom which no one can take away. If, then, I freely resolve to go to Communion and at the same time suffer that terrible void and seeming absence of faith, I shall be doing precisely the right thing by exercising the faith which has apparently ceased to exist. The same method is to be used with the inward prayer: I will stay here, kneeling, trying to speak or keep silent, as the case may be, and the very act of remaining will give testimony before God and myself to my belief in His presence and help. It will be an act of faith, since without faith I would never decide to stay.

Again, specific truths may be assailed by violent doubts. Nothing more fatal, in that case, than to grapple with these doubts. One would merely waste the time reserved for prayer, without ever getting anywhere. These are not justified questions to which reasoning or instruction can supply adequate answers; they are merely doubts, restless, harassing, piercing the heart like the points of arrows, designed only to disturb us, but are never fruitful as the genuine religious problems always can be. One must try to go on praying. It is like taking a walk in the country; gnats and flies buzz around, settling on the skin, stinging occasionally, but who would turn back? One fights them off, and walks on. Just so in prayer. When everything seems in vain, one must keep still and say: "If this be Your pleasure, it is well; but Lord, I believe, help my unbelief!" Perseverance here can mean terrible suffering, but it is a grace indeed to be allowed to persevere.

Almost more painful still are the temptations which result from the experiences just described and undermine hope and trust, and would lead us into despair. The heart had stood in the midst of the other trials, but did it withstand them? Did it succumb or stay faithful? Prayer becomes impossible. Again and again this terrible question rises up: "Am I still entitled to be here, am I not secretly an enemy, cast out? Can God listen to me at all when I am in such a bad way?"

St. Francis de Sales sets down two rules of prime importance: 1) Unless you *know* immediately after a temptation whether you have consented or not, no amount of subsequent pondering will ever enlighten you. Therefore it is futile to try to decide later whether you did or did not yield. 2) If you do not know whether you have consented, you have in fact not done so. Mortal sin is impossible because you would surely be conscious of that. These rules suffice perfectly to extricate oneself from this often terrible predicament. Those who seek God and strive for Him, cannot fall without knowing it clearly and with profound anguish. Anxiety alone is no proof of sin committed; with ardent souls it is, on the contrary, the sign of a great sensitivity, a fear lest the Father in heaven be distressed. Against this type of temptation there is really only one remedy: to throw oneself into God's arms, stripped of all concern for self, blind and deaf and dumb. "There is nothing but Thee, O my God, Thou art all, knowest all, knowest that I love Thee, and want to love Thee above all." Look neither right nor left, consider neither yourself nor the thoughts crowding in upon you; look firmly ahead, into the sacred darkness, and stretch out both hands toward Him. Be assured; He will not repulse you.

Apart from these major temptations with their deeply penetrating agony, there are several others less aggravating, though troublesome enough—those of vanity, for example. We behold our pious demeanor as in a mirror—genuflections, folded hands, reverence before the tabernacle—all importunately vivid in our consciousness, and we seem to enjoy them with complacency, seem to feel secretly admiring glances of others. This is typical of beginners. It is, in truth, indescribably ridiculous and is best countered by laughing at it and at ourselves. The showman that is in every one of us can stand derision least of all; slowly he will beat a retreat. Once, as he was preaching, St. Bernard heard a voice whisper to him: "Bernard, what a beautiful sermon you are preaching." And another voice seemed to say: "Preaching is dangerous for your humility." But he silenced both: "Satan, I did not start to preach for your sake, nor for your sake will I cease." That was all, and the foolish temptation was dealt with. To apply this in practice will, nonetheless, remain difficult.

More seriously difficult is the persistent impression that one does not really love God but is merely seeking oneself. It will be sufficient to recall Christ's definition of the love of God: "to do the will of the heavenly Father." That is precisely what we aim at in prayer, what we try to learn through prayer. It is because of God that I am on my knees and praying—for love of Him. How deep my love? Leave that to Him. "Kindle in me Thy love," and He will do so.

To sum up, the best defense against temptations is never to heed them or to grapple with them but to turn away as resolutely as we can. True, often this will not be possible, but one thing always remains: to make those acts of prayer which run directly counter to the trend of temptation. Against doubts: "Strengthen the faith in me," or simply: "*Credo,* I believe." Against impurities: "I love Thee above all"; "Give me a pure heart and preserve it wholly for Thyself." A glance toward our Lady will here be particularly helpful. Against vanity: "Lord, Thou knowest that I seek only Thee." In this way temptations are transformed into opportunities for doing the very opposite of what they inspire. They become "fuel of love" and the soul reaps sublime rewards from its anguish, including many experiences useful for advising others.

Distractions

Another common difficulty in the practice of prayer is that of distractions. Only voluntary distractions are culpable. They alone can completely nullify our prayer or may even pervert the period of prayer into one continuous act of irreverence and offence against God. One must be on guard against them. They will insinuate themselves under all manner of pretexts: something important occurs to us, an elusive memory returns, a happy inspiration strikes us about certain arrangements, plans or events. Such things may be given to one in prayer, but if we start to pursue and elaborate on them, our prayer time would be wasted. We should valiantly push these things aside and concentrate on our prayer.

Involuntary distractions are those which are simply there, unbidden and unwelcome, even feared and detested. Yet for their presence, too, we are often enough to some extent responsible. We do not live recollectedly enough, are carried away by everything, cannot keep our thoughts under control and indeed do not really strive to do so. Everything gains access to our mind and it is no wonder that when we want to pray, the bustle and noise do not suddenly subside. How incredibly scatter-brained we are is fully revealed only at prayer. To strive for recollection is therefore an important aid for being less distracted at prayer, and conversely the suffering inflicted by distractions is a means of interior purification. If one suffers them in patience, the soul becomes more recollected and detached.

In content these distractions are as kaleidoscopic as life itself. Literally everything can turn up in the form of distraction: events, experiences, bits read or heard years ago, annoyances long forgotten, people whom we hardly know or notice. Of all the unsuitable moments, they crop up now and cause us unexpected pain.

One must deal with distractions in different ways. Some can be brushed aside without much effort; they appear on the horizon, are promptly spotted and ignored while the soul concentrates on the subject of its prayer. Again and again this may happen; they do no harm as long as the soul remains patient and does not get angry at the distraction or itself or God who permits it.

Incomparably more troublesome are the distractions which filter in so surreptitiously that one does not notice their coming. Quite suddenly the realization comes that one is not praying at all but is thinking of something far removed from prayer, although one had every intention to pray and had started well. Here the answer is, quietly and without irritation, to take up the thread of prayer where it dropped. Never go back and repeat; that would give rise to serious interior difficulties. Precisely where we retrieve ourselves from distractions, there we continue, even if the distraction returns again and again during the whole period of prayer. As long as we regain control of our thoughts and return to God at once and, we repeat, calmly, all will be well. Nor should these things surprise or upset us. How could it be otherwise when we are so frail, so fickle, and so untrained in spiritual matters? God knows this, and that is enough; we are sheltered in the forbearance of His love.

But can this still be called prayer? Most certainly, because our will is with God. When starting to speak to Him, the heart offered itself to God, and He lovingly accepted it. Now it remains close to Him, even while our poor head is encircled and overpowered by distractions, for prayer is a function not of the head but of the heart. When distractions entered our consciousness, our will did not let itself be seduced, it rebuffed them, and turned our mind back to God. The will is anchored in God as deeply as when it surrendered itself to grace and began to pray. We may think of a child, resting its head against its mother's breast, knowing that it is protected by a most tender love. Suddenly it begins to dream and its thoughts become confused. Yet there it remains, cradled in its mother's arms and in her love. She would be the last to blame it for being weak and tired, since she knows how frail it still is. God knows the same about us and He loves us in our weakness. Let us bear this in mind when distractions keep recurring and would make us grow weary of prayer altogether. We are truly praying, and nothing is wrong with our prayer, absolutely nothing. This is a real comfort in the midst of these sufferings of the heart, and it is precisely the souls who love God very deeply who will suffer most from seeing that the merest trifles are capable of luring them away from Him. We may carry these comforting thoughts still further by saying that it is the Holy Spirit who prays in us, and as long as we do not disrupt the union between Him and ourselves by voluntary distractions, our prayer continues. God's love and our own are wholly locked together, and no one can tear them apart, no one except ourselves.

Rather than grieve at our weakness, we should accept it in all peacefulness from the hands of our Father. And here the soul will make a wondrous discovery: once it has calmly grasped the fact that even in its weakness God's laws are made manifest, that He Himself is mysteriously behind these afflictions, in His wisdom, justice, charity, loving providence and fidelity, then the soul will encounter Him in its very distractions. If the soul embraces these distractions and, as it were, lovingly draws them close and yet remains wholly filled with God's presence, it will embrace and possess God Himself. And was not that the reason why we started our prayer, that we wished to be close to God and become one with Him as far as possible? After all, there is no more intimate and perfect union with God than in the pure and unreserved submission to His will. Therefore, if He does not want us to be united with Him in ecstasies, visions and perfect recollection, but in that other manner, veiled in distractions, how could we in that instant wish for something "better" or more "useful"? Is anything better than God's will, i.e., than God lovingly giving Himself? Once the soul realizes this, it will at times experience such a great nearness to and union with God as it had never known before, which is the best proof that this was indeed the way on which He meant to meet it and draw it close. This is a great mystery, yet wonderfully simple and intelligible. That this experience should at the same time embarrass and hurt us belongs to the character of penance and reparation which our prayer is meant to have. It is in doing this penance that the soul receives its God and Lover, because atonement is pure and unstinting cooperation with God in that very order which, through sin, became disordered. The abandonment to this higher order, no longer intelligible to us, is the great atonement. In this higher order God is attainable to us, and Christ has pointed the way. His coming in poverty, His passion and death are wholly unintelligible to us and are a "scandal" and a "folly." Our mind refuses to accept that these are the marks of divinity. We would expect to find God in majesty, in exaltation and in ecstasy, but not in nothingness. In the Incarnation God mysteriously became "nothing," and the same mystery lies behind distractions in prayer. There, too, He is truly present for our faith to grasp, for our love to feel. The law of the Incarnation here repeats itself with subtle accuracy and demands of us the same attitude of faithful acceptance. It is only here that we can find God, since it is thus that He likes Himself to be discovered.

Gradually a rather strange interior situation may thus develop. One prays, perhaps with words, perhaps only inwardly. All around lie the distractions; they permeate our interior incessantly. One cannot disperse them nor turn oneself away from them. Inexorably, there they are, seemingly possessing one altogether and leaving no room for anything else. Yet deep within, something wholly different is softly outlined. The heart knows that it is close to God, quietly and full of peace. It is turned toward Him and is met by His gaze. This happens in the depth of one's being, while on the surface there is turmoil. It is like the ocean; a hurricane may whip the waters into a fury, and it would seem as if the entire sea must be in uproar down to its fathomless bottom, but not so. For beneath the mountainous waves, everything is quiet; the great inner currents of the ocean, warm and cold, continue undeflected on their way; nothing alters their direction. Above, movement and change; below, everything remains at it should be.

In prayer we have the same experience. Above, the noise may become deafening, seeming to obliterate everything else; but within, and below, peace reigns. The mind is a prey to distractions but the heart remains in quiet adoration. Whatever goes on above, the heart ignores it as if it were something happening outside, something of no concern to the soul. Therefore the soul may remain untroubled; God is blessing it with His gifts. It feels strangely free, detached, dissociated from the body as from something alien. Yet once again, we must be patient, must not become exasperated by the disturbances nor try to force a change. Instead, accepting these trials, we must leave it to God how through them and in them He wishes to come and bless us.

Aridity

It is difficult to draw neat distinctions between the various types of suffering in prayer. They overlap, and what has been said about one may often apply similarly to another. Yet it will be easier if some attempt is made at separation. Somebody has said most succinctly: "God deals with us like a parent." Children who do not want to eat are lured by their mothers with things which they like and readily accept, such as candy. Gradually, however, she trains them to take other food as well, and in the end the entire diet is wholesome and healthy. The candy was meant to please the palate rather than strengthen the body. At first, bread seems much less pleasant, although it is nourishing; later the children themselves no longer care for the sugary things.

So it is with God. To those who wish to devote themselves to a more intimate and more perfect life of prayer, He gives sweetness. Often it is only with this that He first attracts the soul to Himself, to foster in it the desire to pray more. At times this interior sweetness is intense; one simply loves praying, is drawn to it, and cannot stop. Simply to think of God already fills the heart with a tender joy and emotion. The soul is infatuated as in the first ecstasies of love and indeed there is this similarity between the two experiences: as in the transports of a first love, one far more enjoys oneself in the loved one than cherishes the beloved for his own sake. It is still a very self-centered and self-seeking love. It is pointless to ruminate about this state of affairs; everything has and follows its own laws and inner structure, and progress cannot be made by leaps even in spiritual matters. It is necessary for the heart to be filled to overflowing by this inebriating bliss, for it is so deeply engrossed in self and earthly things that it can only thus be lured away from them and drawn to God. If hitherto it found its pleasure almost exclusively in the things of this earth and made itself drunk with them, it now learns that there exists a spiritual sweetness far more intoxicating. God may regard this initial fervor with benign forbearance; He can wait and can gradually lead the soul where He wants it, where real bliss can be found.

He does so by slowly withdrawing this palpable happiness, this emotional rapture. By now, the soul has become accustomed to Him, enjoys His nearness, but mainly on account of the pleasurable gift. Since, however, this in itself has freed it from many other things which formerly held it bound, that which it relinquished has lost some of its attraction. The soul has grown stronger in its new freedom, and as its resilience increases, God can take away some of the props and prune the soul's young happiness. Now and then prayer will give much less joy and transport; it will seem labored, dry, halting, colorless. It may be that this lack of feeling is a punishment for a relapse into mundane pleasures and for the failure to conquer oneself for God's sake. But even if the soul has been most faithful, the habit of thriving on the emotions has to be broken.

Sometimes satisfaction will suddenly be restored, as if God

were concerned lest the soul, still so tender, might slip away from Him because it finds this new kind of guidance too indistinct or too harsh. Later the periods of aridity will become extended, lasting for weeks and months, or longer still, but not before the soul has achieved natural generosity in giving and in resignation, or has attained robustness under the heavenly Father's wonderfully wise and subtle tutelage. Then the emotions may reappear, but with changed character. The soul has learned no longer to search or even ask for emotional experiences. It does not look to itself now, nor cloak its self-love with the love of God; instead, it looks for what may please Him or what He may desire of it. And if He deems it wise to leave the soul in this spiritual desert, it can now accept His decision and will later thank Him for it. Still later it will ask Him not to send any more emotional consolations but to give Himself, Himself instead of the gifts which were formerly so highly valued.

Before getting this far, the soul must truly suffer much. To remain steadfast in aridity is at first most strenuous, and the desire to drop so wearisome a form of union with God becomes intense. Here the soul will prove whether or not it is worthy of God. If it turns away now, because He no longer offers "sweets," is proof of its unworthiness, of a certain baseness which, while glad to receive, gives but grudgingly, keeping its gaze fixed only on the gift and not looking upwards into the lovable face of Him by whom the gift is tendered and now, for a change, withdraws His hand. The soul looks up and is startled at first to find the hand gone, and with it the gift, but soon it will be deeply grateful because it will behold something indescribably more beautiful and rewarding. Thereafter, its gaze will not easily revert to the hand, though gifts be tendered again. It will cling to the divine countenance, now loving God for His own sake and no longer in terms of self. The ignoble, unworthy soul returns to the "husks the swine did eat"; it does not appreciate the "bread of the angels," that bread which issues from "the mouth of God" and of which

Christ said that it was His food: to do the will of the Father. This is the "will of the Father," that our heart be purified and made holy until it is capable of a love as perfect as God's own. He loves us selflessly, for our sake, and yet what difference to Him whether we exist or not, attain bliss or damnation? True love must always have a clear direction; thus our love for Him must want Him alone, not ourselves, or rather, ourselves in Him, because it is His will that we should be in Him. His will is our measure.

If the heart is docile, it will persevere in prayer in spite of the great strain imposed by this interior indifference. The soul receives its Lover but remains cold and unmoved; everything seems dead and barren. Fear assails it. Has it been forsaken by God, the loving God who used to shower it with gladness? What can have come between them? Examining its conscience, it finds faults as usual, but no new or especially grave ones to warrant such punishment. But God has not withdrawn; He only withdrew the awareness of His grace so that He might come closer to the soul and be embraced by it in a purely spiritual way.

But for this, new "organs" must be developed which as yet lie dormant in the soul. Faith, hope, and especially charity, vouchsafed as seeds and already somewhat grown, must now develop into proper spiritual aptitudes, becoming the eyes and hands of the soul, reaching out to God, holding Him. This growth will take place especially in darkness. Fidelity, then, is of the essence, observing carefully the times allotted to prayer, not dropping a single minute. To give even the smallest leeway to one's whim means to be untrue to God and to oneself. Rather add an extra minute or two, and experience confirms how salutary this is. Read or recite verbal prayers as devoutly as possible, keep on with interior prayer at least in brief acts of aspiration, and if even this is too much and the inner resistance becomes overpowering, then just stay put and occasionally make an act of the theological virtues. Above all, keep calm. One might make it a practice to recall certain thoughts which are helpful or write them in a notebook carried on one's person, because so often they will elude one just when they are needed most. For example, one may consider that the pain of this hour has been ordained by God from eternity in perfect wisdom and in most considerate love and that at this moment nothing better could be found for the soul, or else He would give it. Quietly the heart adores this wisdom and this love so utterly beyond its comprehension. Such acceptance and adoration give great glory to God and the pure love which seeks Him alone here begins to spread its wings. The beautiful Chapter 50 in Book III of the *Imitation of Christ* can be a great help, or sentences from the writings of St. Teresa of Avila, who experienced all forms of suffering and is a wise counsellor. Prayer sometimes became so difficult for her that she kept shaking her hour-glass, hoping that the sand would pass through more quickly and thus hasten the end of prayer time. Once, after kneeling in church and unable to "get anywhere," she was about to leave to do something more "sensible" when she noticed the statues along the walls. Instantly she realized that they, too, do not accomplish anything, are simply there for God's greater glory. "So will I also stay, faithful and still as the statues, giving my Friend this time for which no better purpose could be found than to be with Him and thus to accomplish His will, and it *is* His will that I should be here and yet be useless." And so she stayed. Again, she reminds us that there are two kinds of servants of the King: lackeys, who come forward eagerly but always with an eye to tangible rewards or at least to attracting favorable notice, and noble-men, who hold themselves quietly at their King's disposal, often unobserved, rarely called, but when the need arises, there they are. They give thought neither to reward nor favor, merely wishing loyally to serve for love of the King, not of themselves. So, too, lackeys and knights may be found among the servants of God. The former expect that every little service of theirs should promptly be rewarded with happiness and peace; the latter merely ask: "Do I serve well and truly? Is my duty wholly done?" They do not look for recognition or for gifts; they only want to love, unselfishly. Considering this, the soul will remain faithful and in this true sanctification of its love it will receive a rich blessing.

Boredom

The suffering of aridity may be experienced in various ways. As long as a certain perception of God remains, it is still bearable just to "stay on." But when this is wholly withdrawn, the soul may be seized by a definite boredom. "What am I sitting here for, dawdling away my time? Had I not better do some work, visit the sick, or read a book which would at least yield stimulation? Anything rather than this utter tedium!" Thoughts like these pervade the soul and prompt us to leave. And, truly, it is anything but simple to stay on in this condition and again and again refocus the interior glance on God in brief acts of aspiration, on God who now shows so little of His former attractiveness. Here we must be supernaturally prudent, as natural intelligence alone cannot for long assist us. What is my purpose here on earth? To glorify God. Not to entertain Him; He can well do without my enlightened discourse or my fervent prayer. He does not need me, and whatever I do for Him it does not add one grain to His majesty or to His bliss. And again: "I am not here to 'gain' something, to enjoy myself or spend an interesting half-hour. Why then should I be annoyed that, so to speak, nothing happens? I give freely of my time to Him who gives me eternity. At this moment I am here only for Him, who Himself is always there for me just as if nothing and nobody else existed. I must consider Him worthy of putting everything else aside for His sake and of waiting only for Him, whether and when He will deign to come to me."

Here, also, to think of God's will is extraordinarily helpful. There is nothing more sweet, more wonderful, more holy and adorable than this will which is love. And here this will demands: "Stay with Me and endure, even if apparently I pay no heed." St. Frances de Chantal, in her long spiritual desolations, coined the magnificent phrase: "It is most attractive to be bored in the proximity of one's lover." One cannot adequately translate this word *charmant*, which signifies the enchantment and graciousness radiating from the loved one even when he is silent, asleep or incommunicative. Truly a wonderful saying: "It is most attractive, delicious in fact, to be bored in the proximity of one's lover." If we try to make this thought come to life in ourselves, we discover that the very boredom is promptly neutralized by this attraction and that the soul is now content quietly to stay close to the loved one. Indeed, it learns to take pleasure in this silence and to find a special grace in waiting, the grace of perceiving that our agitation and toil do not bring God to us a minute before it is time, before "His hour is come."

Repugnance

Yet this trial may take on an even harsher and more cruel appearance. Boredom may become intensified to the point of repugnance and disgust. The heart revolts against this inner void and stagnation. It gets the impression that God is tormenting it deliberately, is finding pleasure in bringing home to the poor heart its wretchedness, and wants to drown it in a sea of nothingness. It is almost as if God treated its pain and helpless desire with derision, finding it abject and contemptible. Staying with Him then becomes grovelling before a tyrant, and all that ever seemed dear to the soul is destroyed. Revolt ensues, open rebellion, mutiny, and the soul can barely stammer that it does not really mean any of it. Here we must implore God, not with words, which the mouth can no longer form, but with the very act of kneeling, of hands tightly folded. And so, in spite of everything, we shall stay, shall try not to pursue these rebellious thoughts but instead shall look beyond them to recapture the sight of God's countenance, and simply murmur: "I accept all this, it is well; I no longer understand, but that is not important, since Thou knowest all, knowest me." Often the soul will find it quite impossible to utter or even to think such thoughts; then there is nothing for it but to remain and to wait for the time allotted for prayer to pass. That, now, will be our prayer, and it suffices before God, who looks down on our misery with love, protection and compassion.

Silence of the soul

It is less frightening and wearing, yet nonetheless deeply painful for the God-seeking soul when it becomes quite unable to speak, as if struck dumb. Thoughts do not come and falling back on printed prayers, it finds them empty babble, without rhyme or reason. All seems utterly remote, even insincere, in no way fitting nor expressive of what it wishes to say yet cannot. All is tangled, like a ball of string which can no more be unravelled. Deep inside, something seems to cry out, and at times this cry wells up to the lips, there to be turned into a gentle moan or sigh. To that, the soul is welcome. God hears and understands this sound only too well. Not for a second should the soul voluntarily give in to the thought that now all is in vain, that it had not achieved prayer and that, not bearing any gifts, it had incurred God's anger. On the contrary, it now brings gifts more precious than before, when it was filled with edifying thoughts, with abundant emotion and tenderness. It offers Him its self-will and the desire—at this stage obviously still fully justified—to talk to Him and adore. It gives Him everything, down to the depth of its being, for Him to do with it as He wishes. Here the soul must simply hold on, nothing else. Whether He trim or pare, it is well; whether He loosen its muteness or still leave it dumb, His name be blessed; whether it be brightened by His light or wrapped more closely in impenetrable darkness, glory be to the Father. When the soul can no longer form words of its own, the Spirit groans within it and one day it will know that it had to learn to be silent so that His word might replace its own, transforming it and bearing it upward. The ability to pray, to converse with God will be restored, but now different and more beautiful than the soul could ever have dreamed. The secret is: "In your patience you shall possess your souls" (Luke 21:19).

Silence of God

What we have just tried to outline (and it is almost impossible to describe these things so that they can be grasped by those without experience) can also occur in reverse order, that is, it seems that God has become silent. The soul still manages to say something but it seems to speak against a wall. It hears nothing but the echo of its own voice. God's gaze is averted; He does not look and does not listen; He is wrapped in silence. Is He still there at all? Does He exist? This utter lack of response is a bitter test. But what does this lack of response mean? Nobody expects God to speak audibly or even with sounds perceptible to our inner ear. True, this may happen but it does not concern us here, and to desire or ask for such a sublime experience would be shocking presumption. God's answer consists in knowing that one has been heard and understood. A closer definition is hardly possible. In human conversation a similar experience occurs. We relate something and the other person listens. We know that somehow we have been understood; a gentle nod, a slight change of expression, they suffice to give us that certainty. The union between two people may be so close that even these signs, however sparing, can be dispensed with. The friend understands; his eyes reveal it by the very way in which they are fixed on the speaker. The same thing occurs in prayer. There is little room here for explanation; it is a fact, and the heart knows it, knows it in a deeply spiritual kind of awareness which is of exceptional importance for the soul's further progress.

But it is possible for this awareness to recede or to become obliterated altogether. Then follows that desperate state described above: the shouting which no one seems to hear, the reverberating echo of oneself, the utter desolation. Here our faith is summoned to its highest ardor, the faith that tells us unequivocally that God is there always, that He is always there for me, that He listens to and knows everything, that our cries will never go unheard, and that He is active within us as when we call Him. That is enough, even though it may be most difficult to be content with this. The soul here attains to a very pure form of surrender and self-detachment, to a genuine and unreserved abandonment to the inscrutable darkness, the sacred depths of God's being. Why should God ever grant me a personal and specific confirmation that He hears me? Has He not confirmed it once and for all in that revelation which we grasp by faith and on which rests our entire Christian existence? Can it affect the truth of our being heard by God whether we ourselves are aware of it or not? Might such interior perception not itself mislead us, reflecting some psychological condition rather than a real act of divine condescension? Pure faith is a far more certain guide than any subjective experience. To be sure, such experiences have their place and value, and faith itself will lead to them almost inevitably, but only faith provides true certainty and a firm foundation. Without it our experiences are of questionable and dubious value, however impressive and convincing they may appear. Faith alone must remain the ultimate norm. That is why God teaches the soul for a time to do without experiencing Him, in order that its faith may grow deep and strong, to give a basis for future experiences and yet make us independent of them.

Let us then let God be silent for a while if He deems it well. Let us say, in faith, "I know Thou art there and hearest me; I know it from Thy own word, from the very Word of eternal truth. No longer do I rely on myself and my perceptions, but on Thy assurance alone. Now Thou dost bear me up; nothing within me gives comfort or support." Here the soul achieves great purity and freedom, and its love, which knows and seeks nothing but Him, soars heavenward. Thus these testing periods offer the highest spiritual rewards, and if the soul remains constant it will one day realize their promise and thank God jubilantly. St. Thérèse of Lisieux gives us a delightful simile which might, if recalled in time, help the soul to endure this muteness of God. She describes a child in the nursery, surrounded by its toys—a ball, a doll, a little railway, a box of bricks. The child plays for a time with one thing, then with another. Now it is the ball and then something else strikes the child's fancy while the ball rolls into a corner, forgotten. The child is elsewhere absorbed and it is as if the ball did not exist. Yet later on the child will once again take it up to play with it. God seems to treat us in much the same fashion. At times He showers us with tenderness, making us see and sense a thousand beauties, comforting and encouraging us. Down to the most intimate details His enlightenment comes to teach us how we may best accomplish this or that. So well does He attend to us that it is as if there was nothing else to engage Him. But then He seems to turn away; we lie in a corner, as if forgotten. No glance comes to caress us, no word to comfort us. The blissful intercourse has ceased and we no longer feel the warmth of His fatherly heart. Yet, when it pleases Him—and it is not whim that guides His pleasure, but loving wisdom—He will draw us back into His arms. Then the sacred play of love begins anew, and this time the happiness is even greater.

With this thought the soul smiles again in the midst of its desolation: "By all means let me lie in a corner for a while, my Father. I shall yet know that Thou carest for me and lovest me, not as a little plaything, but as the apple of Thy eye, as a mother loves her child, as a God loves those whom in love He conceived, created and redeemed, and to whom one day He will give all, Himself."

The various forms of suffering which we have here discussed return in all the phases of prayer. The soul itself, and its relation to God, undergo a profound but gradual transformation. In like manner the form in which these sufferings are experienced will change. Yet they are basically always the same tests, and our reaction to them will alter but little. Until the soul is wholly cleansed, freed from self and open to God; until it dwells in a wholly purifed love, suffering cannot be dispensed with. Indeed, it will increase in violence and intensity because as the soul grows stronger under its impact, God can expose it more directly to the purifying power of His love. This is what causes us to suffer so much, but also to be progressively healed.

Although the sufferings experienced in the various stages are closely related to one another, we shall have occasion to revert to them, first, because in entering upon a new stage everything appears different to the soul and it does not immediately recognize the old tormentors in their new setting; secondly, because these phenomena play such a decisive part in our spiritual life that we cannot ever be sufficiently prepared to forestall them and thus avoid wasted strength and tiring detours.

In speaking of stages or phases of prayer, we should not think in terms of areas clearly circumscribed and sharply distinguished. Rather, we should see them as basic attitudes which penetrate one another, though with varying preponderance. Thus, vocal prayer of the set formulas will, if practiced with care, naturally flow into free vocal prayer. The mind will then be arrested by some of the thoughts formulated in free prayer and will become absorbed therein, and thus meditation has begun, later on to be changed into a quiet resting within God's presence, filled with His nearness and love, meditation no longer, but contemplation.

If the stages are distinguished less by reference to prayer than in terms of Christian existence as a whole, one speaks of the three ways: the purgative way, the illuminative way, the unitive way. In the purgative way the soul is more and more freed of itself, partly by its own exertion (motivated, of course, by grace) and partly by God acting upon it, an action which the soul "suffers" rather than participating in it actively. The illuminative way brings a deepening knowledge of God's life and truth, again as a fruit partly of the soul's own striving born of grace, as in meditation, and partly as an influx of divine light, to be received only in quiet surrender. The unitive way culminates in the intermingling of the two wills, the divine and the human, in the perfect *fiat* of a love so pure that it knows, seeks and desires only Him, totally oblivious of self. In each of these phases further subdivisions could be listed, though to little purpose because we would gain nothing thereby and it is always a little critical to try to locate one's precise position on this endless ladder. Only God knows, and that is well. It is pointless to brood over this. If the saints discuss it at all, they do so for reasons of systematic clarity and not to encourage the soul to put itself in any particular stage. Indeed, when it came to this, the saints usually saw themselves on the lowest rung of the ladder, and they were content because it was God's love that kept them there and that same divine love could raise them up to the most sublime heights. We should instantly dismiss even the shadow of such curiosity, seemingly pious and yet secretly self-seeking, and should affirm in all honesty before God: "This is not my concern; my sanctification and my salvation are entirely in Thy hands." Only thus can we achieve inward peace.

Once again, the steps of the mystical way cannot be neatly distinguished. Even the saint, while still here on earth, will at times need further purging, while the beginner, just starting on the purgative way, may experience interior illumination of great significance, so convincingly, in fact, that he becomes wholly fixed on God and his will is directed in surprising concord with the will of God, at least for certain times and tasks. In all this we meet life, life in its highest form. The spirit, consecrated and favored by God, lives with and by God. But life cannot be dissected into its component parts; it forms an integrated whole, though its many facets are highlighted by the constantly changing emphasis. Let us then proceed steadfastly on our way as best we can, paying but little attention to where we are, how far we have come, and what may happen next. Our spiritual director will be able to chart our progress adequately; if not, God Himself will take charge.

Chapter 16

Meditation

Activity and passivity

A mother leads her child by the hand. Not yet able to walk alone, without her he would fall and come to grief. So she holds him fast, and the child, suffering it gladly, now has the scope that he needs. He hops and skips and gambols, pushing against the mother, squeezing her hand or tugging at it, romping in his own way through his own little area but always held by her. While fully relying on her strength, her help and her love, the child pursues his own interests and the mother, smiling, lets him be. She wants the child to develop his powers; always to carry him about like a baby would be denying life its full development.

At another time the mother and child walk through a dangerous moorland. Again the mother holds the child's hand, this time walking ahead on a very narrow path. Following closely behind, the child does not for one moment let go of the mother's hand. No romping and jumping now. The mother's every move is faithfully copied. He does not wish to follow his way, but hers, the only right way just now. Justified and gladly permitted as was the child's relative independence on that other occasion, now the mother would surely look stern and ill-pleased if the child did not follow carefully in her footsteps. No doubt the child still retains a will of his own, but no longer one that seeks its own free scope. Instead, the child's will has become wholly united to that of the mother. She leads and the child lets himself be guided in every movement and turn. Now and then they come to a boggy part or a footbridge across a ditch, springy and too difficult for the child to manage. The mother then takes him firmly in her arms. He looks into the mother's dear face, calm and serene, smiling and captivating. Once more on the ground, the child trips behind as before, and never did he walk so well, so lightly and so securely; never did he feel less fatigued and more safely anchored in the strength of his mother.

In the first scene, if you like, the child was active; in the second he was passive. In the first he did a great deal; all his powers were engaged in lively movement. He lived his own life, though quite close to the mother and with no desire to cut free. In the second scene he allows himself to be led. Adjusting himself to his mother, he adopts her will and assimilates his will to hers. Thus, the child is passive, suffering the mother's influence to reach him and bear him along. And yet there is actually far more activity in this than in the first scene, for such precise compliance and adaptation requires much greater exertion, care and readiness. Seemingly everything here is done by the mother and the child does nothing. Yet all his strength is in operation, in cooperation. Eyes and hands and feet, perception, volition and feeling, all are engaged, though they are impregnated by the mother's example, her will having imparted itself so completely to that of the child that they now are in total agreement. Admittedly it is not an agreement of understanding, for even if the mother attempted to explain the dangers of the moorland and the necessity for the child to follow her closely, he would understand very little. But this is of no importance; all that matters is that the child is not now self-willed but cooperative, and thus he reaches his goal. The child knows that the mother loves him profoundly, and what she tells him must therefore be true. Therefore, without hesitation he surrenders himself to love's guidance, sharing for a little while his mother's life. It is almost like the time that she carried him in the womb, but now in greater freedom and with his own heart engaged.

From this analogy we can easily see the difference between

the prayer of meditation and that of contemplation, frequently referred to as active and passive prayer respectively. Unless we are careful, we tend to dismiss passive prayer as of dubious value and even to warn against it because nothing seems to "happen" in it. We rather feel the soul to be in danger of indolence, fancying itself an object of special grace instead of making an honest effort and thus to work out its salvation. Actually, however, our analogy points the right way. As a child of God, the soul ever holds on to His hand, that is, to His grace which carries and stimulates it, helps and heals. But then different attitudes can be adopted.

Following some inner prompting, one concentrates on a specific thought, works at it, considers it from this angle or that, and derives from it whatever seems best to fit the soul's inner life. This is always done under God's grace, under His blessing and encouragement, in the safety of His good pleasure, but all the same, the soul itself is at work, reflecting, considering, making the different acts. Often a great deal of scope is allowed which it certainly must use fully. Stirred by the will of God, the soul's will is inclined toward Him; it moves, as it were, side by side with God's will.

Matters are different in contemplation, when the soul is being drawn away from what previously had been its spiritual activities. The soul can no longer make its own steps or movements. God wants it to abandon itself to Him to a far greater degree than before. Now it must follow His least inner impulse and motion. No choice or selection is left to the soul, God alone controls the pace and measure and all. The soul surrenders itself, though very slowly and with pain. How good it felt to bustle around, to sing and praise, to enthuse and discover, to beg and atone, according to the heart's inspiration. Now God alone inspires, and the soul has to follow Him. Often it does not even faintly grasp what God is doing or what He makes it do. But this becomes more and more insignificant, as the soul no longer bothers about goals and achievements and deep penetration by the intellect. By a mysterious kind of knowledge that nobody can destroy, the soul knows that it is loved. It knows God's presence, and that He loves and guides it; that He is right in all things, always; and that, apart from Him, no right can ever be claimed. In its abandonment to God the soul finds deep and hidden bliss, for such is love's very essence.

A deep understanding of another person still brings our own ego into play. Love alone takes us out of self, beyond self in a degree and measure and direction determined by the object of our love. Ultimately love does not rely on itself; to follow Him becomes its exquisite delight. It is not easy, but such a strain that meditation now seems like child's play. Although to all appearances the soul is passive, it is as intensely active as ever, since there can never be a more absorbing activity than love. Love is inflamed ardor, infinite impulse, in imitation of the Holy Spirit, who is eternal and blessed ardor. All the mind's powers are engaged, without exception, gathered together from their isolation into complete unity. If ever love was alive, now it is wide awake, sharing the life of God so far as He will impart it. In a higher sense, passivity and activity here merge into one, even as Jesus Christ is passive in that He "cannot do anything of Himself but what He seeth the Father doing" (John 5:19), and is yet so truly active that "without Him was made nothing that was made" (John 1:3). Whatever the Father does, "the Son doth in like manner" (John 5:19). Yet of the Son we hear that "He can lay down His life of Himself and has power to take it up again" (John 10:18), power in the absolute sense and measure, and at the same time complete unity with the Father through the Holy Ghost. Passivity then is the mode by which the divine activity passes into the soul, unites it to God, and thus brings to pure and perfect fruition the soul's innermost power to be active.

If at times the soul is gathered up in the arms of God in contemplation, like the child of which we spoke, is not that part of it all? And even then, was the child really passive, not doing anything? He held on; he looked up at the mother's expression, anxiously, and yet ready to forget all the fear of his heart, loving her and trusting her without restraint. He imbibed love and kindness, peace and security, and his heart was full of it all, too full indeed to express, even if he wanted to, the deep joy of such intimacy and profound trust. Though quietly folded around his mother's neck, did not those little arms express the will to hold on, to draw close, and to stay? And the gaze upon her face, did it not carry the whole of the child's little soul, alert, expectant, grateful and glad?

Are we active only in the hustle and bustle of our thoughts, and not equally in their stillness and deep recollection? Must our heart tell of its love and its trust in so many words? Is it asleep when, marvelling at its own power of love, it is silent in God, caught in His fire and so aglow that its whole being seems to change? In fact, just then are revealed its mightiest powers and its most wonderful glories, glories all its own, revealed in and through the fire of God.

Meditation then is an achievement born of and guided by grace and bearing fruit out of grace. Yet some scope, proper to individual abilities, is left to the meditating person, whose own reflection, inner resonance and conscious acts of the will are called upon. It is a real personal effort in which the will has to determine object, method and desired goals. Consequently, meditation is always exposed to those emotions which are connected with all our actions: eagerness, boredom, anticipation, fatigue. Preparation is needed to avoid using one's strength at random; examination is needed to determine whether the chosen method was faithfully and correctly observed with profitable results. Meditation is an honest achievement, with a definite place in the spiritual plan of our day. It is a matter of conscious self-discipline rather than training by others.

But if contemplation ranks higher than meditation, why not go directly to the former and leave the latter alone? Simply because contemplation must be either a direct gift from God, not in any way dependent on human effort, or it is the ultimate achievement of the effort of meditation. The first we can only hope and pray for; the second may be acquired and will normally be attained by those who meditate well. Without contemplation, however, there can be no full Christian life wholly centered in God, no "heaven on earth," no hand-in-hand companionship with God. Are we to wait for God to give this to us or should we see what, with God's help, we can achieve by our personal efforts? God always wants our own efforts first; then He will take a hand when we realize that we shall always be deficient unless He guides our steps and imparts His life to us. Meditation thus renders a twofold service: it shows us the limitations which we cannot overcome and it enables us to know God in such a way that we shall abandon ourselves to Him and let Him carry us beyond our own limitations.

However, the necessity for meditation does not presuppose a specific and prescribed method. As long as there have been religious people, there have been prayer and meditation. A clearly defined method has been known only since the days of St. Ignatius of Loyola. Comparing his *Spiritual Exercises* with the *Manual of the Spiritual Life* by García Cisneros, which is supposed to have influenced the former, one realizes the distance that had to be covered before a meticulously thought-out system of meditation was prepared by St. Ignatius. But there had always been meditation. Therefore, nobody entering upon this phase of prayer can be committed to a specific method. A method may be expedient, important, and even indispensable, but only for a given time. It will also differ with individual use. If we use a method, well and good, but let us beware of losing our freedom and of binding ourselves slavishly to the method. It must always be left to the Holy Ghost to guide the soul into that realm which it can enter only at His gentle bidding.

Many devout people never adopt a method, yet imperceptibly the Holy Ghost will introduce them to the prayer of meditation. The training-ground here may be the Rosary, which can help to unfold the whole scale of our life of prayer.

[160

Such people use the different elements of meditation informally and naturally, whereas a method would work them out logically and in strict order. And unless we simply live and talk idly and without purpose, do we not all ponder over the affairs of our daily life? Everyone but the most superficial person considers, weighs, searches and makes resolutions. This means *N.B.* exploiting one's experiences and drawing theoretical and practical conclusions. Our concern here is how to apply these functions to the spiritual life. Every normal Christian, indeed every mentally sound human being, is capable of this kind of meditation. The frequent lament, "I can't," is due to a confusion of meditation as such with the use of a particular method which is a help to one person and a hindrance to another.

In later stages meditation will not simply be replaced by contemplation and made superfluous; it will retain its place, not during contemplation, of course, which would be inconsistent, but side by side with it as a help to appreciate its content, and perhaps also for the instruction of others. The matter beheld in contemplation contains much that is of value as an object or directive for future meditation. Once more, the different phases of prayer do not displace but supplement, enhance and support one another, finally to mature in the fullness of the Christian life in God.

What is the connection between mental and vocal prayer? Can contemplation be reached only after vocal prayer has passed into meditation? Not necessarily. God will at times grant contemplation at a stage in which the soul is as yet quite untrained in the spiritual life, to bind it to Himself in early preparation for His later plans. These occasional moments of contemplation may render meditation difficult or impossible. On the whole, vocal prayer will point to meditation, because it produces a growing desire further to penetrate into and exploit the contents of our prayers. Here is the place to recall our earlier advice, namely, to pause and linger over vocal prayer. The soul must learn better to focus its attention on individual aspects, concentrate deeply upon them and thus absorb and fully experience them. The quiet break can even be, or develop into, contemplation; at least it will make us better aware of certain parts of our prayers and thus engender a deeper understanding. Often some text of a prayer lingers on in the mind. One cannot, so to speak, get rid of it; persistently it will reappear, like someone knocking and demanding attention. Then, involuntarily, the soul considers and tries to penetrate it, and it may happen that this fragment proves to be greatly significant as an incentive or a consolation, or perhaps a barrier, a decisive turning-point of the interior life. Alternatively, meditation leading to contemplation also enlivens and enriches vocal prayer. The soul must talk to God of all its findings and make them part of its essential union with Him.

The practice of meditation

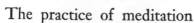

Is meditation really a form of prayer? This may seem a strange question, since we have been talking of mental prayer. But we must distinguish clearly. Can reflection on a divine truth be called prayer? Is a deep consciousness of beauty already a prayer? Is the practical resolution drawn from meditation—to accomplish a certain moral action—a prayer? Yes and no. If prayer is understood to embrace everything by which a person lives entirely and solely in God and devotes all his actions wholly to God, then work, talk or recreation would also be prayer, as are the mental acts that come into play in meditation. Substantially these may be different, though even that does not necessarily follow. If an artist is outlining a holy picture, or someone in meditation is creating a mental image of his subject, are both of these persons praying? If not, is he praying who mentally fashions the images of his meditation? Both, no doubt, pray, provided their activities are focused upon God.

If, however, prayer is understood as looking at, being and acting with God in the union of love, then those incidents just described are not prayer. Neither the artist's creation nor the philosopher's vision of God nor the imagery and perception of him who meditates are true prayer. Ultimately, is it not the heart alone that prays, that "bottom of the soul," as the German mystics called it; its "summit," according to the French; or "spark," in the expression of Scholastic mysticism; that innermost core of the soul mysteriously drawn to God present within it? There, in most secret intimacy and in a union effected in deepest darkness, the human will is blended with the will of God in the love of the Holy Ghost. Was it not this which gave the true character of prayer to all vocal prayer? Without it, all our speaking to God would be mere lip service, worthless and insulting.

Nor can the acts of meditation as such be called true prayer, even though they may be explicitly directed to it or sustain it. The individual acts of meditation are not in themselves prayer in the proper sense; they are a help toward it and to that extent they are good, but they are not what is ultimately desired. There is always the danger that those acts will degenerate into the "acrobatics" of prayer, yielding much pleasure and excitement to the mind. But the imagery remains a playful illusion, the careful considerations turn into brooding and philosophizing about truth and about God, and the resolutions are translated into terms of morality to govern daily life. All that may be good and useful and—save for the complacency which may attach to it—pleasing to God, but it is not prayer.

It is therefore necessary that meditation, directed to God but not yet prayer, be interspersed by prayer. Reflecting on the meaning, for instance, of the phrase, "the poor in spirit," could not be called praying, but we can execute our reflections in the form of prayer: "What dost Thou mean, Lord, by this word? Show it to me. Thou knowest that, left to myself, I cannot find my way. I need Thy light, which Thou hast promised me. Didst Thou mean that those are blessed who are dull, untrained, and weak in intellect? Hardly, for what advantage would that be?"

Addressed to God in this way, our reflections as well as our understanding are submerged in prayer. Each phase of thought takes the heart closer to God, makes the soul reach out for His hand and fix its glance upon Him. And it is much easier and simpler in this way than to be recollected in God while at work. Therefore, in that sense meditation more than work or our life in general is suitable to be embraced by and converted into prayer.

Wherever the opportunity arises, there will be those explicit acts of prayer, especially whenever the Holy Spirit inspires the soul. One should not pursue one's reflections about God, however captivating, when the soul is given an inner signal to halt and to adore that glorious God and Father and offer praise and worship to Him in Jesus Christ. One should not then continue to think of today's possible opportunities to imitate the kindness observed in Christ, when one feels pressed simply to beg: "Make me as Thou art; fashion my heart according to Thine; draw me close to Thee and do not leave me in my wretchedness and insufficiency, in the frigidity and hardness of my heart."

It is only when these actual prayers are woven into meditation that the soul lays itself open to God. And what it has grasped and felt, can now reach its very depth, anchor it to God and quicken it in Him. Neither a theologian nor a philosopher will be the outcome; merely somebody who is able to pray; who loves, and knows that he is loved; who desires God in and above all. Thus one also escapes the danger of considering the fruits of meditation as precepts which, given an adequate effort, the soul could emulate by its own momentum. Praying, the soul discovers that to become as good as it now knows it must be is possible only by the power of God. With Him alone can be achieved the noble end of the soul's new resolve. Then there will not be imitation, but cooperation; not a mere mirage, but reality abounding with life: God in my soul, my soul within God.

If our meditation is thus focused upon God and consequently steeped in prayer, it will itself become prayer. The

[164

goal is not a logically worked-out piece of truth nor one of those well-ordered moral resolutions but a union of love and life between God and the soul, based upon and quickened by the knowledge of truth. Praying, the soul anchors its perception of truth and its good resolutions in the depth of Him whose very being is truth and goodness, who is "the Father of lights" (Jas. 1:17) from whom every good thing comes. And if at times meditation fails to advance, because our heart feels strongly attracted to God and must speak to Him, and goes on to quite different subjects, as "the Spirit moves it," are we then to tear ourselves away forcibly and turn back to our meditation? No more, surely, than one could be expected to turn back from the goal of a journey and retrace his steps once more. Similarly, the soul dare not renounce prayer for meditation out of a misplaced deference to a rule or a resolution. God commands love, nothing else, and lovingly He radiates love into our souls. And if God wanted human beings to devise methods conducive to the greater love of Him, He certainly did not intend us to prefer the external form to the contents, the means to the end, and thus pervert the right order of things. If meditation does not evolve into prayer, it fails its very purpose. But we should in all this not be too active; better to be ready to respond to the way in which God gently moves the soul and leads it on. If we trust Him, if we allow the delicate, increasingly distinct force of God's grace to overwhelm our self-will, then we shall not—or never for very long —come to a dead end of futile attempts. There will, as in every beginning, be uncertainty, error and awkwardness, but gradually our inner eye and our heart will learn to be surer of their ground and single-minded under God's grace, so lovingly infused into the soul eager to "follow the Lamb whithersoever He goeth" (Apoc. 14:4).

Spiritual meditation, like any other, depends on the proper application of the various mental powers to a given object. Not as if first one and then the other works in its own specific area. Our faculties operate rather with and through each other, forming a kind of multicolored fabric whose yarns, to make the pattern, combine now in this, now in that fashion. Meditation is, after all, a vital mental process, and in all things alive there is always interaction and constant exchange back and forth. All the same, there must be an ordering principle. A thing must first be perceived before you can love it, though loving will soon lead to better perception and deeper knowledge. You are drawn toward something only after recognizing it as worthy of affection, although these very feelings promote such recognition and loving inclination. A richly varied activity unfolds, whenever the soul rouses its powers. Once aware of this, we need not fear that our meditation will deteriorate into an excessively conventional and tedious exercise, not even in regard to the "proper order of meditation," which is so much more than a mere system. Only in actual meditation do we realize what a vigorous and prolific exercise it is when compared to a dry description of it, which sometimes may rather deter than attract us.

We pray, or to be precise we desire to pray more ardently, and for this reason we meditate. Thus we naturally begin with a prayer. We pray to Christ, who is our way and the truth whence we receive all. We pray to the Holy Ghost, who enlightens, stimulates and gently guides the soul and ripens the seeds deposited in meditation. We pray to the Father, into whose love everything is to flow just as everything originates therein. We pray to Mary, the Mother of Christ and our Mother, revered as the "Seat of Wisdom," where the Eternal Wisdom itself was made incarnate, that she might bless us in maternal love and teach us the way which she herself traveled in faith and trust and dedicated love. Was not she the great example of prayer and meditation? So the liturgical texts of her feasts tell us that to her was entrusted both the gift and the task of teaching the children of God. We pray to our guardian angel, that he may help to quicken within us such stimulations as we shall presently require. Finally, we pray to the saint of the day and possibly some others whom we especially venerate. Did not the saints live entirely by the divine mysteries contemplated again and again, therein discovering the source of their sanctity and their efficacy? "Thy law my meditation all the day and the night, O Lord" (Ps. 119:97). It is obvious that such introductory prayer must proceed from that reverent and devout recollection of which we treated earlier. It is obvious also that such preparations should not take long, for they are but the upward beat to the essential.

The same applies to the next two stages of preparation. Memory first comes into its own. Out of its treasury it must provide today's subject of meditation. To that effect, memory must, of course, have something definite in store. Hence a good meditation clearly requires careful preparation. Normally this is done the previous night, when the subject is chosen. You read something about it, thus fixing it in your mind; you try to think about it a little, before falling asleep and again when you wake up. Later you marshal the whole briefly before your inner eye. Again, not too profusely, because it is in meditation proper that all the different aspects will be considered. So far you merely visualize the Gospel paragraph, the miracle, the parable in question, one of our Lord's statements, or whatever else. Thus your subject is ready.

Yet, being as we are, we want to see things, hear them, touch them, if possible. The purely spiritual is not our world, and only very gradually do we learn to be at home in it. Trying to start off there would mean to court disaster. In magazines, are not the pictures always regarded first? By many, even exclusively. The same applies to the beginning of meditation. Our imagination creates an image of the subject, visualizing it full of color and movement, apprehending words, touching things, as it were, and perceiving their warmth or coolness, tasting of their sweetness. But this should not be done too thoroughly, or else the soul may be caught by those images and forget to penetrate into their substance. To highly imaginative people this can be a real danger. On the other hand, a weak power of imagination may make meditation more difficult. But then there are ready-made images for every mystery of the faith. However, if we summon up our own images, besides engaging us more easily in meditation, they harness our imagination and assign to it a useful office. Otherwise in its continual ramblings and restless searchings it tends to be one of the main causes of distraction in prayer. But here it is somewhat tamed and occupied and will continue to accompany our meditation. Whatever material the memory brings forth, the imagination will transform into symbol and tangible reality and thus call forth another operation: reflection.

When this third mental power is engaged, meditation proper begins, a serious effort and the real task. Our reason tries to penetrate the meaning and significance of our subject, unfolding it, accounting for motives and aims, and above all, for the interior attitudes of any persons involved in it. Possibly other words or facts not actually contained in our current subject are remembered as points of comparison. Chiefly, however, our reason will probe into our personal life, weighing it against that which our subject has revealed to us—our good works compared to our Lord's love, our striving measured against Christ's indefatigable charity, our ways with others seen in the light of those of the Divine Heart. Trying to judge the great disparity, we realize ever more deeply how wide is the gap. Gradually we gain a genuine understanding of divine truth and hence of ourselves. Ever more unsparingly our true being is discovered to us, but equally in ever increasing amazement, delight and joy we recognize the glory of our Lord and His love. The connections of various truths long since believed are more deeply and better conceived, and in utter wonder we see how inexhaustible they are, though not long ago they appeared plain and obvious. But let us remember that all this should be interspersed with short acts of adoration, love, veneration, remorse, and so forth.

The next powers to come into play are our affections and

emotions. The two are normally distinguished by saying that emotions are a matter of feeling but affections are a matter of spiritual participation and inclination. Emotions can easily be self-centered and sensuous, since they derive from the senses; affections are more detached from self, more directly focused on their object and therefore higher in rank and importance. Now they have their place in meditation. What our reason perceived, impresses the soul, touches and affects it, repels or attracts it. Countless movements of the mind are roused, countless emotions awakened. They are, after all, the life of the soul, its rhythm fluctuating in joy and sorrow, its sympathy and cooperation with the world around and inside us. These faculties must not be neglected in favor of rational thinking, because they take the first place in stimulating our interior life and it is by them that our will is sustained. Here as everywhere else the golden mean should reign and nothing should be overdone. And while a vigilant moderation should make us renounce any exaggerated appetite for interior consolations, yet we should certainly never deliberately suppress the emotional life of the soul. Rather, those who by nature are cold and unfeeling should awaken and train this underdeveloped part of their being through regular meditation. As St. Augustine once said, there is no merit in insensitivity; it is a deficiency.

Now all is set for the final and decisive faculty of the soul to operate: the will. It has been said that the will in itself is a blind force without intelligence or judgment. Fired by a sense of value and by emotional desires pressing upon it, the will rushes toward the target which reason points out. Without that and without the emotional faculties preparing the way and providing the impulse, the will could not begin to do anything worthwhile. The will, however, is the faculty by which we achieve union with something outside ourselves. It is the power that enables us to have devotion, fidelity, steadfastness, since it is the power of love, and on this everything ultimately depends. For love determines and achieves our spiritual position, our target, our eternal life. In the light of this final aim, therefore, it becomes quite clear how necessary it is to engage and activate, prior to the will, all those other faculties of the soul. The more distinctly and profoundly I understand a truth, and the stronger its impact upon me, the more certain my will is to rise in the direction suggested by reason and affection. All aglow, it will run its course. An understanding of guilt and a horror of it will impel the will to flee sin and consequently any occasions of sin. Deeply impressed by the beauty of Christ's self-denying love, the will tears itself free from its egotism. It will long to emulate the divine-human Model, deeply stirred by the sight of Christ's unstinting surrender to the will of the Father in the hour of Gethsemane. The will fashions its resolve after the subject of meditation, and thus our meditation is directly connected to our practical life as Christians. But all this must ever be accompanied by and integrated into prayer—for God's pardon, for strength and courage, for patience, or whatever else it may be that the will lovingly longs to embrace and possess.

Here some points must be stressed. It would not be right to draw out of one meditation several resolutions to be observed simultaneously. We are unable to attend to so many things at once, and thus nothing would come of it all. It is possible, however, to have several different resolutions which apply to various situations. One can, for instance, resolve to kneel at prayer instead of always sitting down, and also not to give curt answers to a particular person but to be gentle and kind to him. But to strive to be loving, patient, prayerful and recollected all day long and all at once, that will not do. Here again asceticism applies: the practice of moderation.

Nor would it be appropriate to forge new resolutions every few minutes, for they are not mastered so quickly. Ought we then to meditate over and over again on the same subject? Perhaps we shall learn this in time, when we like to return to the same subject which has proved rich and full of significance. However, this is a matter of prolonged practice and spiritual experience. Until then, we should deal with different subjects of meditation in such a way that they all help us to aim at the same resolutions. Almost every period of our Lord's life illustrates His love, His loyalty, His wisdom, and above all His abandonment to the will of the Father in heaven. And there is nothing as important as that, since it includes all the rest.

Meditation ends in thanksgiving and adoration, in a prayer for God's blessing and for His forgiveness that we have perhaps not taken enough trouble about it. Concluding our time with God by a trusting gaze upon the Most Holy Trinity, we endeavor to retain, as well as possible, the state of recollection attained, and not to give full reign to our thoughts all too soon. The soul was with God; all its powers reached out for Him, and mysteriously He has given Himself in return. Charity has increased, and thus our meditation achieved its end. More ardently, more lovingly than before, our heart will now turn to God when we pray.

There is not a single subject which would not prove too vast and too deep to be dealt with in one period of meditation. In spiritual as in profane life things happen in much the same manner. To contemplate a picture, does that mean just looking at it? No, it means taking in every detail. The picture is, as it were, dissected, and point by point our eyes study each feature of it, as if it were the only one: each figure, each face with its individual traits and expressions, each movement of hands, of the body, the color and folds of the garments in which so much of the nature and condition of those wearing them can be expressed; then the landscape, the background, the foreground. Only then are relations discovered. Out of the many details the total builds itself up, more impressive in its effect on us according to the measure of the attention given to the details. An overall view of the whole does not usually yield much, except the presumption of having grasped a great deal. Here as everywhere, work is required if anything is to be gained.

That also applies to spiritual meditation. Do not hurry on as soon as some little perception has been granted to you. Not an extensive view, but a profound one is what you desire. What good is there in a quantity of things if there is no quantity of value? No organism can live by nibbling at its food—the soul least of all. How wonderful, on the other hand, when by degrees, the whole of the picture begins to come to life in all its magnificence and splendor! When the parable reveals itself in a wealth of significance and interpretation. When the figure of our Lord in a particular scene is suddenly made translucent to our sight, one word from His mouth giving an inkling of His divinely sublime depth which the soul can but adore in silent rejoicing, marveling that such things can be, and that He, within whom and through whom they are, is its own love, its Lord and its God.

Enough teaching; now for a brief example of the form which meditation may assume. We choose something familiar; often, indeed, too easily familiar, such as the beginning of the Lord's Prayer. Let us confine ourselves to the first word of the Latin version: *P a t e r noster*. We beg of Jesus that, in the love of the Holy Ghost, He may show and lead us to the Father, so that a deep trust and a fervent love for Him may result from our meditation.

There is not much for the memory to do. It merely calls up the subject and the beginning of that prayer which the mouth quietly pronounces once or twice. Imagination has a less easy task. How does one picture God, who is pure spirit and beyond all means of representation? Best perhaps to do without the physical frame of a face or suchlike, unless we fall back upon some work of art, such as Michelangelo's picture of God the Father on the ceiling of the Sistine Chapel. It would probably be better just to imagine God's attitude toward the soul, inclined toward it, full of bounty, a tide of loving warmth surging from the divine being across to me, desirous to enter my soul and dwell there. But there is remoteness, too, a distance born of reverence and of my consciousness of

God being all and I being nothing before Him. Yet here I am, His child that looks up to Him.

Now reason starts and considers the words: *Pater noster*. There is something very subtle in the Latin version. The English language has *Our* Father, unlike Spanish or Latin, where the order is reversed. We are accustomed to make our ego the measure of things, the center of the world. The true order, however, demands that God should come first. So from this manner of addressing God, odd to us but very revealing, we can learn the need for repentance, for reparation, for the repair of our sense of values. God is the beginning of all, the reason and meaning of all that exists. Every distinction is His, all prominence of being and will. The *Pater* is here given such emphasis that the *noster* has little significance by comparison. Yet, it is there. God Himself wants it to be there, immediately after or next to His name. Thus we are shown that we are inferior to God, but also how it would be perverse to cast ourselves away, as it were. God allows us to be near Him and wants us to be there. So let us honor Him by acknowledging Him to be first and supreme, and be ourselves honored and ennobled by the nearness to Him which He grants.

Our heart does not tarry now to marvel at the wondrously deep wisdom of a Father who in two words shows us the order of our existence, fundamentally repairing all our perversity, who admonishes us to say this daily so that it may impress itself ever more deeply upon us and save us from slipping again out of the order He made. Adorable wisdom! Glorious might of the Spirit, both overwhelmingly strong and utterly simple, which teaches and offers to us what, though sublime, can be grasped even by unlearned reason! Does not this one small point fully reveal that God truly is what He makes us call Him: Father—our Father? Now I shall look up to Him with unbounded trust, since wisely, securely and gently He guides me. Reason acknowledges how often it has offended against this convincingly true and sacred order, how harshly it claimed the rights of the ego, in contrast to the generous and indulgent simplicity with which the Father now restores all to order.

Cause enough now for the will to feel shame and sincere remorse; to resolve also henceforth to observe and honor this sacred original order and help others to do so. How and when? Right now; for instance, when the will, refusing to be its own spokesman, endeavors to "hallow His name"; when effort is expended not so much for one's own perfection, but for God's greater glory and praise.

Reason already knows that two words of such depth are too much for one meditation. It therefore returns to the first word: Father. The true infinite God I call Father. I call Him thus because He Himself bids me to do so. My reason must, by His command, say this wonderful word. And since Eternal Truth wills me to say it, no mere comparison, however beautiful and full of comfort, can be intended. This is the truth. Other words come to the mind: "children of God" (I John 3:1); we "have received the spirit of adoption of sons whereby we cry Abba—Father" (Rom. 8:15); in Christ we were given "power to be made the sons of God" (John 1:12), if we "believe in His name" (*ibid.*). Here is so vast a vision that our poor reason soon despairs of ever reaching the end. It hands it over to our heart which marvels, rejoices, adores. Our will, however, harvests of all this an infinite trust. How could it ever waver or doubt whether perhaps God was indifferent and had left me out of His care? Could a Father who is God, who is love and is all, be capable of such a thing? How could I even think it, much less turn against Him, pretending to myself that my fate, my struggle, my joys were of no matter to Him? Deeper and deeper the will now sinks itself into this word, into this being: Father. It abandons itself to Him and rests in His heart.

Once more reason takes up the cherished word, trying to approach its essence, mysteriously remote and yet so close, by a comparison. Surely God chooses the name of Father because of certain similarities between Him and a human father. Otherwise the name would be misleading. What, then, is my earthly father to me? He is the origin of my being, the source of my life. Without him, I could not be. To him I owe existence, abilities, dispositions. Similarly I owe my spiritual existence to God. My soul, and above all the divine life within me, comes from Him whom alone I must thank. It follows naturally that I owe Him obedience as well as loyalty and reverence; that I must labor for His honor, defend it where it is impaired, and within my own state of life always strive to serve it. Is not my family background apparent in my behavior? Thus also should my life of the God-Father stamp my whole being and tell of Him whose gift it is. So far, has anybody been able to detect in me any traits of a child of God? Our heart never tires in savoring this, nor our will to submit its acts, especially that of its complete surrender, to the heart of our Father. Filled with a sacred pride in such a Father, the soul experiences a new strength and assurance; leaning on Him, it will pursue its path. A new and delicious awareness of its filial union with God fills the soul with love, jubilation and gratitude.

Considering now the qualities of God my Father, what wealth offers itself to my spiritual eyes. His faithfulness guiding and escorting me, not letting go of me ever, though I try to withdraw from Him and even to find my own way—and not too good a way has it been. What mild forbearance; no trace of anger, but new encouragement and ever patient warning. There must be firmness, of course, or else my Father could not properly train me. God has tried me with quite a few hard and heavy tasks, has given me short shrift at times, denied me certain things, prevented others. But afterwards I always knew that God's paternal heart had been in all these events, set on my rescue and my sanctification. And I, fool that I am, remonstrated, was desperate, angry; wanted to hand in my notice and run away. My God, how shamefully revealing! And there, above the turmoil, always His countenance, unspeakably lovable; the purest light, the never-ending love, eternal patience, divinely, mercifully waiting for me and trusting that the good in me will persevere and grow in strength at last. This Father, different from the human one, always has time for me. He never turns His glance away from me, always anticipates my problems and requests, and in His only-begotten Son He shows me how much He shares my life. For in His Son the Father came to us to walk with us, to bear and fight and suffer with us, so that beyond all doubt we should know that He is with us and never will He leave us. He always understands. A human father can often understand his children's souls astonishingly well, but not in any ultimate degree, where one remains alone. The heavenly Father sees into our soul's remotest depths.

The soul could long pursue this theme. However, time is up. So, summarizing all, we say our *fiat*. Into the hands that gave this time of meditation, we give it back, knowing that next day, and the next, more may be understood. From that word "Father" a source of living water has sprung up.

Sanctification through meditation

Meditation is a means for the soul to be near God and to grow closer to Him. It is therefore a means of sanctification, since sanctity simply consists in this: to be totally one with God, to be of one will with Him who is holiness personified. In adoration, surrender and steadfastness, this union of the wills is brought about, and this is precisely the object and reward of every meditation. Usually the desire for sanctity is condensed into some clear-cut resolutions. They result from the comparison of our own life with that of the characters considered in meditation, or simply from the deep impression on us of their sublime and noble ways. Earlier we said that great economy must be observed in forming resolutions and, more particularly, in drawing the same kind of resolution for a long time from different meditations. Not to do so means scattering one's strength and fighting a losing battle from the start.

But if our resolution is really to become a sanctifying mechanism in our life, it will not be enough simply to try hard to keep it, nor to think of it anew each day, nor even to pray for the will and the strength to persevere. The point is to give back, in purest self-surrender, this very resolution into the hands of God. As long as it is our primary wish to become holy and for that reason to persevere in our resolutions, as long as we are ourselves the object of our self-sanctification, all is misplaced. Here, too, God must be our aim. It is in fact quite possible—and experience teaches this time and again—that God does not yet want us to attain to any particular virtue which we selected. Months or even years may pass in fruitless but renewed attempts. Rather than improve, things will grow worse, though this may often merely appear so to us who, more now than before, will pay special attention to this failing and seem to meet it everywhere. But the fact is that we do not succeed, and something like inertia and discouragement may come upon us. Well, let it. It comes to give us an awareness of our impotence, of the fact that not even a fraction of our sanctification can be achieved by ourselves. It comes from God, as His gift.

God wishes us to learn this lesson, until we are prepared, in spite of all our striving, to credit Him alone for each particle of success; until we are resigned to the pain and the shame of our unconquered failings, because God knows this to be good for us. Is not a wound sometimes deliberately kept open because the surgeon knows that other and far more important ailments within the organism must first be cured, which would be jeopardized by prematurely sewing up the wound? Here is a person assiduously treating her face because of a few pimples; the doctor smiles and sets to work quite differently, treating the impure blood of which they are a symptom. He lets the patient work away at her complexion; at least she will do nothing to damage it yet further. Once the main cause, known only to the doctor, has been removed, the healing of the secondary symptoms, which do not overmuch preoccupy the doctor, will be quite simple.

God acts likewise. He leaves us to forge resolutions and to exert ourselves again and again; but He does not remove that dreadful fault because meanwhile He, in the depth of our being, must remove and reform some very different thing. That is why we should without reserve leave it to God, where, when and how He will perfect our souls. That He will do so is as certain as His own word: "For this is the will of God: your sanctification" (I Thess. 4:3).

Even if we were to lose courage for any definite resolves, but decided instead quietly to leave everything to God's love, trusting that in His own good time He would make it come right, if we only wait, would meditation then cease to be a means of sanctification, and should it therefore be suspended? Most certainly not. For the very process of meditation is the proper means to sanctity. By it we practice goodness and fill ourselves with love, remorse and gratitude, with the longing for purity. In the process of meditation the heart adores, acknowledges God to be its only good, resigns itself in reparation to suffering and divine dispensations, opens itself to inflowing grace and prays for itself and others and for the kingdom of God. All this may so transport our heart that it never reaches the point of forming a resolution; forgets, in fact, all about it. But why resolve to adore, if adoration is my very attitude toward God? That is why we stress the decisive importance of prayer during meditation. If, in the desire for sanctity, this is well and faithfully done, the effects of prayer will make themselves felt at the opportune moment. Having considered and lovingly tasted the beauty of God, shall we not, at the sight of flowering shrubs and magnificent trees in a garden, remember and praise it and the Creator of whom these are image and likeness? This happens without any special resolve, being the fruit on the branches of meditation, as naturally grown as any other.

Thus the place of precise resolutions is taken by interior attitudes. It is no longer a question of individual acts, but of inner dispositions. Acts come and go, are called forth, reach a climax and disappear. The will can provoke them, even though we may not have much need for the particular virtues occasionally practiced. Dispositions, on the other hand, are something lasting. They fill our inner being and fashion it. From them the act then arises, as the occasion demands. If, for instance, we learn to maintain a holy reverence for God and all that concerns Him, we shall at the opportune moment have this within us, naturally and spontaneously, and there will be no need for a specific act to be made. If faith fills the soul through and through, need it make acts of faith? Will not its internal faith simply reveal itself whenever called upon? Meditation teaches the soul how such dispositions are acquired. Drawn deeply toward God's wisdom or love, God's beauty or strength, and drinking it in, the soul is gradually fashioned according to it, and the features which God wishes the soul to possess are impressed upon it. Later these very traits determine the soul's demeanor.

More especially, when spiritual sufferings and dryness break into our meditations and, to a large extent, turn them to agony, then the steadfast soul will of necessity practice a great many virtues in imitation of Christ, to be, in prayer and suffering, ever more closely fashioned according to the divine-human Model beheld in meditation. The soul will try perhaps to acquire the patience of Christ in the sorrowing hour of Gethsemane. Filled with sadness about its inanity, pervaded by a feeling of unspeakable helplessness and wretched loneliness, the soul actually participates in the suffering of Christ. And in joining His passion to its own, ready to go on bearing it out of love and devotion, in not running away and not giving up meditation which caused all the pain and torment, but remaining faithful and true in spite of temptations, the soul sorrows with its Beloved. With Him it is patient and with Him it is sacrificed in faith to the mysterious and purest of graces, which is the will of the Father.

Distractions may torment the soul. They cannot be mastered or chased away. So the soul accepts them as a participation in that frightful frustration with which human obtuseness, villainy, perversity, superficiality and waywardness met the noblest and purest intentions of our Redeemer, ever solicitous to give of His most precious gifts. Atrocious His final apparent desolation, yet beyond this frustration the Father's blessing turns it to grace and salvation in a way too mysterious for us to grasp. The soul, with the misery of its distractions which seem to nullify all adoration, union with God, and efforts to penetrate truth, now not only looks at the frustration in our Lord's life, but unites its own experience with it. Thus our frustrations, absorbed by those of Christ, turn into purest grace and a love of the Father which creates and transforms. With Christ the soul is crucified, and with Him it gently says: "God, my God, why hast Thou forsaken me?" (Mark 15:34). But with Him also it says: "Into Thy hands, O Lord, do I commend my spirit" (Luke 23:46). It considers the love of Christ in His care for His disciples, His sweet pleasure in children, His patient warning of those in danger. In so doing, the soul carries into the Sacred Heart all those who, through Christ, have been entrusted to its care, embraces them lovingly and holds them up to Him. Thus the soul learns to love as He does, and with Him; grows actually into the mind of Christ, into His dispositions, and lives in and by them. His being imprints itself—if we dare say so—on our souls. We "put on Christ," as St. Paul loves to say. The soul within us is cast anew in His image, and now, in and with Christ, it gradually grows into a true child of God. The glory of the Beloved radiates into the heart of the spouse who in her own right is so very poor, but He gives her beauty. It is well that she herself is hardly aware of it. She could not yet bear it. She would credit herself with what was and ever remains His alone, and will remain His all the more as she increasingly makes it all hers.

As we gradually grow into the way of meditation, our heart will frequently prompt us to continue. This we should certainly do. Contemplating, for instance, the kindness of Christ in one of the miracles of His healing, the soul feels captivated. Let it remain in silent adoration. The fewer its own efforts now, the better for deeper perception of and participation in the subject beheld; the better, too, for a real entering into and taking possession of it, which actually is the best preparation for contemplation. The soul will know the moment when to halt. The Holy Ghost gives this knowing, and the soul must obey Him at once. For His word ever wills and achieves its further sanctification.

All that God is, everything that refers to Him or is related to Him, can serve as material for meditation. The object is always to discover God, to be with Him, to know Him better, and to make ourselves His in increasingly fervent love. Whatever serves that purpose is suitable material. For one person nature can be a mine of rich treasures from which to deduct the attributes of God, which He manifests there. And if the Holy Ghost enlightens the soul, the inner eye will penetrate the veil to find Him whom nature veils and discloses. This is magnificently shown in the psalms, where the facts and phenomena of nature are viewed entirely in their relation to God and become an unceasingly rich source of divine praises. Nature is not here understood as a subject of natural science nor one of mythological interest or magic, but as the world of God. It is His field of activity, "His footstool" and the "place where His glory dwelleth" (Ps. 25:8). Making the psalms the basis of meditation means learning to discover God everywhere around us. Meditating on this sublime and excellent poetry, conceived in saintly people under the inspira-

181]

tion of the Creator Himself, the soul is made wide and deep, and finds a position from which the world is seen to disclose its original meaning anew.

The soul itself is a part of nature, though at the same time it is immeasurably more, especially the soul of the child of God, hallowed by grace. Within its being and in its abilities, in its destinies and in the vicissitudes of life, the soul finds ample cause for reflection and comparison and hence for considering God its Father, from whose love it proceeded and who lovingly carries and guides it on the way to Himself. Above all, the soul realizes and deeply admires the mysteries of God's solicitous providence the more carefully it scrutinizes its own life. By faith the soul knows this as a fact, but how much deeper will be the effect of the actual experience, when the soul by its faith perceives palpably, as it were, that it is being looked after, enlightened and led the right way. The awareness of the heavenly Father's love, born of faith, wonderfully fortifies the soul and helps it to surrender itself to God in filial trust, in spite of all its revolts because of the incomprehensibility of God's dispensations.

Yet in all this God reveals Himself only indirectly, as if in remote transparence, and nowhere quite tangibly, as the soul needs and desires Him. This is not enough, and in the long run it cannot sustain the soul. The soul wants to look at His face, read from the sacred features who He is, what He is, and what it is to Him. So the soul turns to Christ, who assures it: "He that seeth Me, seeth the Father also" (John 14:9). Now at last we are face to face with God! Now the soul may sense His nearness, His beauty and dignity, His love and fidelity. Now it may savor Him truly and live with and by Him. Meditation will always tend to find its conclusion in the figure of the God-Man, our Lord Jesus Christ, who is our Brother and our God, our friend, our master and our consuming love throughout eternity. The Gospel is an inexhaustible treasury for the soul that pines for God and a deeper knowledge of Him. Here are the founts of living water promised by our Lord; here is the justice after which we all hunger and thirst.

It would probably be wise not to start off with the more difficult chapters of Christ's discourses, but first to try those parables and incidents which, since they are taken from daily life, are easily imaginable and comparatively simple. Then come the events in the life of Christ, His ways with different kinds of people, His works, and above all, His sacred passion. Finally the great soliloquies transmitted to us, especially by St. John. Their full supernatural value will unveil itself only after long and intense preoccupation with the other two groups. Only after meditating on our Lord's discourses can one approach the Epistles, for instance those of St. Paul. In their largely abstract thinking they can prove too difficult for the average understanding; a deep knowledge of the truths of salvation is expected from us who meditate upon them as it was from those to whom they were addressed. Whatever the mystery, whatever the depth of thought of our meditation, it will always return to the figure of Christ, to His being, as it were, in time and space. In Him alone can be found rest for the soul and its powers. Christ is its life. In Him and only in Him can it be with the Father in the love of the Holy Ghost.

How do we proceed to extract from a parable or from a discourse just what it is meant to teach us? Some practice is needed for the right use of the sacred texts and for what we call exegesis. No doubt the Spirit of God will help the groping soul. Not least in value are the meditation books in which more or less systematically the whole life of Christ or certain episodes are expounded and counsels are given for directing one's life accordingly. These books differ greatly in value. The affective ones, transforming everything into outpourings of the heart and prayers of affection, are by no means the best, because they do too much for the soul and leave little or no room for the Holy Ghost's gentle activity. The soul should not, after all, feel or say what others suggest, but only what spontaneously comes forth after considering some truth. The slender fare of a more factual exposition can be much healthier, though at first we may not find it much to our liking. Nor should one select only those books on Scripture which are written in a purely descriptive fashion, in the style of a novel. While one need not shun these entirely, they may lead one to dwell excessively on non-essential or useless details. The same thing must be said about some of the works on Christ and Mary composed by certain mystics.

Here, of course, it is not important that everything be meticulously taken to pieces in accordance with the famous "points of meditation" which seem indispensable to some people. No doubt these points have their value, for they make things easy to survey and to absorb, but there is also the risk of feeling impelled to work laboriously through all the three points. This makes for undue haste and for pressure on the spontaneous manifestations of our interior life. Never should we hurry on at the expense of deep concentration. What cannot be mastered today must be left for tomorrow. God can be reached from every point, and that is all that matters. To be with Him, to look at Him, to sink our heart deeply into His love—that must ever remain the primary goal; all the "points" must take second place. One thing is certain: the less material the soul requires, the better for it, and the more proof of its progress. Steadily progressive simplification makes the soul independent of methods, classifications and deductions.

The most valuable books of meditation are those which the Church lovingly offers to us: the books of the liturgy. True, there are no paragraphs or divisions as in the works just referred to, but neither is there anything forced or artificial. All is lucid, full of meaning and life, genuine and essential. Nothing superfluous is offered, and nothing that would be too heavy a burden. After a passage of great depth, like most of the Epistles at Mass, immediately follow others of vibrating lightness, such as the Gradual and Alleluia, and what we have just heard penetrates into the soul not only because of the ease and harmony of its sounds, but especially because the previously heard theme is now illuminated and dramatized by a verse from a psalm or a hymn. Thoughts are organically connected; analogies help to relate one to the other and to unlock their hidden meaning. Take, for example, the Mass of our Lady, *Salve, Sancta Parens,* where the exulting words of the woman in the Gospel, "Blessed is the womb that bore Thee," recur in slight transformation in the Communion verse: "Blessed is the womb of the Virgin Mary, which bore the Son of the Eternal Father." Womb should here be understood as the innermost part of the body. The words of the Gospel thus apply to all who, by virtue of the Eucharist, have within them the Son of God. What a depth of inference and meaning is contained here! There is systematic order, too, not simply reproducing the actual course of events in the life of our Lord, but showing a magnificent conception of the liturgical year, gradually placing it before our eyes, representing it to us beyond time and space in the moment of consecration. For here our Lord is Himself before our eyes, in our midst, in His miracles no less than in His parables.

Here the Church as Bride and Mother speaks to us of the Beloved, and through her He Himself speaks and acts and gives power to His words and His works to be made real in those who "have ears to hear" (Mark 4:23). To meditate on the liturgical texts means to take the hand of our Mother the Church and to be led by her to Christ, who is the goal and meaning of all our liturgy, and through Him to the Father in heaven. Thus this meditation, more than any other, ends in the heart of God.

Chapter 17

Contemplation

Meditation and contemplation

The goal of the soul's interior journey in search of God is contemplation. The term itself says much, yet not enough. In its Latin root there is a reference to observation, vision; the mind observes God and His truths. What is not indicated is that this vision must be charged with love, and that love itself is its culmination. It is an achievement not of the speculative reason, but of the pulsating heart. If in the word itself the stress seems to lie on discernment, i.e., on an act of the intellect, that is because the contact between God and the soul is basically established on knowledge. Everything else is built on this foundation—our love and the life proceeding therefrom. Vision serves as a runway for the plane's take-off and ascent; love, which there begins its upward flight, gradually soars to the most sublime perfection that can be vouchsafed here on earth. Discernment, the intellectual part of the process, must of necessity always remain imperfect, incomplete and provisional; not only because in this life we are meant to develop by merit, which can be gained only in faith (it is hardly meritorious for reason to acknowledge an evident truth), but also because in our earthly state we cannot achieve an unveiled vision of God. Such is God's essence that full vision of it would amount to the ending of our earth- and time-bound existence, and a transposition into the infinite. Hence it is not vision alone which is to be stressed in contemplation, but love. All genuine mysticism—and we have here reached the mystics' territory—always revolves round love, while false mysticism strives mainly or even exclusively for further discernment. It gets caught in the theoretical and provisional and loses itself therein, since invariably its vision degenerates into more or less shadowy speculations and phantasms which turn the head and make the mind haughty, leading it to perdition. True mysticism, on the contrary, promptly proceeds from the objects of its vision to acts of love, warming the heart. It does not engender a vain preoccupation with self but attachment to God and to all His creatures, bringing God to them.

Contemplative prayer, therefore, does not aim at the discerning of "higher worlds" and the like, nor at deepened understanding for its own sake, nor—least of all—at knowledge diversified and studded with "discoveries." As St. Paul states: "Knowledge puffeth up, but charity edifieth" (I Cor. 8:1). Is not God Himself, in His very revelation, most sparing in the disclosure of truths? Christ does not dream of explaining to the Jews the mystery of the Eucharist, in spite of their stunned questions; they are asked to accept His statement: "The bread that I will give is My flesh for the life of the world" (John 6:52). Once accepted, this mystery is to become a source of love and of life, all renewed and transfigured. This is the constant theme: love, and a life filled with love. No explanations as to how He is God and yet man simultaneously, nothing about the mystery of the most holy Trinity, but always just this: that through love we are able to share in this mysterious life. In educating us, His children, God again and again seems to apply this rule: children must obey, not blindly, but with no more than a modicum of understanding, a single beam of light to guide the willing intellect, and so to act in and from the love of God.

We are here already confronted with two extremely important clarifications: first, that on the inner journey we must never cast around for discoveries, never in eager curiosity wait for phenomena, sensations, encounters. We would immediately falsify and disrupt our attitude to God and would thus produce in ourselves effects directly opposite to what contemplative prayer is meant to achieve. With categorical firmness we must suppress all and any craving for disclosures, for individual truths, and certainly for personal revelations, otherwise we shall at this point be open to diabolical allurement. We come back to asceticism, a constant companion on this journey, and here certainly no less imperative than in the earlier phases. Secondly, if even without our encouragement something seems to become apparent, some specific explanation or vision seems about to be vouchsafed to us, then we should want to refuse it and turn ourselves away with all available strength. Yet we should never hide it from our spiritual director. If God should ever wish to grant us some special communication, He will surely find a way to make His authorship plain beyond all possible doubt. The soul must, of course, be acute of hearing, and in this it will find its love renewed and intensified. Think of the revelations concerning the Sacred Heart, which were granted to St. Margaret Mary Alacoque; they were wholly aimed at fanning a great love and at a transformation of Christian existence, while their intelligible content only served as a spur and incentive.

The attempt, still made from a distance and with great caution, to describe contemplative prayer will take us back to the simile which we used earlier to exemplify the difference between activity and passivity, between meditation and contemplation. With the former, the stress was on our own effort, on bringing all the soul's powers and faculties into play so that they would, though wholly resting upon grace, expand fully and be operative in all directions. We saw this in greater detail when we examined the functions assigned to each individual power of the soul in the course of a meditation. Each becomes fully engaged, chooses, directs, commands for a time and then hands over to another, always under the vital and gently guiding aspiration of the Holy Ghost, yet in a consciously experienced freedom of self-determination. Here the soul itself is active; God lovingly renders assistance because He Himself wants this activity. In meditation the soul works like a skilled craftsman, experienced, well-versed and adroit, whose hands fashion many beautiful things in conformity with the requests or designs of his customers, to everyone's delight, not least his own.

But when we turn to contemplative, prayer, the accent noticeably shifts to receiving, to keeping still. One is tempted to say that meditation is masculine in its essential characteristics, but contemplation is feminine. Life proceeding from God is received and here most inwardly absorbed. The soul is not merely guided by God, held by His hand, but now follows Him step by step. It no longer pursues ways or notions of its own, but keeps most carefully in His wake, anxious almost not to make any movements at all unless they be in accord with His. It is like that child who so faithfully followed in his mother's footsteps and never dared to do things differently from her. Or again, it is like a truly gifted artist who applies all the technical knowledge acquired during his years of study and ultimately creates a work of art in accordance with the inspiration received from above and the mysterious guidance to which he owes obedience and to which he may never oppose his own personal conception and self-determined desires. He knows only too well that by so doing he would fail both his calling as an artist and the order of his own existence as one who is "called." His only task is to obey, and even if the vision, the gift of understanding for the mysteries of a higher order, take on his own flesh and blood, that is, even if the manner of their translation into the world of visible things bears the mark of his own personality, yet his work will still be an act of receiving, of pure obedience, a passive response to actuation from above. Even the child, following his mother through the moor, takes his steps in the manner of children, though they copy hers exactly in faithful and obedient conformity. In this way too our subjectiveness is always called in, and it could not be otherwise. Yet it will be appreciated that the subjective element is here no more than a shell, the outward form in which that which is given to us is enveloped, while in meditation not only the form but also the inner substance, down to every detail, comes from within. It is the difference between the artisan, who draws on the knowledge and experience stored inside him, and the true artist, who receives inspiration from above. Is it not highly significant that the man whose work lives by inspiration is called creative, when in fact all that is essential comes to him as a gift, and that we hold him in incomparably higher esteem than even the most studious and intelligent artisan, however gifted with sense of form and with taste? So also does the prophet, through whom God speaks, tower above him who, after careful study and deliberation, proclaims what will always remain God's truth yet what in manner and accent of expression is wholly his own. Likewise contemplative prayer ranks high above that of meditation, since in the former it is ultimately the triune God Himself praying in and through the soul, His own eternal prayer, making all prayer perfect.

The difference between activity and passivity is beautifully demonstrated in a comparison given to us by St. Teresa of Avila. She likens meditation to the watering of a spacious garden by means of a draw-well. One goes to the well, labors with chain and pail, fills the buckets and carries them to the beds which need watering. All this is done as painstakingly as possible, truly "in the sweat of one's brow." Yet in the end one must admit that all this can never be more than a temporary expedient, and the gardener continues anxiously to watch the sky for any sign of the rain which is so long in coming. Contemplative prayer, on the other hand, is like a spring rising in the very middle of the garden of our soul, with its sweet and clear waters flowing in all directions, moistening wide patches of soil. In such a garden, fresh and healthy plants will grow in happy profusion. Without so much sweat and toil, even without effort in the coarser sense, things happen, apparently, of their own accord and yet a great deal is happening, far more, in fact, than when the garden was being laboriously watered by human hands. Here nature itself is at work, doing for itself what is needed, quietly, easily, spontaneously, with beauty and grace both in substance and manner. The manifold efforts made by the powers of the soul in meditative prayer are, in contemplation, replaced by a spontaneity which is far more productive. God's love now pervades the soul in quite a different way, more naturally and lightly and not as before, when great efforts were required merely for getting this love into perspective and for fashioning an adequate response. Now the soul is truly at home in this love, having arrived at last whither it had always felt mysteriously drawn. It is all flame and life, and what more could it possibly be?

Let us try, once again, to delineate these two modes of prayer. When we study a painting, we proceed in the manner already described. First we concentrate on a specific detail, examine it closely, try to understand it in relation to other details, giving ourselves ample time for this scrutiny. Only when we have assimilated sufficient detail can we gain an appreciation of the painting as a whole, grasping its full meaning now in a glance, as it were. But in this one glance are contained all the preparatory studies, the industry and the patience employed to unriddle and master the component parts. In so doing we reverse the process of artistic creation. The artist had first conceived the painting as a whole and had then slowly made it come to life on the canvas, through the various details which he used to build up his composition. But were they his main concern? Certainly not; otherwise the painting would have lost much in artistic value. It might still be interesting, but it would no longer be great. It would tend to distract us rather than focus our attention on the original concept and inspiration. He who meditates—in this case on a painting—starts with the individual details and works through them until at last his mind's eye grasps the whole which had been envisaged by the artist.

Once the whole has been mastered, vision (contemplation) replaces scrutiny (meditation). For brief moments one may re-examine one or the other detail, but in the main the eye now encompasses the whole of the composition. One sees it now (and will see it at other times when the picture is looked at again) in a manner different from that of meditating scrutiny; beauty and meaning of detail recede into the background to make way for the impact, the strength, the richness, the depth of the composition as a whole. Now that the ultimate meaning has become revealed, the detail, which was required only to lead the eye to such deeper understanding, may be ignored. The gaze comes to rest on the picture, or more precisely, it rests on that to which the picture, itself a means to an end, wishes to direct our mental eye. The glance is at rest, it searches no longer because it has reached its goal. The glance is not rigidly staring or gaping, but free, vital, almost fluid. Perhaps one could describe it as "circling tranquillity." The eye encompasses all, now from one angle, now from another, but always as a whole. Excessive attention to detail would destroy the unity of composition and would disturb the deep joy and tranquillity of this vision lost in contemplation. If we come back to this particular painting later on, we need not do the work of careful scrutiny again. Once having gained the vision of the whole, we possess it forever, though we may advance to even deeper understanding if the picture be full of meaning and our soul be sensitive enough. But it is as a whole that the picture has so much more to tell; that whole which our gaze continues to circle, in which it dwells and knows itself to be at home.

It is not difficult to apply this to the two modes of prayer. Contemplation means to come to rest, to repose in the whole. It is no longer concerned with details to be examined, compared or elucidated so that the truth contained in them may become apparent. All that lies behind; it has been mastered before. Now the harvest is come. That very truth is now at hand and is itself the object of the soul's tranquil and steady gaze. The soul lives and moves in it, not toward it, as before. It circles round it and penetrates ever more deeply into it. It no longer considers Christ's charity as manifested in His attitude to the children; instead it grasps this charity itself, is seized by it, loves and adores it, and gradually makes itself conform to this divine-human love, almost without realizing it. To put it differently, it is no longer the soul which is active, but that truth now acts in it, directs and animates it, while the soul responds with all its powers jointly so that it experiences that truth as a force of life. Certainly, the soul will also have occasion again to meditate, but it will be less and less successful in doing so since it has been too much seized by the truth and come under its spell, and it is impossible to meditate and contemplate at the same time. Each of these two modes of prayer wholly absorbs the soul; to try to force them under the same yoke would spell the death of both. When we walk, we cannot be on two different altitudes at the same moment. To leave the one means to take up a position on the other, and one readily descends when at last he has reached the summit.

Perhaps it will cause surprise that we have made such ample use of pictorial similes at the very place where we are dealing with man's most highly spiritual aptitudes. Yet this is part of the universal law: the more spiritual His message, the more does Christ use parables to make His meaning clear. For example, the kingdom of heaven, a concept essentially not of this world even if incorporated in the here and now, is portrayed by numerous parables of sense images so that we might obtain some kind of perception or inward vision of it. And He Himself, God made man, reveals God's presence in human nature so that God might be touched and seen and heard by us in a manner suited to the limitations of our being. Thus we may use similes as a means of evoking in the mind images of spiritual realities whose radiance the similes reflect. But the likeness gradually recedes until it fades totally and the soul draws its life directly from that spiritual realm to which the similes were meant to lead it.

Images also present themselves as aids to deeper perception while contemplative prayer is already being fashioned within us. They are helpful as expedients, and in passing. Therefore the soul may accept them once they come. If, however, it has already reached the level of contemplation, or if it is just about to do so, then the soul must never turn to them with interest and joy, though this was quite lawful and even necessary in meditation. Instead, these images must be used in the manner of stepping stones on which the foot rests but for a moment, leaving them instantly behind. The former was necessary to make a start, the latter for making progress. In place of images, brought to life by the powers of imagination, we are to experience a far more spiritual kind of awareness. In the early stages, for example, the memory of a beautiful painting may be instrumental in making the face of Christ rise before us, and in focusing our inner gaze, but we are not to cling to it. Later, His face will be present, and we will know that it is there, without anything being consciously perceived by our imagination. And our gaze will rest on it, though not as on the Eternal Word within God, but as on the human face of the Word made flesh.

All this almost defies description, especially if one addresses people who have never yet experienced it. He who has, will understand at once, and for the inexperienced ones our text may at least serve to sketch the outlines so that on entering into the realm of contemplation they may know their way and not be afraid, but proceed with high courage.

Acquired and infused contemplation

If contemplation is so precious and sublime, why do we not aim for it immediately instead of spending such long periods on vocal prayer and meditation? Does that not mean a waste of our time? Why climb about laboriously in the face of the mountain when real enjoyment can be found only on the summit? Contemplative prayer is God's work within us. Therefore we cannot simply rise to it as we would like, but must wait for it to be given to us when it pleases God. Though certainly we may strive for it as best we can, moving toward the desired end; but to gain it is not given to us except by God Himself. This is so even in the field of natural perception. There are days when we seem able to penetrate without effort the things that happen to us, to grasp their meaning, joyfully reading them like a book open before us. Everything is clear, self-evident, straight-forward. And there are other days when the book is sealed. Impossible now to gain access to those depths which had already become so familiar. It is as if we had been dreaming, had imagined things, while in fact the grim realities of life continued to face us impregnably, shutting us out, leaving us desolate and poor, and helplessly searching for the ultimate sense after which our mind hungers. On such days it is useless to try to force an approach; the feeling of distance, of exile and disgrace will only be heightened. The revelation of God before our mental eye is an act of grace, a pure gift granted only to him who, though full of longing, waits in utter patience or to those to whom it is given more quickly and are even more deeply aware that it is a gift.

That is why contemplation cannot be acquired, although there are books in which a distinction is made between infused contemplation, given by God, and acquired contemplation, made possible by our own efforts. Therefore we repeat that contemplation cannot be acquired. One can dispose oneself in the manner of a person who gazes at a painting and gradually re-creates the composition as a whole from the wealth of component detail until the underlying concept is fully disclosed, until the painting surrenders itself in an act of self-revelation. Yet the painting, like any other inanimate object, can never really speak or give itself to us, but a personal being has self-consciousness and thus the power to concede or deny access to its inner essence. It can be approached from outside, but only up to a point; beyond that it must disclose itself in the gift of voluntary self-revelation, if one is to penetrate to the very core of its personality. And how much more is this true of the most sublime being, the triune God.

Our task is limited to tracing the likeness of Himself which God has instilled into nature and into ourselves; to listen to the truth He teaches in the revelation of His word, and to

195]

respond to it by faith. Beyond that, He Himself must unlock the mysteries of His heart, must open the door and disclose Himself to us. Often He will do so in answer to the soul's deep and patient fidelity in study, suffering and prayer. In that case it may be somewhat justified to speak of "acquired" contemplation, though only in a most limited sense, as the expression might be used in connection with a beggar who again and again presents himself at the rich man's door, stretching out his hand in supplication and trying to make himself agreeable by attitudes of respect and zeal, so that he might "acquire" a more generous gift. But the word cannot, in this context, have its usual meaning; there is no element of claim or right, no relation between what the beggar did and what he received, and the gift remains so gratuitous that the rich man would not have acted unjustly if he had ignored the beggar's supplication altogether, or sent him away with no more than a pittance. If God reveals Himself to us in contemplation, He acts in the most complete freedom. Nothing constrains or obliges Him, nothing except His own charity and the desire to grant us the happiness of union with Him. He "infuses" contemplation into us, gives it to us from above, as rain falls to refresh the fields. The fields, too, have done nothing more than lie there parched, waiting, and needing the rain, if ever their crops are to ripen.

We can turn to vocal prayer and meditation at any time, as we see fit, but not to contemplation. That we can use only when God gives it to us. The achievement of contemplation therefore implies vocation, though once called we can hardly ever lose this state of grace again. But we must beware lest we treat this sublime gift with carelessness instead of turning it to fullest account to gain that eminence of the interior life which God, through this gift, holds out to us.

Must we assume then that only a few are predestined to receive these special graces? Certainly not. More and more has the view been accepted that the mystical life of grace which reaches its apex in contemplation rightly belongs to every child of grace, to everyone reborn in Jesus Christ, because it is, in reality, nothing else but the perfection of the three theological virtues in us. The theological virtues—so called because they are centered upon God Himself, upon His truth, His beauty and His love, because they move toward Him, reach out to Him and attain Him—are infused into every baptized soul as a truly divine dowry, enabling us to sustain the life of Christians. And God Himself deepens and strengthens and kindles them in us. The soul can dispose for this with the help of God's grace and create favorable conditions, but the increase itself, the growth in strength and maturity, is never the fruit of the soul's own efforts, unlike the natural virtues, which the soul itself can practice and perfect. God alone infuses the theological virtues and the more powerfully these three, faith, hope and charity, are activated in the soul by God, the more closely do we approach the state of contemplation. Always, however, this presupposes that the soul has been faithfully submissive to the gently guiding direction of the Holy Ghost. It is this fidelity, we repeat, which constitutes our contribution, and God demands it.

It is not, though, as if God needed such fidelity. He could bestow the gift of contemplation on someone far advanced on the road to perdition. Thus it has happened that people who, a moment ago, were deeply immersed in sin, suddenly receive the grace of a contemplative vision. Is it perhaps that only the full impact of the love of God could so captivate and engross their hearts that relapse into sin became morally impossible? It is not for us to question why God grants His mercies in seemingly contradictory fashion, showering one person with gifts although he never did anything to "earn" them, while another, who always did his very best, is kept endlessly waiting. Whichever way God chooses, we must be certain that it is the best, the wisest and certainly the safest way for the soul, and in following it trustingly, the soul will be sanctified in the measure ordained for it from all eternity.

This, too, must be said: method or system have nothing to

do with the call to contemplative prayer. God makes the flow of His love and grace independent of such expedients, as if He wanted to demonstrate that He bestows His gifts with complete sovereignty. True, often enough God makes His action in us follow the pattern of certain methods, observances, etc., which in their final form bear the mark of sanctity and as such have been approved and recommended by the Church. They also are in accordance with His holy will, since He is a God of order. But this order must not turn into a kind of spiritual bureaucracy, a barren system by which we think we can ensnare and hold God's grace. If that happens, God will direct His gaze away from such all too human endeavor, to let it rest where apparently no achievement had prepared the ground, but where, in utter freedom, it pleases Him to perform the works of His love. This will be a salutary experience, and we must bow to His mysterious judgment.

It is possible, for example, that someone appears incapable— for want of the most rudimentary education and suppleness of mind—ever to achieve meditative prayer. St. Teresa of Avila tells of an old lay-sister in one of her convents who complained that she had never been able to meditate and, consequently, could never hope to attain contemplation; vocal prayer was the best she could do. What had she then been praying during the long hours reserved for prayer by the rules of the Order? The Our Father, nothing else. St. Teresa plies her with questions: how did she do it, and what were her experiences? In the end the Saint discovers that this humble old sister, who believed that in matters spiritual she could utilize but the most simple tools, had in fact attained to one of the most exalted forms of contemplation, utterly without method, without recourse to the finely-spun system of spiritual progress which so many bemoan as being too difficult. That is why we have, in the previous chapters, insisted so strongly on the need to let oneself be guided in vocal prayer, spiritual reading and meditation by the often almost imperceptible suggestions of grace, by the "aspiration of the Holy Ghost"; to stop reading or meditating as soon as this tender "halt" is sensed, the gentle tightening of the reins which foolish zeal is so prone to ignore and to dismiss as an idle fancy, deeming its own deliberate effort and striving far more important and reward-ing. In halting, in keeping still, we may, if only for seconds, experience a foretaste of contemplation, a first glimmer of the essential presence. We may find ourselves in touch with that reality which stands behind text, thought or image and which now comes across to us. We may for the first time experience or taste God's truth, and thus Himself, since truths do not float in space by themselves; ultimately they are but the mode of our perception of God or of His self-revelation. He is the truth, and thus in all truth seen with our inner eye we already behold Him. God wants this loyal obedience to the aspirations of His Spirit first and foremost, since it is by it alone that faithful observance of our duties as regards the times and content of prayer becomes meet and just, leaving behind the standards of self to cling only to Him, the ultimate measure, even, and indeed more so, when none of it seems to make sense.

Thus, contemplation may arise amid the other types of prayer, touching them with a first glimmer of its radiance so that the soul becomes aware of something new, something more beautiful and arresting waiting to strengthen its desire and to draw it still closer to God. In this form, many devout Christians may be granted a degree of contemplation even though they do not recognize it and, in their ignorance, fail to nurture it in any way.

But when the soul senses more and more that this new form of spiritual experience becomes a necessity and that it ardently desires to possess it forever, then it will enter upon a way of suffering, a veritable crucifixion of the heart, and it is essential that the soul should be prepared to accept this even if it does not know how such pain can possibly be endured. But what may later be required should not alarm us now. God wants no more than that His appeal be heard, and that the soul be resolved to faithfulness; He will sustain it. The soul need but reach out to Him with both hands and say (even if all its strength barely suffices to formulate the words): "Take me and guide me, I surrender everything to Thee; all my life and being, in time and eternity. Thou alone shall lead and direct. Teach me to follow blindly and to let go of myself that Thou alone reignest in me."

If the soul thus responds to the first experience of contemplation, then the essential pre-requisite has been furnished, without which God cannot accomplish His ultimate purpose in the soul: gradually to transfigure it, to make it "divine," without ever suspending its state as a created being. Patience, however, must be the soul's equipment. God Himself will grant that virtue, will so train the soul that its patience will ever increase, for it will need it in abundant measure. Contemplation does not come ready-made; it is a vital thing and as such is subject to the laws of life, implying movement, progress, change. It is a gradual deepening of familiarity with God and first of all one must become accustomed to a new spiritual environment which, vague as yet and causing distress, will at the same time attract and repel. Above all, the soul must learn to wait; otherwise it had better not kindle hopes of spiritual progress which can never come true. Especially one should keep well away from mystical books. It is actually dangerous to try to acquire by reading what one is destined to live. Determination here means, not "I want this to happen," but "I will wait for Thy grace to make happen in me what pleases Thee." Of all explicit petitions it is perhaps that for the gift of patience which should least of all become muted in the soul striving for union with God, a patience which is a passive surrender as much as an active effort, an offering of self in utmost concentration, yet full of peace.

The suffering of contemplation

The suffering which must inevitably be encountered on the way of contemplation will be accepted by the soul only if it has begun to see contemplation itself as something vitally necessary. But cannot eternal bliss be gained without contemplation? No, in actual fact it cannot. As the subjective experience of God's holiness and as the perfect joy derived from knowing that God has at last and forever come into His own in the soul and that henceforth His will alone will be fulfilled in and by it, beatitude presupposes that anything which might at any time have stood between God and the soul should have been removed utterly and completely. Countless times the mystics have affirmed, following Aristotle, that the ailing eye is not capable of absorbing the full radiance of the sun's light and of seeing all other things in this light. Instead, the impact of light will cause pain, the eye begins to water, and instinctively turns away as much as possible, seeing even less now than before. The sick eye of the soul, that is, the soul which is still beset with sins, deficiencies and evil inclinations, is incapable of opening itself to the truth of the divine essence, to the supernal brightness and purity of the triune majesty. It must turn away. That is why those who are eternally damned will forever turn themselves away from Him, because for them, and due to their own faults, to behold God is a greater torment than the renunciation of His love. For our physical well-being a hot bath of 100 degrees is agreeable and just right, but let the heat increase to the boiling point and we are scalded and cry out with pain. What then shall the soul say when the glowing radiance of God sears into its chilled wretchedness? Or again, in a dimly lit room it is relatively unimportant whether a bit of dust remains or not; it will not be seen anyway. But when the lights are turned on, every speck is plainly visible, patches of dirt or things left lying about are awkwardly prominent, and the whole room which, a moment ago, seemed habitable enough, now fills us with disgust and with the desire to run away. When the incorruptible light of God flows into the soul but the soul itself is still soiled by its attachment to earthly things, by infatuation with self and contempt for others, by lack of devotion and loyalty, must it not then flee from itself and clamor for the earth to swallow it up? The soul that is not purified down to its innermost recesses simply cannot endure God's close proximity, and yet it is to that very nearness that the soul has been called from eternity, the ultimate meaning of its creation and of the embrace of God's love. There, in most intimate closeness to God, near to His heart, the soul can find its eternal abode. There alone can the aim and scope of its existence be fulfilled.

But this purification, without which there can be no perfect union with God, do we not achieve it by means of asceticism? Is not its whole purpose to take ourselves to task, root out faults and vices, bad habits and dangerous inclinations, and at the same time strengthen and confirm all that is beautiful and holy? True enough, we shall never reach down into our secret depths, the most secure and indiscoverable hiding places for everything that is perverted in us. Who we really are and what we really look like, that we shall never see. And it is kindness indeed, the kindness of our heavenly Father, that our real countenance remains forever veiled to our own eyes. He knows that the disclosure would hurtle us into despair, precisely because we could never muster the strength so radically to transform ourselves that our features become molded in the likeness of Christ. He lets the dark and truly horrifying recesses of our soul lie hidden under the veil of our ignorance, out of mercy, as if He Himself placed a hand across our eyes lest we collapse. And collapse we certainly would, should we ever see ourselves as we really are. Because there is literally nothing in us that is not impregnated with self-love, that arch-enemy whose works are cloaked in the mantle of concern for our well-being; with the terrible pride which self-love begets and so thoroughly disrupts our relation with God and with our fellow creatures; with that avidity, possessive and gluttonous, which recoils from the very thought of sacrifice and so utterly debases us.

No; we ourselves can never accomplish it, this thorough cleansing and purification. We shall die miserably in our state of wretchedness without ever having seen it completed. But where do we go from here? If this be final, then we shall never be close to God, never possess His life as our own. Until love has been made perfect in us and our whole being has been reformed in the likeness of God through love, we shall not see Him as He is, that is, as love itself. Asceticism is vitally necessary, is unavoidable and imperative, but of itself it is not sufficient, not by any manner of means. It extends our energies in the direction of all that is good; it awakens in us longing and zeal; it will push us to the extremities of our own strength; but there we come to a halt, sadly ignorant of what to do next. At this point we must open our arms wide in ardent supplication for His help, which alone can complete the task which He Himself began. In asceticism, under the stimulus of divine grace, we progress as far toward God as our own abilities permit, now He Himself must lift us up, drawing us to His heart, since that is more than our powers can ever achieve, even if strengthened by His grace. And it is well, since in this we learn—and forever—that we are nothing, and that God is all.

"And the truth shall make you free" (John 8:32), Christ tells us. Shall make us free of everything that fetters the soul and holds it back from God and from flying into His arms. All sin, and everything connected with it as cause or consequence, hinders the soul on its upward flight. Every inclination, though lovable in itself and as such without any baseness, will yet become a grave obstacle if the soul is improperly cleansed, remaining wedded to things which it secretly cherishes and tries to shield against God's "jealousy," dreading the moment when He will ask: "Give this to Me, too."

How fond we are of everything around us, how fond of ourselves. And how natural it seems to us that it should be so. How deeply are we revolted by the suggestion that we should renounce these attributes of human existence. Fetters everywhere, enslavement wherever we look closely. Things and people chain us down; ideals even and the very striving for sanctification can become bonds of slavery if our desire and efforts are prompted by self-love, by the pleasure with which we regard ourselves, instead of springing from a pure love for God and from the ardent wish that His will alone should be done. Even the most noble and exalted thoughts and tendencies are enmeshed in this web of bondage, and we do not even suspect them. That we should be made free of all this is the promise contained in the Gospels; it is the essential meaning of the evangelical message of glad tidings. Is not freedom the gladdest message of all? Freedom which will permit us at long last to become truly ourselves in God, and thus wholly to belong to Him?

The truth will "make us free"; but what is truth? "I am the Truth," is our Lord's solemn declaration. From Him, then, will come our freedom. Not by our listening to individual truths, which in faith we accept and upon which we meditate in order to draw practical conclusions for our life and conduct, though all that is necessary and in accordance with God's will. But it is a beginning only. Truth as such wants to enter into us; truth wants to penetrate our being and thus evict all untruths, all mendacity, all furtiveness and dishonesty. Not all at once, of course; that would be impossible. But by gradually seeping into us, the truth which is Christ and the life of the triune God in Christ wants to impart to us, to implant in us, that divine sanctity to which our own endeavors can never attain, not even with the help of grace. And it is this, all this, that happens in contemplation, in contemplative prayer. Only there, and only by it, does God convert the soul to Himself, transform the soul into Himself as far as is possible, and who would point out its limits?

So true is this that the soul which did not arrive at contemplative prayer in this life, to be made perfect by and in contemplation, must with absolute certainty undergo the cleansing processes of purgatory. In purgatory we are purified because the eye is still ailing, the inner temple is still strewn with rubbish, or too much coldness and rigidity remain in the soul, making it hypersensitive to heat. There is no essential difference between the processes to which the soul is subjected

in purgatory and the sufferings imposed upon it in contemplation. There as here it is the truth which will bring freedom
and thus make the soul ready for the life of the children of
God. With this distinction, however: after death all this will
happen without merit, since it no longer stems from the soul's
freedom of choice. After death the soul wills nothing but
that God's will in it should prevail, wills this purification and
this manner of being purified because it has utterly surrendered
itself to God and knows that only thus can it attain its goal.
And because it cannot, in fact, will anything else, since its
closeness to God now allows of only one direction for its
striving, nothing is left that could possibly distract it. In its
earthly existence the soul always remains free to choose, to
say yes or no, to hold back, however ardent its love for God.
It retains the freedom of betrayal, of desertion, of transferring
its allegiance elsewhere. But since it is this very freedom of
saying no to God which, in His eyes, constitutes the special
value and merit of the soul's acceptance of His will in action
and in suffering, to be purified here on earth by the pains and
raptures of contemplation will gain something for the soul
which the same purification after death can never give to it.
Though the process and the aim—sanctity—are the same, how
different the depth of feeling, of enjoyment, of positive bliss
with which the soul will one day realize its sanctity.

We would surpass proper limits by saying more about it,
though we may perhaps point the direction by a simile. Someone may find a budding crocus as the first sign of approaching
spring, and his joy is tremendous. Another picks a bunch of
rare flowers, yet they move him but little; his delight is half-
hearted and short-lived. Two souls with a wholly different
resonance. The soul which has acquired greater merit will,
though in all other respects its state of perfection is the same,
possess a much greater capacity for ecstatic joy, and will be
more easily stimulated, roused, enchanted. Because it gave itself
to God of its own free volition, not holding back the heart
but surrendering it to Him that He might transform it, must

not this love, more tender and quicker to respond, endow the soul with greater sweetness, maturity, translucence, sensitivity? Thus we gain incomparably more when in this world we reach the state of contemplation than when, after struggling against it or failing to direct our whole life toward it, we must yet undergo the same or even worse suffering in the next life.

Finally, what else is the terrible torment of the soul in hell than the eternal vision of its own repellent hideousness, illuminated from above by the light of truth undimmed and undeflected? Is not that the reason for the lost soul's indescribable pain? The light of God's truth breaks in upon it, searing and scorching, because the soul is hardened against it and forever unyielding. And therefore, through all eternity, the soul can never be healed. God's holy presence and the radiance of His truth, which the lost souls abhor, are agony indeed, and if they were exposed to the full glare of God's wrath they would burn up and perish altogether. Thus, in His light they do not see Him, but see themselves, though void of meaning, condemned by their own fault, which yet, in their untruth, they will deny forever. The light cannot cleanse them because they have chosen, once and for all, a life without charity, the perversion of the divine order of values. As the bliss of the blessed derives from God and through union with Him, so does the torment of the damned also derive from God, through disunion. The former hasten into the light of truth and are transfigured; the latter stand in opposition to the light, and thus remain what they are, only themselves, for all eternity. Thus, it is the truth of the divine essence from which come bliss, justification and judgment. He who believes shall be blessed, and he who does not believe "hath one that judgeth him" (John 12:48). To be allowed to see the truth because one ardently desires it, is purification and blessedness; to have to see it even though one does not want it, is judgment and damnation. Need more be said to make clear why it is all-important that the soul should put no obstacles in the way of contemplative grace and should, when it is given, accept it with all its heart?

Signs of contemplation

If contemplation in its fullness were to be granted all at once, little more would have to be said; the soul would instantly understand what is happening and would know how to react. But the first stirrings of contemplation are usually so deeply imbedded in the life of prayer and normally so brief that the soul is hardly aware of anything new. And since the effects produced by this coming of God are often the very opposite of what the soul expected, it is all the more perplexed and does not know what to make of its condition. Nor does it help that these phenomena are ambiguous. If experienced singly, they could belong to earlier stages of prayer without in any way preparing a new development.

Thus many are prevented from properly understanding what is beginning to manifest itself and from adopting the proper attitude. Though called, they make no progress. They lose the way, and in the end they may even give up the practices hitherto so faithfully observed. Or they may attempt, with obdurate persistence, to continue praying as before, to force it even when they sense most clearly that it will not work. They smother the new growth that is budding in the soul, while at the same time the familiar methods of prayer become sheer agony. They are utterly in the air, and their state is indescribably desolate. If they fail to find inner clarity and order, theirs will be sheer martyrdom. In the eyes of God this may have high value indeed, but it singularly fails to lead the soul to that consolation which was to be vouchsafed to it.

That is why an attempt has been made to enumerate the signs by which the advent of the grace of contemplation may be recognized with certainty. Probably they were for the first time clearly and validly defined and interpreted by St. John of the Cross, the Mystical Doctor. With superlative mastery he treats of these most difficult matters, and if the soul entrusts itself to his guidance, it cannot go astray. We shall follow his teaching.

The first sign is that the soul no longer takes pleasure as before in what is beautiful and lovable in the world around it. It senses, faintly at first, then stronger and more frequently, that somehow all this is too little, not good enough, insufficient. True, the soul already knows that these joys could not satisfy forever and, trained in devotion, it had automatically related its enjoyment to God, discerning Him in the beauty and purpose of nature. It rejoiced in Him, but its gladness sprang from created things: flowers, stars, and people, music also and art and poetry, noble thoughts and noble actions. Now all this becomes stale, insipid, flat. The soul feels emptiness and disillusionment when dealing with the things previously so dear and familiar, and at times this may reach the point of positive distaste coupled with deep sadness. Not always, though. The soul is still capable, occasionally, of being wholly captivated by a brilliantly written book, transported by the strains of a magnificent symphony. But suddenly these joys are cut short, sometimes right in the middle. Everything seems wrapped in a grey shroud, despoiled and devalued. The soul knows that what it needs and looks for is something quite different, something other than all this. And since the soul is at home in its relations with God, it will soon enough realize that it is He for whom the heart searches. Indeed, the quest may become a desperate cry.

Walking through meadows profuse with flowers, the soul comes upon a rare plant, long and eagerly looked for. But what happens? There is no sense of joy, but a feeling of pain. Listlessly the soul turns away, or stands unseeing before this tiny miracle of creation, while something seems to whisper deep inside: "Is that what Thou givest me? Only that? Why not Thyself?" It knows, of course, that God is present and that the very flower which arrested it proclaims His wisdom and beauty. Yet the soul wants more, wants Him.

All this is obvious, and kindred experiences may occur in other spheres. A person filled with deep love for another will sense that all other people fail to bring comfort. It experiences an utter loneliness in the midst of their laughter and kindness. It longs for that one Person whose presence alone makes life worthwhile.

It is unlikely that the truly devout and prayerful Christian would ever undergo this experience in its extreme form, since he will know that no created being can bring fulfillment and that God must forever remain the ultimate goal. But he, too, may become saddened by a feeling of insufficiency and by the longing for something more perfect, though this need not necessarily foreshadow the call to contemplative prayer. In that case, however, there will be hardly more than a diffuse pain, a sad withdrawal from everything, an aimless longing for something. On the other hand, if the experience is meant as a first step toward contemplation, the pain and the longing will gradually become so intense that they will almost break his heart, and they will ever more clearly converge upon God. It is love that here begins to stir, the deepest love of the human soul, calling for Him whom it needs, the Bridegroom for whom it was created, to share in blissful companionship the eternity of His being and operations. One is less weighed down by a heavy heart than moved by a secret restlessness, driven by a ceaseless quest, as was said of the bride in the Canticle of Canticles. The contact with things which unexpectedly remind the soul of God—be it only the beauty of a flower—may suddenly make this pain so intense that the eyes fill with tears and the soul must avert its gaze, otherwise the longing would become unbearable.

The same thing can happen when the soul prays. Faithfully doing its duty, it is suddenly stung by the fear that this kind of prayer is a wall between itself and God. He is behind that wall, while the soul needs to see Him face to face. Can this be prayer at all? If only the soul could be still, lost in His embrace forever, all would be well. Yet, the tremor may pass; it may have been no more than a fervent surge of the emotions, gradually subsiding to make room again for a more tranquil life of prayer. It is only when this happens again and again that it acquires the significance of a "sign," though even then it will be valid only in conjunction with the other two.

Different from the first sign, which can become apparent anywhere and often does so quite suddenly and unexpectedly, the second sign occurs only in connection with the life of prayer. Here something very strange occurs. It is as if the soul found speech difficult, the tongue seems half paralyzed, thought is inert and sluggish. The soul tries to pull itself together, to take new life from truth by meditation, and thus to stimulate the heart and rekindle its love, but in vain. Things will not work that way any more. The soul still speaks to God, but haltingly, without order or resonance. Formerly, religious experiences were accompanied by appropriate emotions, lending fervor to gratitude, zeal to remorse. Now something has gone wrong. All seems strangely dull inside. Feeling no longer responds to what reason laboriously tries to demonstrate. The soul endeavors to take refuge in action, in acts of faith or adoration, calling upon the will to step into the breach. But there, too, success is partial at best, as if something was pinning it down and preventing it from spreading its wings with the accustomed ease. By a tremendous effort it can perhaps move just a little, but all buoyancy, all life and fervor have gone. Or so it seems. It appears to the soul as if it had been partly deprived of the power of self-determination. Maybe this experience will presently subside, leaving things as they were before, but it is also possible for it to be repeated, and to increase in intensity, so that the soul feels practically paralyzed. It is seized by an inexplicable helplessness at the very moment it tries to settle down to prayer or meditation. At all other times, when dealing with people or studying, the soul can move as freely as ever, can expound, interpret, proclaim, and even compose prayers for the edification of others. But as soon as it wants to do anything for itself—and it feels driven to interior religious activity—its ability evaporates. It is impossible to make things clear to oneself, to develop thoughts for one's guidance, to find words of encouragement or com-

fort for one's own requirements, as was possible previously
in meditation. Indeed, there is now no pleasure at all in any
form of prayerful reflection. The soul is under the impression
that all this ground has been covered, so why go over it again?
It senses that somehow God's eyes are upon it, and in that
instant it becomes utterly superfluous to meditate upon Him.
Just as it would be superfluous, and even ludicrous, if the
bride, while gazing into the eyes of her husband in the embrace
of love, were to wonder why he brushes his hair in a certain
way or why a line on his forehead has an odd twist at the end.
To do so would be to betray love for the sake of non-essentials.
Not that they are always out of place, for the soul is certainly
entitled to think about God and to read about Him. Indeed,
one should cultivate spiritual reading and the study of the
Scriptures, but not now, when we are at prayer. This is the
moment when one should encounter Him face to face in love.
It is this that the soul now strongly feels, and with increasing
clarity. It is not a time to think or ponder. All action becomes
distasteful, and the time will come when the very acts which
the soul had previously sought with such eagerness are resented
as unwelcome interruptions.

Here we have already implied the third sign which comple-
ments the other two. The realization of the insufficiency of
everything and the strange paralysis and utter impotence give
the soul the experience of a new way of being drawn to God,
and this is the third sign. Somehow, God is felt to be there,
though there is nothing as yet to be seen clearly, nothing to
be discerned. Yet the soul is captured, arrested; it cannot and
would not move. Nothing specific is happening, yet the soul
is stayed because there is something which claims it altogether.
Not as if the soul could not budge any more, let alone that
the body's ability to move were in any way affected. That,
too, may happen, but normally it is simply that the soul has
the impression, in greater or lesser degree, of being incapable
of anything except to stay, to wait, to look and to leave all
else to Him. In this it is right; it is meant to keep still in this

attitude of suspended animation. Something is coming across to the soul from Him; He Himself is approaching. There is nothing to see, nothing for the imagination to lay hold of, and certainly no visions, apparitions, or the like. There is absolutely nothing for the spiritual or physical faculties to grasp. And yet the soul is profoundly conscious of His being there and looking upon it, and of itself being turned in His direction. It is also conscious of something which links the soul to Him. There is utter darkness, yet in it the soul sees in a manner wholly spiritual, sees Him for whom it has waited so long, whom it loves, and by whom it is loved ineffably.

The first sign may deceive, as we have indicated already. It may be no more than a passing lassitude of our powers of enjoyment, a disappointment leading to a sudden sense of utter loneliness. This is not to be confused with weariness of life. The deep sorrow caused by their insufficiency does not make the things of this world distasteful; they remain God's creatures, His signs and gifts, and as such are essentially lovable. Yet in this love there is much sadness, just as there is sadness in listening to music which was dear to someone deeply loved and now gone forever; sadness, certainly, but not disgust. The weariness of life is experienced also, and indeed pre-eminently, by those who live licentiously; they are tired of everything until their vices regain vigor and attractiveness under some new aspect. The sorrow of the insufficiency of every created being is something utterly different.

The second sign, too, may mislead one, especially when the feeling of impotence is experienced not only during prayer but also on other occasions, interfering with the fulfillment of one's duties. There are cases, it is true, where God seizes the soul with such overpowering force that it is for a time completely removed from the world around it, cut off from reality like a fool, an object of derision. But in most cases this state will be due not to the action of divine grace but to some physiological defects which have nothing to do with the life of prayer, and they should be tended by a doctor. If, however, this seeming paralysis is experienced only when the soul collects itself for prayer and especially for meditation, or in the course of praying or meditating, then indeed it is highly probable that it betokens the beginning of contemplation.

It is in the third sign that the growing probability is at last turned into certainty. The third sign is infallible. Of itself it would be sufficient evidence, but in practice it cannot appear unless the other two have previously been experienced. The heart that harbors and holds to things other than God—though in a manner wholly innocent and in no way sinful—cannot possibly be totally recollected in Him as its one and all. The purging experience of the insufficiency of the created world is indispensable to make the heart's most inward yearning turn away from them, to make it reach with open arms to the one and only good which is alone worthwhile. It is the question of serving two masters; nobody ever can. Nor could it be argued that the soul may love these things in God and with Him. That is a fallacy here. The soul still loves the world *and* God, but not yet the world *in* God, even if many are under this delusion. That sublime stage is possible only in and through contemplation. Only when the soul has become deeply immersed in God, has sunk its roots in Him and thus has penetrated, as it were, to the primeval source of all creation—so deeply that everything has been passed by and left behind, has been hated in the sense in which our Lord used the word— only then is the soul capable of rediscovering the world *in* God and of loving it in Him. But before this can happen all things must have become as remote as if they were in no way the soul's concern, with the single exception of those which have been specifically entrusted to our care by God, and to these we will then turn truly for love of Him alone and not for love of the things themselves. It is in contemplation that the soul gradually progresses from the "also" to the "in Him alone."

In like manner the soul remains incapable of truly waiting for God and for His moving toward it (as will happen in contemplation) as long as it continues its self-willed activity, conscious reflection and acts of the will. In them the created being merely asserts the belief that its own active contribution is important or even indispensable, thus interfering with the Creator's own designs and with the works that He alone can perform. The soul, the little busybody, with its anxiety to please and even with the real merit of faithful performance of its duties, must first be brought to silence. The emphasis is shifted; hitherto it was the soul itself that was active while God merely assisted; now He Himself takes over and the soul is left to cooperate in self-surrender, to be guided and trained for a new form of action, action in God.

When the soul has rejected all other attractions for the desire of the one, all-consuming love of Him; when it has renounced possession of itself to be free for the sway of that overpowering majesty which is now approaching; then it is prepared for the encounter with the very presence of this sweet and dominating power. It is prepared at last to enter into contemplation.

The three signs are by no means always felt with equal intensity, nor need they be present simultaneously, except that the second must always appear together with the third. The first sign will be experienced mainly in the beginning, when God is gradually detaching the soul from what, before, it loved so dearly and even considered indispensable. At this stage it predominates. Again later, when the same process of liberation is repeated in successively deeper layers of the soul, the first sign will reappear. In the interim it may be hardly felt at all. So thoroughly have the things of the world been divested of their previous attractiveness that they can no longer tempt us to distraction. They leave the heart so cold that one can only marvel faintly how they were ever able to cast such a powerful spell. Yet quite suddenly the searing desire for God and His nearness may pierce the soul, since the heart, though already far removed from created things, is not yet "with God"; it is still "in between," desolate and poor and sore, like an open wound.

The second sign will always be encountered when the third makes its appearance. At first the experience will be extremely short-lived, lasting for seconds only, and thus hardly notice-able. It is like a catch in the throat, after which normal breath-ing immediately continues. Yet once the soul is thus "arrested" by truth—however briefly—it is imperative that the powers of the soul—imagination, reason, will and feeling—should in-stantly abandon their free and deliberate activity; otherwise the gaze of contemplation will not be possible. This does not mean that these powers will no longer make themselves felt during contemplation; on the contrary, their activity is likely to continue, involuntarily and on the surface, and this con-stitutes one of the deepest torments of the soul on this ascent. But here we are only thinking of what one does voluntarily, of the deliberate use of one's powers, and of that we say that it is incompatible with the contemplative act.

Again, there are marked differences in the degree of intensity with which the truth seizes the soul to transport it to contem-plation. They are, in turn, the measure of our sudden im-potence. At times, the pull is very gentle indeed and hardly felt. The soul will then remain capable of cooperative action and of quietly resuming its normal activity after each such interruption. This capacity for intellectual and emotional re-sponse and for acts of virtue is perfectly proper, if we avoid strain. To use force in spiritual matters is never beneficial, and in most cases it is positively harmful. It will take a long time before contemplation grows so strong that it pervades the life of prayer altogether, and on this arduous way one will often falter or even lose sight of the goal. But of this we shall speak later.

We have seen how the experiences of growing detachment from all created beings and of burning desire for a wholly different manner of possessing God are in no way tied to the accustomed times of prayer but may seize us quite unex-pectedly in the midst of work or leisure or conversation. In fact, they may permeate the whole of our life. In the same way, contemplation itself, prepared by these experiences, will not only be a new stage of prayer but will gradually become a new form of existence. It, too, will not be limited to the hours of recollection; indeed, it is possible that it will be less prominent then but at other times lay hold of our heart quite irresistibly. Thus, one may have spent a period of time before the tabernacle; the heart was able to say a few things to God and to lift itself up in certain acts, but hardly any attraction was felt. Afterwards one goes for a walk, and quite unexpectedly the presence which only a moment ago was so sadly missing, is there. It embraces and pervades and calms the soul, and instantly all reflective and affective action ceases. In this state—which may last for quite some time—all desire for personal activity in relation to God is stilled, and if things do continue to happen in the soul, they are felt as irksome and painful. Thus, contemplation will come to be diffused through our whole life, occupying more and more of the spare moments of our days and nights. It finally leads to a permanent presence before God, a constant recollection within Him, and thus to continuous prayer, to prayer as the essential manifestation of faith, its original purpose and ultimate fulfillment.

But does this not mean the end of all other forms of life, of "life in the world?" Does it not remove the Christian from the mundane tasks which, after all, were set by God Himself, or render him unfit for their proper discharge? Quite the contrary, it is precisely in this state of being God's prisoner that the soul is at last free to attend to the things which are truly His desire, and not merely the soul's own. In the strength of its union with God, attained in contemplation, the soul will henceforth do what it must, better than ever before, free from all waywardness of the ego, in pure love of Him who entrusts His tasks to us and to whom we return their fulfillment as the fruit of our love and of His. Not less will be achieved, but more, because now God Himself is at work in the soul which no longer in any way obstructs Him, but in Him and by His grace cooperates in ultimate self-fulfillment. Perhaps very few ever reach this stage. It is not for us to decide this question, but merely to try to offer our heart to God so that He may use it according to His pleasure. That final state of the contemplative life which we have just described is perfect sanctity; the purest love, wholly lost in God and His adorable will, offered by the soul which has been admitted to the "kiss of His lips."

Chapter 18

Obscurity of Contemplation

RATHER than try to describe the way of suffering by which God leads the soul once He has called it to contemplation, we shall now treat of contemplation itself in its essence, in spite of the fact that for the beginner the sufferings occupy a more predominant place as opposed to a clear understanding of contemplation itself. For how is one to bear such suffering without knowing whether it is an essential part of the way and must, in fact, be considered as part of contemplation? Once reassured, we shall have more courage, more willingness; for the goal is so marvelous that for its sake we shall be prepared to accept real hardship. We shall venture to say, with our heart trembling: "Make me holy, Lord, at any price whatever!" And that which causes the pain and leads to the final goal will give the supernal strength for the ascent of Mount Carmel. Hence we shall treat of contemplative prayer as if it unfolded unhampered and undisturbed.

We have already distinguished contemplation from the lower grades of prayer. It is not vocal prayer. The lips are, so to speak, sealed up the moment contemplation begins. They are capable only now and then of an ejaculation, but not of any organic coherent prayer. Nor is contemplation affective prayer. On the contrary, it is more likely the death of all sentiments and feeling. Finally, contemplation is not the same as meditation. All the powers called into action in meditation are now removed from their office, confined to silence, deprived of their former noble operations. Consequently, contemplation is not a kind of perception in any way related to the imagination,

[218

emotions or thought. The soul sees nothing. Were it to see at all, one could not speak of contemplation. God and His metaphysical reality are not revealed in this world in a manner corresponding to the normal way of the senses.

This is no place to consider what we call visions; suffice it to repeat the strict admonition to avoid them with all our strength—even though they be truly God-given—and once more to point out the duty to call for advice from the spiritual director. Many visions are delusions, mirages of genuine spiritual experience, or else they may be of diabolical origin. In a sense they are always somewhat imperfect, compared to purely spiritual perceptions, and to wish for them would not only be presumption, but folly as well, for they can so easily lead the soul into error. One should not pay any attention to them until advice has been sought. If a person fancies that he sees apparitions or figures of light, or hears words, phrases or exclamations, he is certainly not engaged in contemplation; very likely he is a victim of hallucinations. If in prayer one seems to feel that he is touched or embraced by someone or something, he is not in contemplation, but very far from it, though such phenomena can enter into contemplation as disturbances. In themselves, however, they have nothing whatever to do with contemplation.

Then does one see nothing? Nothing whatever. That is why we speak of obscure or dark contemplation. Does not God always remain in "light inaccessible" as long as we live in this world? Not even the Mother of God ever saw Him in His divine spiritual essence. True, the Only-begotten of the Father has made Him known to us, but that is different from actually seeing God. That is hearing of and believing in Him. But does not Christ say: "He who seeth Me, seeth the Father also?" So we do, by meditation on His human nature. There the life of God is reflected brilliantly, but we see it only indirectly, never directly. The works of Christ are the works of the Father, His charity is that of the Father, and in that sense we can see in Christ the Father's acts and His love, transposed into our own idiom, into the nature of man. But as spirit, God remains un-seen, unapprehended; flesh and blood cannot grasp the spiritual.

The mystics have frequently repeated the exquisite thought that God in His essence is light. Christ loves to refer to Him-self thus and how often St. John repeats it. He is spiritual light, purest truth, luminous clarity, resplendent, immaculate holi-ness! Images only, no doubt, but they point to something con-crete, and thus also to what in the essence of light corresponds to the essence of God's being. Brilliant light cannot actually be seen. If you try, you will at once experience darkness, sim-ply because the eyes are not suited for such abundance of light; they are not equal to it. Only gradually can the eyes accustom themselves to the light, conquer their inferiority and, through light itself, grow strong enough to look at it, thus finally learn-ing to contemplate what before they could not behold.

In contemplation the soul turned toward the essence of God is infinitely less equal to that resplendent light than the eyes are to that of the sun. If we want to gaze upon intense light we use tinted glasses which dim the light. First we choose very dark ones, then, progressively, lighter shades. For the eye of the soul there is no equivalent, but God Himself dims the light of His presence, to make it bearable for the soul, though often enough it remains painful and almost annihilating. Were God to come all at once, the soul would perish. Only gradu-ally, over a span of years, some faint light appears, as the soul has been trained to it, or rather, as it has been progressively purified, healed and strengthened. Even then the term, "ob-scure contemplation," will yet apply, because the light of truth, the eternal splendor of divine truth which the soul has begun to perceive in a purely spiritual way, is still infinitely remote. Even St. Paul, to whom it was granted to behold so many and such sublime things that his lips remained sealed about them, did not, according to generally accepted doctrine, see God Himself nor the glory of heaven such as it really is.

In all its stages, contemplation happens in darkness, in the darkness of faith, but—and this is essential—in a new kind of faith which no longer is merely a simple and firm acceptance of truth by the will, based on God's revelation and its trustworthiness, which our intellect, enlightened by grace, understands. This is an entirely spiritual experience of the core of the teachings of faith.

Take an object firmly in your hand. Then start to handle it until your grasp helps you to understand its specific essence. To hold the thing firmly is the first necessary act but it does not suffice to give you an essential knowledge of the object. A consistent effort is needed to reach full comprehension. Thus, apart from the grace which calls it forth and sustains it, faith begins by a firm grasp of the truths of faith by the will and by an instructed reason. But from here we go on. The grace of faith grows and develops, so that the individual tenets of faith form a vital union with it. The objects of our belief grow into something concrete and real to our spiritual perception; something which has its own presence and efficacy, by which we Christians live. Now it no longer is as if we dealt with mere concepts, communicated to us by God and apprehended by us in the virtue of faith, but with substantial realities, facts with a life and impulse of their own. At times the soul feels as if walking through a wide open door into a spacious hall where, though its eyes cannot see, everything seems to be strangely familiar. With rare powers of perception, the soul senses the truth, the impact of what it blindly believes, full of beauty and life and perfection, shrouded mysteriously in invisible light and unspeakable radiance. The soul has long ceased to make any acts of faith. In deepest joy its faith is dumb before God. It has entered the realm of vital knowledge of Him, an essential experience of His divine word and being.

Here the words apply: "Taste and see how sweet is the Lord" (Ps. 34:8). This is not only acknowledgment born of belief, nor merely enlightened faith in the sense of knowing, keeping its tenets, and acting accordingly by instruction, prayer and conduct; it is a much deeper concern, a spiritual participation which grants a genuine experience, an interior knowing vouchsafed to the soul from the heart of its Lord and its God. This is something which cannot be thought about, nor even actively felt. It has its own vibration, its own life within the soul, now closer, now more remote, in its mysterious presence, sensed not emotionally nor speculatively, but in a purely spiritual immediacy which excludes the perception of the senses. These will again come into their own at a later stage of the mystical life, when they have been totally purged and thus become capable of participation—within their own measure of strength and grace—in the purely spiritual experience. Yet all this ever and solely is under the veil of faith, in darkness or, if you prefer, in an early dawn of light. Faith as such will never be superseded, never be made superfluous. Right to the hour when, as finally perfected beings in eternity, we appear before God, faith will remain the form of our beholding Him. Within faith will happen that progress of inner perfection which we are here discussing, from obedient acceptance of the tenets of faith to the life-giving, profound experience of faith itself in contemplation. This again proves that the interior contemplative life does not violate the norm of Christian existence as conceived by God and made manifest in His Son through the Holy Ghost. It is, rather, an essential and wholly organic, if ultimate, evolution of Christian existence. Unless we achieve it, something was deeply wrong with our Christian life.

Generally speaking, the most adequate description of contemplation would seem to be: a glancing upon truth, though with unseeing eyes, and an awareness of its existence. At one time or other the soul becomes conscious of truth as a presence. That is the moment of knowing. This is new; it is different from anything ever experienced in the soul's contact with God and the things that are His. The ways by which the soul enters into relation with this new presence vary greatly; love knows countless ways of encounter; not one of them is likely to resemble another. One can, however, distinguish two principal modes of contemplative realization.

First, this "other," which is God, is simply felt as a presence, and as soon as the soul turns toward it with its inner attention fixed upon it, perception is granted, interior contact is gained. It may happen that the soul, preoccupied with its daily tasks and diversions, is completely forgetful of the presence. At the early stages of the new way this will often enough be the case, because the soul has not yet acquired the habit of turning its gaze inward as often as possible, to contemplate God. Later it will do so spontaneously or by a conscious act of the will, and each time God will be there. He looks at the soul, truth converging upon it as the soul is focused upon truth. A vital encounter, face to face. All this happens quite simply, almost "naturally," as it is for two people in love to look at each other and know that they are deeply united, that they live for one another. No need for mutual assurance, for any words; it is a vital fact, unquestioned and unreflected.

Secondly, and this is the more intense mode of contemplative realization, the presence moves toward the soul, and in this encounter there is a much stronger impact of attraction and fascination than in the first. In a rare manner of knowing, the soul is conscious of God's nearness, of His presence within it. No need now to turn its gaze toward Him to contemplate Him. Rather, it is as if God now forced the soul to lift its eyes so that it cannot help regarding Him. There is nothing violent, nothing laborious in this. Gently, lightly and tenderly it occurs. It is difficult, if not impossible, to express the experience of intimacy which contemplation can afford in this experience. It is as if no distance whatever remained between God and the soul, as if He were one with the soul, welded to its innermost essence, while the two yet remain individual beings. This experience can be so strong that the soul, even though it might so desire, can no longer avert its gaze. For hours or for days on end He accompanies the soul, and one day perhaps forever.

In this condition, whatever the soul does, He will always be there, very noticeably. It is as if one were working in a room with another person present. Whether he will or not, he senses this presence, no matter how engrossed he is in his work. So alive, so possessive, so flaming is the regard to that divine love that the soul is powerless to escape it. This is perhaps a little like being in heaven. So much of the soul's longing for God is now filled that it might easily think that there could hardly be more to expect. This seems to be supreme bliss, until the soul understands that even this is but a phase, until the receding of the divine presence makes the soul deeply aware of the imperfection of this preliminary union of love. So close can this union be that the expression of being touched seems more adequate than that of beholding, though this is apt, too, in that the divine regard and that of the soul seem deeply immersed in one another. But let there be no mistake; all this is mere figurative speaking, because there is no other way to speak of such things.

At times it seems more the spirit, at other times more the heart which senses the closeness. God touches the foundation, the pinnacle of the soul, that "point" where it originates from Him and His eternal creative love. Called and guided by Him, the soul returns to its own initial place in eternity, to its prime origin, to encounter God at the source where it ever proceeds from Him. With all its being, the soul reverts to Him by whose glance it is fully encompassed, loses itself to this glance and, in it, to the essence of God.

Here is the soul's true abode, its home, its love without end. The soul knows it, feels as if its spirit, its innermost self no longer belonged to it, as if it were no longer itself. It is as if He had taken its place, filled it to overflowing; as if the soul were no more than a manner of His being within it. All the same, the soul knows quite clearly that it remains itself; that it did not—absurd error of thought—itself become part of God's being. But it is like a no-thing, living, but lived in solely by Him.

Again it may happen that the emphasis of the encounter is entirely upon the heart. If in what we have just described, the accent was on the beholding and on truth—though, of course, aiming at and ending in union—here love is the decisive factor from the start. And here the expression of being touched is particularly fitting. It is as in the beautiful myth of Amor and Psyche. Psyche—the soul—does not see Amor—her love. Whenever Amor is with her, it is in darkness. He has even ordered her never to make an attempt to see him, until he deems the time is right. So Psyche senses him, feels his presence, his tenderness, and her heart is filled with unspeakable joy. He must be the ultimate good, the purest, the most lovable being. Such is her experience of him, and it leaves her heart well content. Had there not been alien insinuations, seducing her to inquisitiveness and even to doubt, so that she schemes to see Amor, thereby bringing catastrophe to their love, Psyche's happiness would have remained unalloyed.

The soul's experience of God touching it in contemplation is very similar. It does not see God, yet its heart is filled with love, not only with its own love for Him, but especially with God's love for the soul. And the soul is contented, saturated with love, free from all further yearning. But woe to the soul if, yielding to the mind's temptation to see and to understand, it were to try to lift the veil of blind faith. Here is the open road to all those disastrous practices already mentioned: to the experiments of vision and speculation, to the desire for clever deduction, for shrewd expositions of mysteries not proffered by revelation, or to philosophizing about those which Holy Scripture reveals. Experiments of this kind would break all contact between God and the soul. He wants the bridal veil of faith, beneath which the soul is to experience the miracle of His love, until that day when the soul will have been made perfect and He will Himself lift the veil and reveal to the soul and to all the world this love so unspeakably pure and tender and chaste, so devoid of selfish desire and ever ready to give His creative love which will then have achieved its work in the enraptured soul.

Contemplation, whether for short spells, for long periods or as a permanent spiritual condition, will always consist in this: the transcendent, the eternal, the totally-other, the one truth, God, is present to the soul in a spiritually perceptible way. Touched, startled, seized, arrested by that presence, the soul always recognizes it without further question or thought. In a manner of complete simplicity, yet vital actuality, God is inclined toward the soul and the soul to Him. This is a possessing and comprehending of one another, a dialogue of the heart, a song without words. It is a knowing without instruction, an abandonment of the will without hesitation or fear, but all stillness and peace. Nobody could persuade the soul that God is not present to it; it knows better, and none but the soul itself knows this at all, since this is the secret of a love confined to God and one individual soul, as if no other being existed throughout the universe. True, somebody else may be able to confirm and explain the experience, to explain, if need be, how to conduct oneself in it, provided the other person has had the experience and has already been initiated into this life of "God and my soul."

Now let us insist once more: all this comes from God alone, never from our soul and its own wisdom and knowledge. The soul cannot give this life to itself; it must be given by God. The soul can only dispose itself and remain quiet, and even that, God must grant and stimulate. Nowhere else can we realize so well that all, quite literally all, comes solely from God, nothing from ourselves or from any of His creatures. There is but one source of being, of life, of action, of love; one source of contemplation: God alone; and whoever shares in these, does so through Him. In this "God alone" and "God-all" the soul finds its bliss, for in such realization love is truly made pure.

The experience of totality

Let us carefully advance further. We have said that meditation means a close examination of details taken one by one, by our powers of imagination, memory, intellect, and so on, individually engaged. From the single features of the subject under meditation there will slowly emerge a harmoniously co-ordinated whole, and only gradually will our mental powers reach, as it were, a place of appointment where they are no longer kept apart, but together attain to tranquillity within that one whole. This is the contemplative act, in which the subject of meditation reveals itself in its entirety to our inner perception. Meditation has come to an end; contemplation begins.

Contemplation is directly concerned with one whole. Details are no longer focusing points. As parts of the whole they continue, of course, to exist, but they are immersed in the whole which they help to establish and which, in turn, is the reason as well as the form of their logic, order and union. And it is no longer first this, then the next mental power which steps in to fulfill its function; they are now jointly centered upon that whole and they repose in it. The same thing has occurred in two correlating spheres: arriving at contemplation, meditation has reached to the essence of things, which, though expressing itself in individual features, lies beyond them and is more than their sum or their combination, just as the essence of a human face is certainly more than the total of all its individual traits. The essence is within or behind them, belonging to a higher order than the appearances which we behold and by which its presence is made manifest. Similarly, the soul is more than the sum of its faculties; more also than their combined activity. It, again, is behind or beyond all that, its faculties being merely the manifestations of its life, the manner in which the soul links itself to other forms of being, welcomes them into itself or participates in their existence. The soul is, of course, present in its powers of will, emotion, or reason; but it is more, infinitely more, than all of them together. Once it has, therefore, by meditation on the details and individual features of a subject, reached through to its essence, the two face one another; the essence of the soul facing the essence of that subject.

This is the decisive point in contemplative prayer and life.

The entire soul stands in the face of the entire truth, indeed, in its innermost core. It faces the undivided God, entire, not manifest only in detail nor revealed in part as previously. This also applies when the soul does not actually contemplate God but one of His attributes such as His wisdom, or the adoration offered by the Sacred Heart to the heavenly Father, the purity of the angels, the dignity of the soul reborn of grace. In each instance the soul is faced by an entirety. It does not, for example, scrutinize the manner of the divine-human adoration, nor when and how the divine and the human nature blend into one another. The soul may perceive this, too, but not singled out as a part from which to begin the scrutiny of the whole. The soul's regard is, as it were, held by and within that whole, and only thus—if at all—can all the rest be included in that comprehensive glance. Neither does the soul actually wish for nor is it usually capable of anything else. It must remain still, captivated by that totality.

Here it is important to note that all individual truths which the soul can ever behold as one whole are in a manner of speaking always God Himself. Whatever is truly essential about them, comes out of or is the essence of God. True, you can look at God's wisdom as if it were an entity by itself, but in so doing, you know at once that it is God Himself you are contemplating, though under the aspect of His wisdom, God as wisdom, if you like. Thus, one may consider some person's entire face as the dear, the serene, the reserved face; not reserve as such is what one here perceives, but the reserve of this particular face, this face, in fact, in its essential reserve. Abstraction and differentiation belong to the realm of philosophy, not to that of loving regard and communion with a cherished personal being. Again, when we contemplate our Lady or consider her, for instance, the Virgin Most Faithful, the same will apply. The soul's glance always embraces the specific entirety, and in this glance is itself always entirely present.

But in all this God is the soul's true concern. One day we

may perhaps learn to behold all beings and things of creation in this same essential manner. Our soul's regard will then reach beyond first perceptions or aspects to inner being and essence, and there it will find God. That is the meaning of seeing things within God and also loving them within God. Here the soul comprehends them within their own origin, as we have shown when explaining the soul's self-recognition in God, and in the entirety of each thing so perceived, the soul contemplates and possesses the entire God. In this process of contemplation the soul participates in the works of God made manifest in every object and being as well as within the soul itself. It participates in their creation, in their infinite generation from the love of His infinite will, in their being and breathing in Him, in their roots within Him and their desire for their return to Him. To share in all this is our soul's true calling.

This experience of totality may, with equal right, be called life or tranquillity. Tranquillity does not exclude life; rather it is the most vital life identical with the most perfect tranquillity. Thus we read in Gen. 2:2: "On the seventh day God rested from all His works"; and Christ said: "My Father worketh until this hour" (John 5:17). The tranquillity of the soul in contemplation is life, a life filled to capacity, the very opposite of lethargy and inactivity. But it is not, as we well know, activity in the usual sense of the word. Rather, it is a consent to the activity of God within us, and by reason of the consent, a cooperation with God. Christ, continuing in the sentence quoted above, says: ". . . and I work," namely, the things, "that He seeth the Father doing" (John 5:19). Here contemplation and action have become one manifestation of life: tranquillity of self-abandonment and vital self-realization. Hence in contemplation the soul is not as if stupefied, incapable of all inner motion. While its self-appointed activity is rendered difficult and later impossible, until the soul leaves off altogether, action as such does not cease within it. But it is God's action now, the soul being deprived of its own, in order that He may rule supreme and invite the soul's full cooperation. It takes time, though, for the soul to comprehend this, and more time till it has learned how to respond to this experience. We shall have to examine further that condition of the soul in which nothing seems to stir or respond within it, an initial stage of contemplation or else one of transition. In reality, contemplation in all its stages delivers the soul from any fictitious life, to lead it to that true life to which Christ, in the words of St. John, so often alludes and for which He became man, in order to impart it to us in all its fullness (John 1:16).

The contemplative act

Contemplation means the closest proximity between God and the soul. There are moments when the soul feels spread out before Him completely, as if it tried to expand itself as far as possible so that it might both capture the abundance of light that radiates from God and be itself in constant readiness for Him. Not some part of the soul, but the soul in its entirety presents itself to God. Certain schools of philosophy like to distinguish between the appearance of a thing and the thing itself. Philosophical perception is sufficiently astute to establish that the thing itself always lies behind the phenomenon, but the intellect lacks the power to seize it. The intellect can but trace the boundaries but is unable to cross them. Not so the heart, which transcends all boundaries in the high flight of love. It leaves far behind the appearances which reason ponders and soars to the reality of being, the ultimate substance of the soul encountering the ultimate substance of God. By this we mean the core or essence of being and we would not venture to use this expression were it not that St. John of the Cross justified it and employed it as the most apt term. We could hardly hope to find a more apposite formula for the harmony and union with God which are granted in contemplation.

In these very words, "substance" and "essence," that blessed fullness is encompassed. The contemplative act, far from being something monotonous, something that ever simplifies things or reduces them to nothingness, is an experience of totality, of tightly condensed reality. Instead of parallelism or divergence, even of faculties and of attributes, a unity is experienced, far richer than all multiplicity. In the beginning the soul hardly perceives this. True, it has been arrested, but it still finds everything much the same all the time, though the attraction may vary in degrees of intensity. Slowly the plenitude which that unity contains, emerges. It is as if the soul, quietly and without any effort or intent, directed the searchlight of its contemplative gaze upon this mysterious multiplicity within the unity that has captivated it. One moment the soul rests in the wisdom of God, the next moment in His love; now in His power, and now in His providence. Without effort it can acquiesce in an interior beholding of God's attributes, provided God frees the soul of an incapacity which at times chains it completely. If the soul may use its freedom, of which an inner certainty will always inform it, it will recognize without doubt that those attributes which it beholds are the manner of God's coming and His self-revelation; that they are inseparable from the essence of God; are, in fact, God Himself to whom the soul is forever inclined. It is as if in this way God slowly displayed the entire and infinite wealth of His being, ready to impart all of it to the soul without reserve, and in it Himself. He treats the soul like the bride of His heart whom one day He will call to the wedding feast.

It is certainly not out of place to repeat that all this occurs entirely within the order and frame of truth as revealed once and for all in and by Jesus Christ. On no account need it ever transcend that given order. Whether it can or may do so or ever did, must not here concern us. The calling to contemplation is not given to us as a means to acquire new truths, but to recognize better, to absorb more deeply, to assimilate lovingly those that have been revealed. Christ declares explicitly that He would send the Spirit not to teach something new but "He shall receive of Mine and shall show it to you" (John 16:14) and thus "teach you all truth" (John 16:13).

This showing and teaching happens above all in contemplation. There it will be given the soul to absorb into itself in ever-increasing measure and ever-growing depth the treasures revealed in the faith; to incorporate them, as it were, or to be transformed by their impact. For this is the soul's final calling: gradually to attain to that purity, beauty and virtue, that perfect glory which will make it worthy to be the bride of the Lamb and to appear at the throne of the Father in heaven.

An exactly corresponding experience, however, occurs within the soul's own being, as it is before God and with Him, in the plenitude of its substance; no longer in single, separate acts but as an essential presence which fills every act of the soul with the whole of its being. Thus the soul may perceive that its actual being with God at this particular moment carries the accent, the slightly predominant note of adoration. Not in the sense of making this an individual act, as in affective prayer or meditation, but in its entirety, as one who adores, the soul is now before God, with the whole of its being absorbed in this one attitude. The soul is itself adoration. In like manner it may become trust, gratitude, loving surrender, indeed, any act of virtue in which the soul's life and being can become manifest. Not so much adoring as being itself adoration, yet immediately and simultaneously, though less prominently, the soul is also gratitude, supplication and the rest. Easily and without strain the soul shifts the accent, either prompted by inspiration or freely choosing one or the other adjustment. Thus the soul seems to unfold before God the wealth of its own potential in a manner corresponding entirely to the call of His love which, as we have seen, is the revealing phrase which signifies that the human soul is "*quodammodo omnia*." It is, in a sense, everything. It is the image and likeness of God, responding along the whole breadth of its being to the call of His love which, as we have seen, is the revealing of His essence to the soul. And thus, finding Him, the soul finds itself, comes to itself, becomes itself, is made perfect at last as the precious thought, full of bliss and delight, which God carries in His heart from all eternity.

Deportment during contemplation

It will not now be difficult to answer the question concerning the attitude to be adopted during contemplation. We shall not yet deal with the sufferings of contemplation, which must be expected, but with the contemplative state as such. In the beginning this will be granted but rarely; as a permanent condition of the soul, it will be attained only at the end of a very long journey.

The first point to note is attention for the actual moment when contemplation begins. This is the moment in which that particular concentration, that recollectedness, makes itself felt, which is like an inner urge to remain utterly still. At this moment it becomes irksome, even unbearable, to persevere with the usual practices of prayer; the feeling of empty words prevails, of superfluous words, which neither capture nor convey the essential meaning. At the same time a gentle force withdraws the soul away from all that is not God and draws it toward Him. This can be experienced often, as we have said elsewhere, while one attends to normal prayers conscientiously, faithfully, with appropriate intervals and earnest recollection, or at any one point of meditation or spiritual reading. It is imperative to obey this gentle urge at once, even though it may last but a few seconds or less, and even when nothing seems to happen within the soul. It will then suffice simply to wait for that force to subside, when one can continue with prayer or reading, without the sensation of doing so in spite of something, of having to oppose something.

Frequently this phenomenon of distaste for all further words, this feeling of being attracted and pulled, comes upon one in front of the tabernacle. Small wonder, for here God not only acts as the sublime Spirit, but also by means of His sacred humanity which two thousand years ago exercised a most powerful influence on those who encountered it. How powerful this was, St. John testified once and for all in his beautiful and deeply convincing description of his own first meeting with Christ, and his first epistle still rings with the memory of that encounter. One must carefully re-read these two passages in order to feel how the mysterious power of our Lord's sacred humanity bears upon the soul and holds it spellbound. Again, that force may be felt during Mass, at Benediction or any other devotion. And when it comes, one should surrender to the quietly insistent force. The same is true before or after Communion.

It would be quite wrong to persist in one's habitual prayers once that gentle coercion is felt. It would mean giving preference to our own way of prayer to that which God desires and suggests to the soul. On such occasions He obviously does not want our effort, our action, our method. He wants His own and wishes to lead us into it. No doubt this means renunciation of one's own will, and in this renunciation lies the secret of spiritual progress. This denial of self engenders total adherence to God, to which pure love attains. If we refuse it, we should not be surprised that we make no spiritual progress and consider as inaccessible all that we read about the soul's life in God. Moreover, we lose all taste even for our familiar ways of prayer and finally become sullen and arid, when we should be like a flame, like a light, like a fount of living water (John 4:10–11). There are, of course, those who know no better. They oppose grace without knowing what they obstruct. But if fundamentally they are truly willing, God's love will guide them safely past the reefs.

The second point is to will nothing, or rather, to will one thing only: to be simply ready for God and for His work within the soul, although for the time being this is quite imperceptible; and to suffer this seeming inactivity. The soul often feels strangely awkward when, having yielded to that pull of grace and now waiting in some suspense for something to happen, nothing at all occurs. Nothing, that is, as far as the soul can perceive. Then one might easily wonder whether one should not, after all, try to do something rather than sit about limply, waste time and possibly end up by offending God rather than serving Him. This can hardly be helped, having so far trained oneself to do things for God, to spur oneself on when feeling distracted, tired or listless. One might perhaps worry at this new inertia, since one has not yet grasped that the whole of one's being is to be transported into the being of God. Yet this can only happen by slow degrees, which makes progress hardly perceptible. Here we need much patience, and watchfulness too, especially in the beginning of the contemplative way, or else we might be in danger of actually being slothful and far from ready for God. The heart must remain awake to the truth, to the presence of God, to His calling.

There is a kind of test, which can help to discriminate. If, when one feels this inactivity, he returns to methodical prayer or meditation, he will soon enough know how he really stands, for he will not succeed. There will at once arise an inner resistance against those forms of prayer, and somehow the soul will know quite distinctly that all is well after all with this inactivity, this keeping utterly still. Or one decides to end the attempt to pray, to go away and do something else for the greater glory of God. Again, the same resistance which rose against reverting to former methods of prayer, will now oppose this decision. This inner resistance arises in that part of the soul in which God's regard rests upon it, where the soul is, by creation and more so by its regeneration through grace, irrevocably linked to God, and whence He will gently conquer the whole of it by His love. This is the depth of the soul, the spark of the soul, the pinnacle of the soul—expressions which clearly show that it is not something easily seen or grasped, but concealed, appearing only occasionally, until at last it will emerge from the depth, enkindle the spark, and descend from the high pinnacle.

There may be those who, when reading about these things, shake their heads doubtfully. And yet, a sudden flash may light up the obscure images, explain the clumsy words, and make it apparent that what they try to convey has long been a familiar and precious possession, though expressed in an unfamiliar way. Basically, the experience to which we are led in contemplation remains in all its width and breadth and depth and height something essentially one and the same, enjoining a uniform standard upon all and joining them all together. It is precisely here that all who are called to this way will meet, when at last the many different similes, paraphrases and methods, necessary though they were for self-expression and mutual understanding, will have been transcended and left behind. There is multiplicity of idiom, but only one divine message inspired by the Holy Ghost.

Once that gentle urge has completely subsided and the previously mentioned "counter-check" does not reveal God's continued demand on the soul, one should quietly revert to the former method of prayer, reading or meditation. And if in these one finds little or no consolation, then the rules regarding our demeanor in the trials of prayer will apply. The special case, when the inner urge is not felt and no kind of active prayer seems possible, belongs to the particular trials on the contemplative way, which will have to be dealt with more fully.

The third point is that once the soul is pervaded by a certain stillness which makes action appear pointless and wearisome, it should quite simply and without any forced effort merely look upon Him or upon the phenomenon that holds the soul thus. At first this is never easy, because our physical eyes, not knowing quite what to do with themselves, keep trying to act after their own fashion. It is best then to keep them quietly fixed on one point, while the soul is at the same time directed upon the essence behind it. If that proves too difficult, a crucifix may help to fix the eyes. Often one may desire to close his eyes, which should be done so lightly that it is hardly felt. By all means he should guard against any strain or tension. It soon spoils everything and leads to a deadlock. The eyes must retain their natural scope, and one should exercise them a little when becoming aware of a rigid fixation. Likewise one should relax the eyelids when noticing that they are tightly compressed, just as one would release any other taut muscles. Otherwise part of our strength will go into this completely wasteful effort, and the soul's own way will be obstructed. The more naturally and easily the soul controls the body, the better the soul's freedom will be safeguarded. These things must be carefully watched especially in the beginning, when one does not yet really understand the spiritual life. Otherwise he might form bad habits which lead to blind alleys.

In the tranquillity of the soul's union with God there is no curiosity, no expectation of anything special; there is only the desire to love. Recognizing that gentle inner force as an appeal of love, a calling in the depth of the heart, the soul submits to it by its ready response to love in return. The truly loving heart is unassuming; it craves neither intellectual nor emotional experience; it has but the desire to love and to be loved. And that is what occurs here. There is an increasing desire for greater depth and tenderness and power of love, but it is love itself that makes it grow, love alone which matters. Hence the soul must not look for anything else nor respond to whatever might be offered. To remain tranquil will at first be no easy task. On either side of the inner way all sorts of impressions, thoughts, hopes and desires seem to spring up, sometimes in such abundance that the soul longs to escape. Its sole task, however, is to treat all this as if it did not exist and not for an instant to pay the slightest attention to it. At least, not deliberately, for the turmoil is hardly ever within the control of the soul. It must continue in the tranquillity of its union with God, must proceed on the way, as one would walk through a haze of dust whirled up by the wind. You turn your back on it as best you can, and momentarily you may shut your eyes, but you walk on. The assault of these eddying emotions, pictures or other impressions can become an unspeakable mortification, but they can never become a fault or an offense as long as the soul does not deliberately respond. This applies even to pious thoughts and emotions, in fact, particularly to these, because they have no place in contemplation. Later we shall consider the kind of thoughts that can become a legitimate part of contemplation. Those, however, which merely tend to deflect from quiet recollection and the simple contemplation of truth are ways of error and temptation. Much patience and tenacity will be needed, and it is well to pray hard and trustingly for the grace resolutely to shut one's eyes and steadfastly to persevere.

Whether disturbed or untroubled, the soul can remain for a long while in this condition, possibly all the time originally allowed for prayer. When the time has run out, one should go away in gratitude and in peace and not examine what the soul may have perceived, learned, experienced, or least of all what it may have achieved in the past hour. Formerly, in meditation, some results could be listed as good; but not now. This mutual love yields no results which could be counted or put into words. It carries all its significance within itself. The fruit which it yields is of a different order altogether, and the soul will appreciate this soon enough. What was it the soul had been doing, where had it been? Deep in the contemplation of Him whom it loves, and offering itself to Him. Being with Him, is not that love to the full? Even though unaware of it, the soul is filled with love. Or did the soul perhaps feel it? Please God, it did not; otherwise this would mean that one had, after all, responded to the urge of engaging one's faculties—in this case the emotions. But the soul must learn to love in a purely spiritual way, that is, without sentiment. All this is at first very strange and somewhat unlikely, until the soul learns to appreciate this as the true love, the love which God intends and wills for us, the love which is God Himself. Thus we might at the end merely ask ourselves whether we earnestly tried to be with Him, to cleave to Him, and not to concern ourselves with anything but His holy presence. If the answer is yes, then that hour of contemplation was well and properly spent.

This keeping still in the presence of God, this complete inactivity on the part of the soul, which at first would appear so difficult and even wrong, has often been compared to the stillness to which one has to submit when posing for an artist. The portrait will never be a success if the model were constantly to shift this way and that, to interrupt the painter, to try to direct the artist. After all, it is not the model but the painter who is the master here. All that the model's interference will achieve is the bungling of the picture. But who is the Master that models and shapes the soul to become the image and likeness of Himself, to reflect the face of Christ? Only God, through the Holy Spirit, whom we call *Digitus paternae dexterae*—Finger of the right hand of God. Is the soul likely to know the plans of God, "whose thoughts are not our thoughts and whose ways are not our ways?" It knows nothing except this: that it must reach perfect sanctity and that no one can give that but God alone. What good can our interference do, our bustling activity? As long as certain handyman's jobs are being expected of us, well and good, but after that, better to remain still. The soul must practice mortification, keep its appointed times of prayer, make resolutions and examinations of conscience, cultivate vocal prayer, and all the rest. But then the time comes when the soul can do no more without endangering the work, the real work which is about to begin. Will the soul be so foolish as to insist on its own activity when the Artist bids it keep silent and quietly wait? He will tell the soul how to pose for Him, how to look at Him that He may catch its glance and hold the soul well within His own. Would you call anyone indolent and inactive, who poses thus for his portrait? If he dozed and fell off his chair, yes; but if he steadily maintains the posture indicated; if he resists the desire to look out of the window, the urge to approach the easel and get a close view of what has so far been done; if, instead, he remains quietly disciplined and attentively looks at the painter to catch any new directive that might be given, then surely that person is very much "on the job." His faculties are concentrated on the painter's activity, whose great work of art thus becomes in some measure that of the model also.

The soul has done all it could; what follows is no longer within its power. Therefore God makes the soul understand that from now on it is He who will act. Not without the soul, which in complete concentration of all its faculties upon God must be entirely at His disposal and alert to His every favor. Here activity is in full union with passivity; this is the active form of total submission. Is that not enough? Is it not, in fact, more than what previously we used to do of ourselves? True, the soul could not have caused this to happen before the Master deemed well to begin His work in it in this particular way. Now it must let it happen, and accept it all in deep gratitude. If we remember this analogy just when, during contemplation, we find it especially difficult to keep still, we shall probably smile a little at our childish zeal and our soul will gladly return to its quietude.

But is there really no question of the soul ever being active except in this total submission? This is difficult to make out from the first. If the impulse which comes from God is strong enough from the beginning, and if it remains persistent, then the soul is neither permitted to nor in need of being itself active. Rather will it remain in this attitude of tranquil attention, of loving regard and readiness which we have just described. Otherwise the following will be observed.

The fourth point is that the soul may have begun with a prayer or a short meditation when that gentle impulse is felt, that pull toward God, to tranquillity, to inner silence. It should be obeyed at once. In such a case God's activity relieves that of the soul. If it now feels that neither vocal prayer nor meditation is likely to succeed, the soul will be well advised to make a few short introductory acts of faith in the presence of God, of trust in His help, of submission to His will and readiness to be completely guided by Him. An act of acceptance also of all the trials and hardships which this hour may now impose.

Quite often the very first of these acts provokes that inner stillness which renders the soul unable or unwilling to continue in this way, and compels it wordlessly to regard Him whom its act of faith acknowledged, or to whom it offered itself lovingly as His very own. If after a while the impulse subsides, one can repeat the act which so quickly resulted in the soul's interior recollection; not too soon, however, lest it anticipate God's activity. One may also fall back on a passage from the Scriptures, and ejaculations from one of the litanies, or some other suitable help for inner enlightenment.

It has been aptly suggested that one should here proceed like someone about to kindle a fire. There is a good deal to be done first: collecting the wood, piling it up, squeezing bits of paper and straw between the logs, lighting them, jogging them, and blowing up the flames. Once it is well ablaze, one cannot do much more about the fire. When it subsides, a fresh log is shoved on top, and it continues to burn, warm and glowing. Thus the soul—unless God deprives it even of these preliminary tasks—must first do a certain amount itself by making those acts which we already mentioned. But when the sacred flame has been carried into the soul from above and has kindled itself, as it were, on the material previously gathered, then the soul should do no more. It is now aflame, warming itself in the love which had been the very motive that made the soul light that fire. Therefore, when recollection seems to cease altogether, when the attraction from "beyond" recedes and the heart appears to be cold, the soul will put a new log on the fire. It will repeat a short act of faith, of love, of resignation, or recall a word of our Lord. No more, though, for already its fire is blazing again. The more often the soul keeps these times of contemplative prayer, the less will be the need to renew its active efforts, until they are hardly ever required even at the start, because the soul is at once entirely in the presence of God. The sacred fire is now always ablaze and the soul's entire attention and consciousness is forever engrossed in it.

There is yet another activity of the soul in contemplative prayer, which is the fifth point that we have to consider. A new kind of action is being born in contemplation. Generally this takes a long time to happen, for the soul must first undergo a basic transformation at the Master's hand. Occasionally, in wonder and sacred joy, first tendencies can be discerned. In a manner of speaking, God has deprived the soul of its powers and faculties and absorbed them into His own self. Now they are truly and utterly at His disposal. What the soul has persistently prayed for and deeply desired, what it tried to facilitate by the offering of itself, is gradually becoming a reality. God has become the soul's life, accomplishing His works within it and inviting the soul to cooperate. No longer mere stillness and wait.

The blessed life of the triune eternal harmony now passes through the soul and carries it forth. Formerly, that most holy life had also animated the soul, but it then lived a separate life of its own, alongside, if one may say so, the spiritual, the supernatural sphere. Now that is totally changed. Thanksgiving, for instance, will suddenly rise up in the middle of contemplation. This is not now, as before, due to an impulse on the part of the soul, a resolution, or an act of the will; it emanates from within, from an interior depth so far quite unknown. At this moment the soul's very being is a thanksgiving. And He who gives thanks is Christ, doing this within the soul in such a way as to induce the soul's cooperation, to envelop the soul entirely in His eternal thanksgiving before the heavenly Father. This is His thanksgiving and also that of the soul, for here is now one act, born of one love, moving and kindling two hearts in unison. This is what Christ meant when He said: "Rivers of living waters shall flow . . ."; to which St. John added: "Now this He said of the Spirit which they should receive" (John 7:38,39). Divine life within the life of the soul. Divine action in the action of the soul.

Thus the mystery of its transformation unveils itself to the soul in the power of contemplative prayer. And it may not refuse this newly arising activity as it had to reject its own when God began His work within it. Now again is the time for the soul to join in. This is no longer distraction, disturbance and immature meddling. This is the manifestation of contemplative inner life; the unfolding of what, in the silent depth of the soul invisibly, incomprehensibly came into being under the life-giving breath of the Holy Spirit of love. This is the fruit of the tree which the hand of the Lord "has planted on the banks of the river," the fruit of sanctification and everlasting life. These acts, which should perhaps properly be called interior states or conditions rather than acts, are in themselves perfect, since they are God's own acts, bearing, if one may say so, a divine-human character. They form the spiritual countenance of the soul. In each one of them the soul is wholly present as the adoring, the loving, the thanking soul. They are in a way the continuation of the divine life of Jesus Christ in His members, the life of the vine in the branches.

Chapter 19

Passive Purification

FROM earliest times the strange and almost alarming metamorphosis of certain insects, above all, that of the butterfly, has been taken for a symbol of the redemption and transformation of the soul to a higher, purer form of existence. First there is the caterpillar, plump and hardly jointed, lazy and insensitive, earthy, and cleaving to the ground with eight pairs of legs. It is nothing but body and mouth, with no more to occupy it than feeding and growing fat. Sometimes a few early signs of beauty appear; a little coloring, small dots, or stripes. But there is much ugliness, too, and occasionally even some poison in the hairy coat of the body. Sometimes, rearing up, as it were, above its humble station, the caterpillar stretches itself, gropingly; then, finding nothing, it returns to its habitual ways.

Now and then certain changes occur: it stops feeding; it does not move; it shrivels up until its skin splits open and it emerges new and fresh—the same larva as before, only bigger and more greedy than ever. Finally it reaches the limits set for it. It is seized by a strange agitation, as if it no longer knew what to do with itself. The most tempting food, so far voraciously absorbed, is now scorned, never again to be found acceptable. With astonishing speed the caterpillar scurries about hither and thither, as if the earth had become repulsive or uninhabitable for it. Finally it inters itself in a hole or wraps itself up in a self-made web; or else it suspends itself from a wall, head downwards, as if it were outlawed, condemned, sentenced to death. It then becomes uglier than ever, quite repellent, in fact. It hardly stirs and could easily now be taken for dead. Only occasionally the body contracts as if in pain. And then, unexpectedly, the skin splits open from one end to the other and falls off the creature like an old, tight garment; and there is the pupa, a different thing altogether!

The pupa has neither legs nor a greedy mouth to feed; and no need of either. It does not stir. Where it is, it stays, and to change its position by force would harm it. It is exposed, defenseless, except for an armor of self-woven fabric which, though finely spun, is a firm protection against injuries or hostile influence. Mostly it now appears quite motionless, and one might easily think it had perished. Now and then it makes a few violent movements, turns or even throws itself this way and that; then, once more, immobility. This condition may last a long time—weeks or even months.

Gradually a further change can be observed. Something like color begins to shine through the grey or brown unpleasing armor. The colors grow more distinct, until a patter of lines and spots can be discerned. More accentuated, too, are the folds of the skin, where the colors show most, like a promising, though as yet undefinable light breaking through the small creature which is seemingly held deeper than ever in its rigidity.

At last the moment arrives when this cloak, too, must split and drop away. And out of it a completely transformed and new being emerges. Had the pupa been opened by force before those specks of color became visible, only a shapeless, yellow-green substance would have been discovered, amorphous, un-identifiable as to its further purpose. But now a new being which in no way resembles the former larva or grub is resur-rected as if from a tomb. Carefully at first, and as yet awk-wardly, the small creature climbs up and suspends itself from a twig. And then that strangely creased skin with the colored stripes and dots, so crumpled and unsightly, begins to unfold itself. It stretches out, smooth and lovely, until it is shaped into wings. The long and delicate weevil, with which the creature will daintily sip fragrant honeyjuice, coils and uncoils as if to test itself. Suddenly all is ready; the creature takes wing, and a butterfly, full of life and agility, color and beauty, flits through the air in blissful anticipation of flowers and the company of its own kind. All memory of the past is so completely extinct that the butterfly will never waste time with a caterpillar, let alone any other larva. It will feed on flowers and will live for love. Light, fragrance and joy will be its element.

How could we fail to marvel at this transformation which, by the Creator's wisdom, mysteriously foreshadows the destiny of the soul that He loves? For here is truly a prototype of the soul that is to be changed into something new and exalted; to be liberated of its feet of clay. Through all the stages of its transformation the soul will certainly remain itself, but looking back, it will hardly recognize itself in the early phases of its lowliness. It had its own nourishment—spiritual instruction and reading—and eagerly it absorbed it all. There had been some aspects of beauty, but a great deal more had been vile, repellent, ugly, hard to endure. The poison of malice would surge in it again and again. There were times when the soul knew this well; times of heart-searching and grief, of disgust at its insufficiency, of discouragement to continue in its habitual ways. But once these moments had passed, the soul had been as before, only more hungry than ever and grown, in good ways and bad.

Then the hour had come when the soul could no longer tolerate its accustomed spiritual existence. Its very being was in revolt. Tired, exhausted, incapable and unwilling to move, it was forced to keep still, to wait, motionless and yearning for something which it could not imagine. There it was, as if suspended between heaven and earth, not yet received in the one, yet driven away from the other. Where did it belong? With its faculties suspended, it seemed horribly like being delivered up to death. And withal the soul remained strangely immune to and strangely safe from all manner of influence from without. A superior law which it did not understand, yet by which it was clearly sustained and protected, governed the soul.

In this utter inactivity it had to remain a long time, possibly years. Seemingly useless, it could do nothing about God or for Him; nothing but continue to wait and keep still. There was complete chaos within and it was impossible to distinguish anything in its interior. Where were those virtues which the soul thought it possessed? Where were its merits? What had become of the many inner experiences which now threatened to fail it completely? Was this annihilation, perdition, an inner death infinitely more horrible and merciless than physical dying? The soul did not know, could not make it out. Nor could others help. It was as if some evolution of the soul's spiritual life was now in progress, and yet there was so much ugliness and incomprehensible deformity, so much confusion. At times there was a peculiar beauty, too, in the soul's remoteness and silence, in its abandonment and its despondency. From time to time some light would seem to shine through from the depth of the soul, clothed in some word, some gesture, some quite simple, yet inwardly animated action, but as it came, so it would fade away.

Then, when the last stage of this dying was reached, when disintegration seemed certain and nobody would give a penny for its survival, the soul was in reality very near to its final perfection. Everything in it had been transformed: its former ways of thought, judgment and prayer; its faith and its love. All has been fundamentally changed, melted down and newly created by that sovereign power in whose hands, in whose loving heart all is safe. The greedy need for food, for instance, has ceased. The soul contents itself with one word, one single thought, and in long draughts it now savors the newly discovered exquisiteness of the one and only who gives it new perception, a new grasp of Himself. Previously the soul had constantly needed new and different pastures. Now it always and gladly returns to the same bloom whose innermost core seems inexhaustible. If it so wishes, the soul is once more free to return to earth—on wings, as it were—with different aims and desires, with a new way to move lightly, delicately and unfettered. Only in so far as its new law of life in the pure light of God and His love bears resemblance to the soul's previous state, must this now concern it. Its life now is love; not ambition, not possessiveness, as before. Freed of selfishness, the soul now seeks beauty and goodness for their own sake. It has abandoned itself to truth, and that now is its life.

Thus it has developed new means of perception, of receptive and active powers. Even the old ones have been transformed, like the delicately jointed legs of the butterfly compared to the short, stumpy limbs of the grub. The soul thinks, but how much more spiritual, lucid and animated are its thoughts. The soul wills, but how completely is the will subjected now to divine guidance. How gentle it is, yet firm; how pure, yet stirring. Nothing convulsive, nothing exaggerated, nothing bigoted about it now. From its most profound depths, where the soul suffered its transformation, these powers have been awakened, and give genuine expression to the new being that has emerged. And just as it is not the larva but the butterfly which is prolific, so the soul now possesses true supernatural fecundity as it lives in, by and for love alone, conceiving from God the Son, the Eternal Word, and giving life to the truth in all things transmitted to its care, to fill all their life with God.

It is difficult to assess whether the process of evolution means pain and suffering to the insect itself. There are transitional stages, when everything seems so violent, awkward and irksome that one feels moved to pity for the tormented creature. But this may well be no more than a semblance to render more perfect the analogy to the soul's transformation. For the pilgrimage of the soul is a way of torment, indeed, a rising from perversion, a penitent's struggling return from wrongness of life and perception and deed, a liberation from shackles which must first be shed before a new kind of existence can come into being. Thus, in great pain—of emotion, of intellect, will and being—the soul must suffer a rebirth. Yet there is bliss in this torment, for the soul knows that this way will lead straight to the goal, even though in a darkness deeper and more impenetrable than that which enveloped the larva. And just as the chrysalis has its peace and its gentle rest in the quiet of death which engulfs it, so the soul in the midst of its dying to self knows a sacred peace. It experiences a certitude that will carry it through, the certitude of an ultimate crowning glory in the love of God.

The soul's awareness of its moral nothingness

Many are the sufferings of the soul on the way of contemplation. Some of them will be mentioned here for the sake of better orientation and perseverance. The suffering, like everything else, can be explained merely in general terms. Each soul has its very own experience of the love of God, and it is in this love that these sufferings have their beginning. Much will remain for each individual soul to learn by itself, to suffer alone, with no one to lighten the burden or even to point the right way. Understanding will be given only by the enlightening love of the Holy Ghost.

If a dark room is suddenly filled with light, anyone in that room will, no doubt, perceive it. But there may be no chance to enjoy the light on account of the squalor which meets the eyes at the sudden illumination. Unwillingly fascinated, one cannot avert his eyes from the disgusting sight, and he feels as if the world all around had nothing but dirt to offer. This is precisely the soul's experience as the presence of truth breaks in upon it at the moment of contemplation. Hardly able to look at the light itself, the soul feels as if that light entered obliquely or indirectly, in a manner revealing everything except the light itself. In this light the soul sees itself. The implacability with which the soul must now recognize itself as in a mirror, the inescapability of that spectacle can be a pain of untold severity. The soul had always known that it was imperfect, that it had countless faults, more obvious at

certain occasions than at others. It had fought them, had re-
pented, had made a new start, and for a while all had seemed
well again.

Earlier we saw that such efforts reach a limit which the soul
cannot surpass. In contemplation, in the light which it bestows,
it is God Himself who now takes over the soul's purification.
It brings pain and deepest confusion, but also the compensation of leading the soul to its goal. In this light of the mysterious
presence of God, the holy, the ineffably pure God, the soul
is faced with itself quite unsparingly, but in a manner which
does not reveal too much at a time, for the soul could not
bear it. That is why this purification will often recur, subside,
and after a while begin again, to continue in ever deeper layers
of the soul's being. Each time the soul will perceive more evil
within itself, though never enough to destroy it.

But what it is forced to behold is, indeed, hideous. From
every nook and cranny it surges up, lowly, mean, unkind,
selfish, insidious. Having fancied certain aspects of its moral
life to be in good order and quite commendable, the soul now
learns that all, all without exception, is contaminated, polluted,
corrupt; impregnated by an immoderate love of self; made
cheap by an unspeakably narrow and parsimonious heart. It
discovers that its love is impure, a perverse distortion of what
it should be; that its fidelity is like a reed, its devotion mere
pretense. The inexorable light reaches down to the soul's
foundation. For the first time the soul knows, or only faintly
surmises, its true nature and is filled with horror and disgust.
Nauseated, it would like to escape, but that it may never do.
Wherever the soul turns, there it will meet itself—a monster of
ugliness and depravity—in order to imprint upon its forgetful
memory this true picture of itself and thus rid it forever of
the sorry pride of excessive self-esteem. In the end, nothing
remains for the soul's presumption. With unspeakable clarity
it now knows that all its unworthiness and baseness come from
itself, and all its goodness from God alone.

From a merely worldly point of view this may sound excessive and even unbalanced. But then, had this not been the soul's own point of view up to now? What of it? The soul has been led elsewhere, to a position from which everything is seen in a completely new perspective subject to totally different standards of judgment. The soul now appreciates that it had once been as blind as those who now wag their heads at its new comprehensions. It knows so much better. No one will ever again dissuade it of this new certainty of its nothingness in the moral order, of its basic unworthiness, its essential impurity. For the soul does not now compare itself to other people. It perceives itself in the light of God and knows itself as measured against His holy majesty. What then will be left to the soul's credit? Before His face it cannot "speak and desire to reason" (Job 13:3).

Thus truth leads the soul to inner sincerity, to the vision and the acknowledgment of things as they are. It is not as if the soul had but newly fallen into this deplorable condition; it merely recognizes it as a fact and is thus saved from a terrible self-deception which would obstruct the way of its further perfection. Being thus made sincere in its naked prostration before God and itself, the soul begins to be humble. Humility is the acknowledgment of things as they really are; of the place which, in the proper order of values, one must allocate to oneself. It is the fundamental condition for the work which God will accomplish in the soul. Without humility, the soul could not bear this; it would perish of its continued wrong judgment, by which it would attribute to itself what is wholly the work of God, and would thus prevent God from accomplishing the task. "The higher the edifice, the more deeply secured must be the foundations," says St. Augustine. The more beautiful, the more holy the soul is one day to be, the more humble it must first become. For that reason it now receives a most telling lesson in humility, which will convince it forcefully of its nothingness. Slowly the soul makes ready to shoulder that burden of misery. No more rebellion against the abhorrent sight; no impassioned attempts to deflect its attention from it; no denying; no tentative justification. There is only acknowledgment and acceptance of its cross, the most heavy of all the crosses which the soul has ever carried. For the first time, accepting itself as it is, the soul says its *Confiteor* in utter sincerity, makes it well up from the innermost depth of its being. Thus will be conquered the soul's fatal disease with its twofold menace of either wanting to be different or desperately trying to be this or that. Accepting itself as it is in the sense of resigning itself to the place that it actually holds, the soul at the same time ardently wishes that God would endow it with a new and holy being. For humility is full of hope. For a scant moment only does it look down to earth in acknowledgment of helplessness and ineptitude, only to raise its glance upwards at once, knowing that from God's love it will surely receive what of itself it could never, never obtain.

Now also the familiar and ugly habit of preferring oneself to others, secretly or openly, of considering oneself better, more capable, more efficient, or even more favored by grace, will gradually disappear. Pride before God has been vanquished, and so now has presumption before one's fellow-men. The soul no longer dares to weigh and to measure, to pass judgment. It leaves all that to God, just as it ceased to assess its own value, preferring to put itself entirely at His mercy.

The breakdown of the soul's haughty pride is one of the most important results of this kind of interior suffering. It is a purification to the roots of its being. It will have to happen many times before the soul is truly transformed and the hidden remnants of evil will no longer produce new shoots nor re-establish their rule.

Gradually a great silence will possess the soul. It lives in the knowledge of its indigence, resigned, contented. It has resolved to defer all judgment and abandon itself to God. Its very annihilation will give birth to that quiet trust which looks only at God and is purest hope. And what of the soul's demanding insistence of earlier days? That, too, gradually ebbs away. No more terms laid down as to when and how God should

grant this or that spiritual favor; no more conditions set as
to the time by which certain resolves must have been mastered.
The soul no longer implores God to concede it any particular
measure of sanctity, any spiritual prerogatives. With ever-
increasing serenity and deepening peace it can leave all that to
God, knowing that He will not merely take better care of it
all, but that He alone can and will have it in safe keeping.
Thus the soul detaches itself more and more from its own
ego, renounces itself and sides with God. He is the measure
for all, as He alone is good. He the beginning of all, the life
of its life, the light of its light. What more could the soul
desire?

To what purpose should we continue to analyze all the
gain to be drawn from this bitter pain of moral self-recognition?
This should suffice to encourage perseverence in this inner
struggle, to dispel despair and dismay. It is as if God had
forsaken the soul because He made it see how ugly it was,
how unworthy of Him whose bride it was destined to be, and
to show that the soul must give thanks for the immensity of
God's grace, born of His love for the soul; that it must desire
to achieve what He has the power to grant: that immaculate
beauty for which the soul longs. Indeed, the soul must give
thanks, and soon it will do so, passionately convinced of the
long-suffering mercy which patiently bore with the soul for
so long before risking to begin its purification and to provoke
its hypersensitive love of self. From the valley of death through
which the soul had to pass, the miracle of a spiritual spring is
born, whose beauty and vigor the soul could never have
known. From the mystery of its own passion it learns to
understand the words: "Ought not Christ to have suffered
these things and so enter into His glory?" (Luke 24:26).

The soul's awareness of its essential nothingness

Under the ardent and consuming light of truth the soul
recognized its moral nothingness. By degrees this experience
takes complete possession of it and it is by no means confined

253]

to the hours of prayer. Rather, in God's own time, it develops into a permanent condition of the soul, engulfing it with particular intensity and severity in the wake of any sin or offense. The soul lives, as it were, in this new consciousness, the opposite of that sacred life of contemplation which is waiting for it at the end of the soul's interior way.

There is no need to trace in detail this self-recognition of nothingness, granted to the soul by the light of contemplation, nor is it possible. We shall study only the major aspects. The effect, in any case, will be an ever-deepening humility, an ever-intensified rooting out of pride, of false self-confidence. That this process should begin in the moral field is obvious; it is there that we are most perniciously sullied and most highly sensitive. In that interior mirror of our conscience, what we actually did is measured against that which we ought to have done; our actions are confronted with the truth to which they did or did not conform. If our striving for perfection is genuine, we come up first against our misdemeanors. Into our conscience, therefore, that light will fall first with unbroken force. But then it pursues its way right down to the innermost core, to the roots of our being. The moral law reveals the existing true values, and thus also the power, the authenticity, the excellence and beauty of the ultimate being whence they originate and in whom they are made manifest. Therefore, when in the light of contemplation the soul's very depth is laid bare to itself, the soul cannot but recognize itself as essentially nothing. "I am nothing; Thou art all." That is how the soul now sees it. The two are connected; the nothingness of the soul is contrasted in that inner vision to the majesty and plenitude of the essence of God in the same way as, in the light of contemplation, the soul recognized its moral unworthiness as the counterpart of God's holiness and justice. In an interior experience the soul is made conscious of the immensity of God, of His absolute power and omnipotence, of His irresistibility and His pre-eminence. In this inner vision it apprehends—though in an indirect manner—that God is being in itself and of itself, neither bound nor indebted to anyone. Free, magnificent, glorious, unique—such is God. And the soul? The very antithesis. It sees itself in its total subservience, its complete dependence on God. This conception of nothingness does not signify non-existence, which would be untrue and a contradiction, for what does not exist, cannot conceive itself as nothing. Only in the infinite distance of being, which distinguishes the soul from God, it knows itself to be nothing. Measured against Him, it is nothing; or rather, it has being only in and through God.

Seeing itself against His light, the soul realizes this deeply. It understands that it has its roots not in itself, but in God, in His creative and sustaining will, that is, in His love. If at first it perceives its moral nothingness with horror, the recognition of its essential nothingness will fill the soul with profound stupefaction, mingled perhaps with a faint terror at the sight of the abyss beneath it. But if God at the same time grants it to perceive itself created and sustained by His love, then from the recognition of nothingness a great joy is born, a joy hardly impaired by the memory of so much revolt which emboldened the soul to pose as "something," with rights and a will and a way of its own.

The fruit of this period of suffering will be the soul's full abandonment to the power and dominion of God in a blessed certainty of its being in and of God and, therefore, of its being safe and protected. On the other hand, if left to itself, it would always have been the victim of uncertainty, apprehension and a sense of perdition. There is a truly wonderful happiness in the experience of this accurate equivalence; the more clearly the soul recognizes itself as nothing, the more deeply it knows itself rescued and anchored in God. Thus, as if directed by a new signpost, the soul strides away from itself and makes its way toward God, not to diminish its strength but to multiply it beyond measure, securing it in a foundation which will never give way.

No doubt the soul knew all this long before; had mentally

appropriated it by faith, prayer and meditation. Yet the interior experience of it is incomparably more. It means to possess the truth, to be saturated by it, to look at it face to face. It means having it in the blood, as a second nature and one of a higher order. It no longer means definitions of the brain or the mind in its diverse faculties, but it is an essential knowing.

The soul's awareness of its ineptitude

However deep the experience of its essential nothingness, the soul must yet pass through a supplementary phase which usually proves particularly hard. It must be faced so vigorously with its own ineptitude that it relinquishes any claim, however remote, to being capable of anything. This conviction may well derive from the experience of essential nothingness, but as such it would remain a logical deduction rather than become an essential knowing. Therefore, this bitterness, too, must be tasted.

To this end the soul is sentenced to a more or less total ineptitude during its spiritual exercises. We have seen that as a consequence of incipient contemplation, which excludes all autonomous employment of the soul's faculties, the mental faculties are, according to the degree of contemplation reached, either partially or totally numbed. The soul can no longer activate them to advantage; they can no longer be instrumental to interior progress. But withal a tense anticipation of the truth beheld in contemplation may well, and normally does, prevail, as the soul vaguely knows that something is happening interiorly. That, however, does not worry the soul, reposing, as it does with love, trust and gratitude in that truth that represents God. At this moment the soul is content not to be able to activate its own powers of reason, will, and the rest; for they are being used, they are being drawn into a mysterious activity called forth not by the soul but from above, by God. But then it may happen that this innermost certainty also disappears.

Now, as we have already explained, one applies the test: an

act of prayer, an attempt at meditation. But it is impossible. One feels as if paralyzed, unable to move in any direction. Something inside seems to stand still. The mind does not work; the heart is as if dead. There is no vibration, no resonance within, nor the slightest hope of autonomous interior activity. One tries to concentrate on a thought but it is scattered before it can begin to take shape. One tries to make an act of faith or resignation, but they elude his grasp. This condition can reach such a pitch that one not only feels as if in a narrow dungeon, too narrow to move a limb, but as if asphyxiated. Annihilated in utter helplessness, the soul seems nailed to its cross, expelled from the earth as from heaven, and it cries out in unspeakable pain. Indeed, it cannot even cry out. It would form the word "God," but not so much as a sigh escapes the soul. Only one thing seems possible: to keep still; to let things remain as they are. In its most profound depth the soul may know that it is safe in God's keeping and that all this has to be. At times indignation will rise in the soul like a flame, a furious will to revolt against this deathly rigidity. It may be a nervous reaction or a satanic temptation. Let the soul then keep still to the end of the time appointed for prayer. Then kneel down, kiss a crucifix—wordlessly, since no word will lend itself—and go about its duties. It can be certain of God's infinite compassion on the soul which, in its bitter pain, He ineffably loves. He holds it fast to His heart, or else it would invariably lose all hope and perhaps even cease to live, yielding to that strong temptation which at times becomes so insistent during those terrible torments. "Could I but die; could I extinguish my life!"

Heaven continues in silence and the soul continues to live; or to describe it more aptly, it experiences the words of the psalm which St. John of the Cross loved to expound: *Ut iumentum factus sum apud Te;* "Like a beast of burden have I become before Thee."

This interior consciousness of annihilation or total abandonment can also penetrate into our daily life and for some time become the permanent condition of the soul, though fortunately, not always in the same intensity. The soul would hardly be able to bear this. The soul continues in this relentless experience of its nothingness. It pervades everything and has nullified everything. It knows that in the natural as well as the supernatural order it can act solely by God's grace, and never more so than in this particular stage of its spiritual way.

There is one more aspect to stress. The condition just described can possibly affect all religious activities, such as spiritual reading, conversation or all manner of private prayer. However, it will not affect the performance of one's duties if they have no definitely religious character. This means that a person in the midst of this experience remains perfectly able to perform the exercises incumbent upon him in obedience; he can even pray, though inwardly he will be as if dead. Were the described condition to affect and inhibit normal activities also, some pathological phenomenon, possibly of a nervous nature, would no doubt have to be inferred. And while God may well use this on the way of contemplation and mystical sanctification, it has in itself nothing to do with either and should be referred to medical care.

Here we mention something which is frequently overlooked. There are a number of constitutional dispositions, pathological tendencies or abnormalities which, to a certain extent, can run parallel to and be mistaken for mystical experiences. It would be as wrong on that account to interpret mystical facts as pathological phenomena as it would be to deny to the genuinely infirm the possibility of simultaneous authentic mystical experiences. God neither needs our infirmities as a means for our sanctification nor is He hindered by them. The paralysis of the mind during prayer time may well be nothing but fatigue or strain, in which case it will persist at all other times as well. But even if it is a case of strain or fatigue, there can simultaneously be genuine contemplation. And if contemplation occurs in normal circumstances, it can rightly be supposed to happen as well in those of physical exhaustion. If for natural reasons our faculties are unable to function, God need not suspend them, but He can grant contemplative grace and accomplish His work in the soul, both of which can prosper only if the soul's faculties are not engaged in autonomous activity. To distinguish accurately may often be hardly possible, nor is it of major importance, since what really matters is the way as a whole, which can always be recognized, though sometimes only after a very long and patient wait. One thing, however, clearly follows from this: much prudence is needed in assessing the nature of the phenomena, especially when denying them the character of genuine signs of contemplation. "Great is God in His saints" (Ps. 107:36).

Temptations

This much is evident now: all the trials discussed in previous chapters, which from the very beginning can and frequently do attach to our life of prayer, are somehow comprised in the preceding section. As in former stages, so on this higher level of our relationship with God, they are an aggravating burden but at the same time a source of profuse grace, provided they are accepted in the right spirit. Now another kind of spiritual suffering, closely related to that of one's ineptitude, re-emerges: the pain of temptations and of actual faults.

Temptations can, of course, be of a greatly varying nature. It depends on the kind of impurities which still remain rooted deep down in the soul and need to be consumed by the mysterious fires of love kindled by contemplative grace. Thus, temptations may be tests of faith or of trust, of perseverance or the purity of the senses. They can often assume the nature of a terrible weight, obnoxious to the soul's natural vitality. "Is not all merely a mockery? Why hope for salvation? God may love others, but why should He love me? Worse still, He loves me but I do not respond, and therefore everything is in vain. Erring as I do in every respect, I have lost my way. If someone in the name of God were to tell me that I am doomed, I should not really be surprised. What else could I expect?"

At other times impure thoughts and images torment the soul. Whatever it sees or hears is almost automatically perverted. Neither prayer nor reading makes any difference. The whole organism can become so involved that one believes that everything is hopelessly lost in the abyss of impurity, lust and lewdness. No escape from this horrible state seems possible. No diversion will help, at least, never for long; neither books, nor music, nor entertainment of any kind. Momentarily all those ugly, lurid or wretched associations may be relegated to the periphery of one's awareness, only to repeat the assault and occupy the mind as if by exclusive right. Sometimes the soul is tortured by the fancy of having consented to it all. Groaning inwardly, it is again submerged in the sea of its grief. Months and years can pass thus. Yet deep down a rare certainty persists, as if with all the hidden forces of its being the soul were secured fast unto God; as if all that loathsomeness with which the soul seemed identified did not concern it at all. There are hours when, in the midst of gravest temptations, the soul suddenly feels far removed from it all; it is unable to touch the soul whose innermost being is in God's arms. Sometimes, while actually hearing that low interior voice whispering of its perdition, the soul may be seized by the knowledge: "God loves me, and nothing can ever befall!" Sometimes, while in the throes of an impetuous desire to cast away all, even its very life, the soul may, with a wan smile, trustingly form the words: "Never; for I am Thine." Or again it may, amid burning temptations of impurity, cling to God, behold Him in unspeakable clarity and know unerringly that it is safe in the Trinity, drawn into that blessed life as never before. In such moments the soul begins to grasp that its sufferings are a necessary transition and that it will survive all their perils. Slowly, or all of a sudden, the whole ghastly nightmare may disappear. The soul feels as if called from the tomb; it is amazed at the new look of the world, at its own deliverance, its freedom. All the turmoil within, which had been pressing upon it, has ceased its assault and no longer torments the soul. This is, of course, not the moment for self-assured daring or the delusion of being safe, for throughout this earthly life we can fall. But the very experience of these torments has made the soul deeply distrustful of its own strength; has taught it neither to rely on nor expect anything of itself. More than ever it is on its guard and so will pass through all fires without being touched by the flames.

A special type of temptation is sadness. Like an immensity of gloom it can weigh down the soul, and this again year after year. Whatever one does, wherever one goes, all is enveloped in sadness. Nobody may notice; people may even envy a seeming joy, a ready wit, a happy disposition, while in reality the soul is like a pit of sorrow hardly ever reached by a ray of light. Neither beauty nor purity nor exquisite goodness; neither the great solemn feasts of the Church nor the nearness to God in Holy Communion are exempt from this mantle of sadness which could tempt one to go in search of wild pleasures to escape that new pain or break through it. One would seek consolations, if any could be found, where the senses are aroused and at last those detestable fetters would fall. The soul must persevere in steadfastness; it must, as we said before, be ready to enter and stay of its own choice in that garden of sorrow where our Lord suffered the bitterness of His friends' desertion. Obviously, no other person must know of this misery, except one's spiritual director, who must be told of it as of other temptations and trials. Nor should one be on the lookout for more or less petty comforts, but abide by one's cross, taking its almst unbearable weight to the foot of the altar. "Thou, my Lord, knowest all." And the soul will thank Him for being allowed to accompany Him into His loneliness; for being permitted to sorrow with Him who sorrowed, whose "soul was sorrowful unto death" (Mark 14:34). And the soul will then learn of its participation in the redemption of those whom He mourned. But one day that, too, comes to an end, when the full force of contemplative grace will have conquered the heart.

Actual faults

Even in its temptations the soul retains an awareness that it belongs to God and that nothing can separate it from Him. Actual faults cause much deeper distress. It may be assumed that grave transgressions are not likely to be committed by any person who has been guided for some time by contemplative grace and has been endeavoring to lead a life entirely centered on God. And even fully deliberate venial sins will be a rare misfortune, if they happen at all. But not so those borderline faults which are so difficult to recognize and whose relation to our free will is so hard to assess. For the God-loving soul, this incapacity to judge can become a most cruel pain. In fact, the less we love God, the less censorious will be our judgment of our faults; the greater our love, the greater our heart's anguish about them.

It is no longer so much a question of ourselves, of our being so imperfect, so full of blemishes, but of God, and because every one of our faults so painfully proves the dismal deficiency of our love. Yet the soul desires to love; would want nothing more than to love, and love God alone. It would do all and suffer all for Him, and on no account commit anything likely to offend Him in the slightest. It would obey every hint of His will and abandon or readjust all its ways for the remotest suggestion that such was His desire. And what happens instead? Faults and more faults every day. Some of them—conditioned, though not excused, by temperament and personal circumstance—pierce the soul like pointed arrows. A thousand resolves and as many expedients have not helped in the least. Once in a while the soul succeeds in being gentle instead of rough and off-hand in manner; once in a while it remains serene instead of flying into a temper as usual. But how rarely! And even if one fell but once a day, could any bride bear to distress her beloved as often?

Yet the soul must endure its proneness to evil, though year after year may pass without any apparent improvement. The soul may have prayed and sorrowed and done all it could, but to no avail, until it becomes very still and accepts these faults as its daily cross. Gradually it will learn to appreciate how great, how unselfish must be the love which in divine forbearance continues to tolerate and forgive a thousand times, without anger, without reproach or censure. Ever and ever God draws the soul close to His heart when it looks up to Him, mortified, from the pit of its wretchedness. It must become meek in its failings and learn to bear them with patience while trying to conquer them. Thus the most profound roots of excessive self-reliance, self-love and impatience are being weeded out of the soul. There is untold bitterness in this mortification, but it makes the soul's love deepen and grow. It is like a healing potion, and the soul will be restored by it. In His own time God will lift this burden also.

One should not be alarmed at the seeming deliberateness of one's faults. One did, of course, feel the inner check that tried to prevent an outburst of temper. Even while he gave way, it was as if someone quickly caught his sleeve to restrain him. But he disobeyed. How could that happen? The soul does not, and perhaps never will, understand it fully. This is a stage which cannot be surmounted; a reef which no navigating can avoid; a concealed threshold impossible to traverse. The soul must resign itself and accept this; it must fight and pray and trust. Were it not for its shocked awareness that it should and could have responded very differently, there would be little cause for grief. But to have had and missed that genuine alternative, that is a torturing pain to its love.

Death of the senses

Further spiritual sufferings to which the contemplative soul is subjected originate in its various faculties. Like other trials, these too had been experienced from the start, but now they are brought to a climax. The emotions attach themselves to everything, surround everything with glamour and joy, and cling with a subtle tenacity. In secret or openly they are out for enjoyment, and with unsurpassed cunning they know how to make use even of the religious life, even of God Himself. Quite ingenuously, too, for is not God the true cause of joy? A monstrous egotism lurks behind our emotions. If our love is to be made pure—and how else could it ever be real love—our emotions must be severely purified in contemplation. The aridity and desolation experienced in previous stages have but prepared the way. Now the soul is, as it were, laid utterly barren. It may concentrate on the most sublime truths but the emotions do not respond. This is all the more trying when one is accustomed to sentiments easily aroused. More sober souls have an easier time. All revelry and excitation, all rapture and ecstasy are easily expelled.

What has truth to do with this intoxication of the senses? There is, as we know, a purely spiritual inebriation, but the soul is brought to this only after the sentiments born of the nerves and the senses have, so to speak, died away. Occasionally, when the soul is too much in danger of weariness, it may be allowed some measure of feeling. God then gives it the crumbs of consolations, for His tender patience will bear with the soul's debility, and the weaker the soul the more gentle will be God's forbearance. But as far as one can renounce all longing for sensible consolations, he should do so, for they slow down the pace of the soul's inner way. The harder that way and the steeper, the more rapid will be its ascent.

In the first stages of contemplative prayer the soul knows little of the "spirit." Consequently, the fading away of every sentiment that had hitherto been the primary means of the soul's encounter with God will prove a most irksome transformation of interior prayer. Here again nothing can help but quiet resignation, until a new vision of God, a new form of possessing Him begins to develop. All feeling of the senses must die before the spirit can manifest itself in its own proper manner. Only then will the soul realize the completely different deeper intimacy between God and itself in this new experience, even if measured against that of the most ardent emotions. In them too, the soul had found God, if it had sought Him sincerely, but in the same way as one has an encounter with God in a flower or in a drop of dew. Now the soul begins to possess God in the spirit, that is, in a manner essentially appropriate to God, who is Spirit.

St. Augustine recalls how long he was on the way to rid himself wholly from any spatial image of God, until at last he could grasp His spiritual nature, and he was a man of outstanding spiritual gifts. To this the soul will penetrate only by shutting off the emotions by deliberate mortification. Later, in contemplation itself, this will be advanced and perfected by God. We should add that even at this stage mortification has a place of its own. Not infrequently it happens that the emotions are suddenly and forcefully aroused in and by contemplation. The soul's interior vision in obscurity impresses and engages it so deeply that its entire being is as if transported. Inadvertently the whole person is caught up in this experience; tears may start to the eyes and something, one knows not what or how, seems to contract the heart. Here one should offer resistance. Such emotional outbursts, though different from those experienced prior to the soul's initiation to contemplation, hinder its progress and the further perfection of its love. At first this seems unlikely, until the soul consents to suppress its emotions. Yes, to suppress them! It must control its feelings, recover its tranquillity, and offer its heart calmly and without constraint to God. He will soon take matters in hand and give and reveal more than that which had so unexpectedly fired the senses.

Torment of the faculties

If the soul suffers from the apparent death or extinction of the emotions, it will be tormented by the unbending dominion of the rest of its faculties. Sometimes the mad dance of images, thoughts and inclinations enters at once into prayer, and it is like a true deliverance when at last they subside and gradually give place to the desired inner tranquillity. But the process can

265]

be reversed. At first peace and recollection; then the turbulent onslaught begins, advances upon the soul's very center, and finally dominates the whole scene so mercilessly that the soul can but look on, impotent and defenseless. True, the soul is and remains with God, but its interior vision is troubled by that ceaseless whirl and confusion, often without coherence. It is as if memory, imagination and reason combined to jumble up tiny pieces of rubble without design or purpose. The soul does not know where to turn. For a time it tries to master the situation, but soon it realizes the futility of the attempt. Then only one thing remains: to accept it as a pain permitted by God and beneficial for the soul through the very act of acceptance.

Regarding the proper demeanor in this predicament, the essential has already been stated. In contemplation above all, the soul learns that beneath all the turmoil its union with God persists and quietly deepens, untouched by events on the surface, which are of no matter. The greater the soul's indifference, its contempt even, and its refusal to take any notice, the more appropriate its bearing. It knows that "the foxes come to the vineyard to destroy the bloom" (Cant. 2:15), but they will not succeed. The soul's love of God and its fidelity are unshakeable. Nothing can drive it away; nothing can tempt it to voluntary distraction. Even if such a state should persist for a long time, leaving one with a feeling of total failure, there is no need to worry, as long as the soul truly desires to be with God. In spite of everything, the heart will be at peace, will rest in the love of God, and from His heart will receive in this hour what it needs to live for Him and to love Him forever.

Thus the soul learns to give itself to God, whatever its inner condition; to trust God and no longer to try to determine the form of its union with Him. Most important of all, the soul realizes how, while all its faculties are actively engaged, the heart can be somewhere else, can truly be with God. This simultaneity is, of course, not only a matter of thought and desire, but of experience and practice; the latter being irksome, no doubt, but equally profitable. One day our life in the love of God will consist in this: to be conscious, always and in everything that we do, of His regard, of His presence; to act in submission to Him and with complete dedication, though never at the price of a narrowed horizon, a distorted vision of our tasks in the here and now. These, on the contrary, we shall recognize and fulfill appropriately only if we realize that, as they are given by God, so they will lead back to Him. To grasp the self-evidence of this connection, to concentrate on the two planes simultaneously, and to live this creative union is something so new that, unless as an exception the soul were allowed to see it all in one flash of divine grace, it can but slowly take shape. In the relentless turmoil of its faculties the soul begins to acquire a double vision, as it gradually learns to keep its gaze upon God, unperturbed by the rest which continues to claim its attention.

Concern for self

A further pain, related to the one just described, originates in the already deepened love of God. Profoundly dismayed, the soul feels how rarely it is truly and wholly with Him. Even in actual prayer this is often rendered most difficult. But then there is some consolation in the thought that it is God Himself who abandons the soul to darkness, fatigue and helplessness, while He could so easily restore it to a worthier condition. To accept His will proves helpful and is usually rewarded by at least an occasional moment of true recollection. But throughout the day, at work, in conversation with others, is it not always I who act and talk and listen, sleep and eat and enjoy myself? Yet God should reign supreme within my soul, which knows from actual experience that this condition is possible and should, therefore, persist without interruption. The soul longs to be always with God, to live in Him, to wait for His instructions, to fulfill them under His eyes and saturate its every act with the love of Him.

Is not a loving wife always thus secretly, wistfully united to her spouse, so that somehow he is with her in everything

she does, since she does it for love of him? Attending to the
daily tasks, even the most trivial and least attractive domestic
matters which she used to despise and even try to avoid, she
now finds all quite changed, elevated into a different order,
charged with new values and the predominant thought of her
husband's good pleasure. This is precisely what the soul now
seeks with growing passion and increasing consciousness, because it loves. It is now, through contemplation, being transformed more and more into love and its gaze is being totally
drawn into God. And yet, no sooner is it once more engaged
in its daily tasks, when all this seems forgotten and the soul
is again "only itself." True, it reminds itself sometimes of God,
offers Him something, whispers its consent; but there is not
that constant union, that fulfillment in God which the soul has
recognized unequivocally as its innermost calling and supreme
form of existence.

In this more than in any of the preceding trials the soul
encounters the indigence of its love, the weakness of its devotion, the immaturity of its strength, the distance between itself
and the acknowledged and desired goal. This causes the soul
unspeakable sorrow, softened only by the secret yet firm hope
that one day God will accomplish this victory, too, as He has
achieved everything that the soul has ever attained. For, surely,
He did not call it, raise it from the dust, draw it to Himself,
reveal to it His mysteries and His very heart and shower it
with ineffable love, only to bid it run half way to the goal.
What God begins, He will complete; that is the soul's con-
soling faith, by which once more it learns as best it can to
leave to God alone the chosen moment, when He will crown
the soul with final glory; when He will raise it to that perfection which He alone knows and the soul is to share.

Closely connected with the soul's sorrow at the as yet unconquered predominance of self in its relation to God is a
distress which is characteristic of bridal love: the frequent
privation when God withdraws from the soul, often enough
without any evident reason. Of this, however, we shall not

treat, as it is but the reverse of an incipient happiness. It is a pain which carries a rare felicity of its own and masters itself in a mysterious manner appropriate to love.

Physical and social suffering

One further observation appears important, namely, that on the whole the evolution of contemplative prayer seems to be accompanied throughout by physical sufferings and by bitternesses deriving from human society. These, too, are dispensed in ever varying patterns and degrees of intensity. In a truly wonderful way God's wisdom administers to each soul precisely what it requires to attain the goal assigned to it personally. It is never too hard to bear, although at times it tries the soul to the limits of its endurance.

It would appear that a robust and healthy physique without any cracks is too homely a vessel to enable the soul to achieve, or even to want to achieve, the break-through to the world beyond. While a beautifully serene, truly edifying and deeply Christian life may indeed unfold under ordinary conditions, progress on the contemplative way seems to begin only when the body's natural equilibrium has been more or less weakened. It is as if a kind of cleft were necessary, to enable the supernatural light to break through. Ordinary experience as well as the lives of the saints show that physical sufferings are somehow an integral part of the contemplative state. They are by no means always grave or chronic; indeed, there is often an interminable chain of ever varying kinds. No sooner has one of them ceased, when another sets in. Of course suitable remedies should be applied, but one is certain that they will not break that mysterious chain. Then comes the time when the soul no longer desires to escape it. Willing to suffer, though by nature perhaps cowardly and but little resilient in the face of physical pain, the soul accepts suffering to the point that a day without discomfort could trouble it, as if something might be remiss. It is most characteristic that these afflictions do not generally reach a degree to incapacitate one to attend to one's daily tasks. Frequently, one is surprised that at the given moment a given task can be mastered, though not long before it had seemed wholly beyond one's strength. To credit this to mere nervous energy would in many cases fall short of the facts.

The trials resulting from social life can also differ greatly. A slight, an intentional insult, complete incomprehension, antipathy and opposition, or even slander may make one feel as if ostracized, even if friendly appearances are preserved. The soul feels hurt, wretched and lonely. Even those who appear genuinely sympathetic do not really understand, and the soul knows it. Thus, to fit into life with others becomes problematic. One is shy, uncertain and awkward; at least, so one appears to oneself, even if others are not likely to notice. Solitude seems the best refuge. But then there is the distressing thought that this proves the soul's lack of charity; its distaste to care about others; and the fact that one is, after all, the hopeless blunderer that others have long since discovered and shunned.

Things need not always come to that pass. Nevertheless, some of it, though not always felt as acutely, lingers at the periphery of the soul's consciousness, ready to intrude and cover everything with its cloak of despondency. Somehow, this has to be. The soul must, in some measure, be uprooted. Its pleasant security, its natural and unperturbed contentedness must be disturbed, must even be destroyed. Neither may the body give any assurance of strength, ability or achievement, nor will human society sustain, acclaim or satisfy the soul. While it is possible that the "hunger and thirst for justice" called "blessed" by our Lord may, by the impact of grace, also be roused in a soul otherwise perfectly well established in this world, it is not likely to happen. The soul must first experience its own limitations, and at as many points as possible. Then only will it become deeply aware of the insufficiency of this life, and then that "hunger and thirst" will arise. Then the soul cries out for God, and soon that interior way may begin to shape, which we have more precisely marked by the three signs. And in order that the soul may never content itself again before it has reached that goal which alone can answer to its infinite desire, God leaves open its wounds or will cause fresh ones to bleed. Henceforth the soul will cry out for the only good which can bring to a blessed end so tormented a life. Such is the nature of man; unless it be furrowed, it cannot receive the good seed. Suffering, be it caused by our body or by our fellow-men, ploughs up the soul and carries the seed into its deepest grooves.

By these two kinds of suffering the soul is made insecure and looks for a firm support. It is detached from many things in which it would otherwise have taken great pleasure, much to the detriment of its attention to God's inner presence and of its loving contact with Him. How easily are we preoccupied with our loved ones, with friends, with books and music; how well we can live on love and appreciation, on achievement and success. So well, in fact, that we hardly ever lift our eyes beyond these things, as if they could never run dry. Though regular care be given to religious exercises, they are no different from other duties and, like them, they are attended with equal assurance and aptitude. But this will never lead to the greater love, to the ultimate ardor of the heart; not before all else has become questionable and its spell has been broken.

Only gradually will the soul grasp the magnitude of grace vouchsafed in these trials. Then it will never again renounce any of them, but embrace them all, thanking God for them. It realizes that God could not bestow a more precious favor than to force open the gates, uproot the soul, and expel it from its terrestrial paradise. It learns to comprehend that this already is, in its particular way, the imitation of Christ. It affords the chance to prove in a thousand ways its genuine love for Him. Would a bride wish life to be sweeter for her than for her husband? Nothing could cause her more shame. So the soul begins to love its cross jealously, as a perpetual salutation to Him whose light penetrates even into the closest darkness. Here is the chance to do penance and to cooperate in His work of redemption. The soul will be permitted to learn that in His heart its sufferings are being transformed into pure grace for the world; for that world which it seemed to have left so far behind and to which in Christ and through Him, the soul remains bound with all its strength. In suffering the soul is made into love for God and love for its brethren, and it perceives how thus begins that same resurrection by which, for Christ and in Him, "the sufferings of this time" are transformed into "the glory to come" (Rom. 8:18).

Indestructible certitude

The way of contemplation will lead the soul through the various degrees of suffering according to its endurance and the measure of perfection to which it is called. It may know conditions which feel like purgatory, and others that seem more like hell—such distance from God, such abysmal wretchedness, such horror of self, and such overpowering awe of the holiness and inaccessibility of God that without His grace the soul would certainly perish in final despair. In agonies of helplessness, abandonment and exhaustion it passes through something like death, and there is no way out except to surrender itself to God's mercy, but that always means an infinite abundance of grace. At times it is as if the soul could tentatively lift its eyes and abide for the briefest instant in the presence of God. Then even this small consolation is denied. Something monstrous seems to force the soul's gaze back into itself, and it has no choice but to wait and keep still, while an eternity seems to pass.

These are truly terrible hours, but they teach the soul more and fashion it better than all consolation and inspiration combined. Here God takes possession of the soul to its innermost point, seizes it by its roots and, purging it, makes it His own, unless it resists. Now at last it begins in a mysterious way to become detached from itself and to choose God for its ultimate measure. With a valor previously unknown to the soul, it makes ready to plunge into the obscurity of His being, to be engulfed by it without further resistance and with no wish of its own, except that "His will be done on earth as it is in heaven." This is where self-love is sentenced to death, and the soul, while still bridling in natural defense, rejoices. Its salvation is near, Advent is truly come, and there is not long now to wait for God to be born in the soul.

All the same, the soul could not bear its cross were it not for an indestructible inner certitude. It is difficult to explain how and why it is there, often hardly perceived, yet the soul lives by it and proceeds on its way. It sees its faults, its wretchedness; it knows that it has nothing to expect of itself; that it is like an outcast without any right of hope. Stripped of all manner of merit, the soul is conscious of having always failed badly; of blundering even at this very hour. It knows that it does not faithfully cooperate with grace; that is repudiates the hand of God a hundred times a day; that it errs and stumbles; that its judgment is like a night-bird's vision in the light of day; that its will is infirm and perverted. And yet it continues on its way; continues as if this were well-known country, though it has never walked it before; and the descriptions of others never seem to apply when the soul would be glad of their guidance. A fool in its own estimation, it walks on like a sage; it seems deranged to itself, yet pursues its way straight and without vacillation. It does not stop for reflection, it does not turn back; the very thought would spell dread for the soul. At rare moments a sudden light, unhoped for, reaches it; a word of God, as if He wished to assure the soul very explicitly of His presence no longer felt. "To whom shall we go? Thou has the words of eternal life" (John 6:69).

Nobody can dissuade the soul of this inner certainty; at the most it could, in some measure, be confirmed by others. For it is not born of the soul nor of any human wisdom or subtle knowledge. Born entirely of God, this certitude is the theological virtue of hope, growing ever more strongly within the soul and carrying it along steadfastly through all darkness and destitution. Deprived of every natural support from reason or will, the soul is no longer grounded in this world. Grounded in hope as only God can teach it, it lives from His sustaining and attracting strength alone. And so its love, its relation to time and space, its orientation toward all that exists is being transformed in essence. Slowly the soul reaches the state of being "beside itself" in the wondrous and truly authentic sense of being freed from the insufficiency of all things created and winning its final haven: the heart of its Lord and God.

One must pray for divine support and perseverance. Often this will be possible only by a silent offering of the heart. What is there to say, since God knows all and only desires the soul's compliance with His will? It prays without words; to continue on its way *is* the offering of its faith, hope and love; of its requests and thanksgiving, all in one. God has called the soul— of this it is strangely certain—and it must go to Him, whatever the price. "Joyfully have I offered all! That "all" had been the ego, to which, consciously or not, the soul had hitherto related all. The soul has now surrendered it joyfully, and in its place has enthroned God as the center of things, as the power that generates, maintains and sanctifies every created being. The soul has begun to know this, and to know that all is well.

Chapter 20

Contemplative Love

"Who cometh across the desert" (Cant. 8:5)

Now we shall consider with all due reverence and holy joy
what occurs between the soul and its beloved Lord when the
veil of darkness and the wreath of suffering are lifted, at least
for a while, and the soul begins to savor that life for which
it had been thirsting and preparing itself. Not much can ever
be said about this, for the relationship between God and each
soul is unique, as each soul is a different mirror of His loving
presence and responds in an essentially different way to the
call of His love. Besides, who ever would describe this mutual
love? It is too deep, too rich, too immense, too tender and
chaste. This love can be spoken of only to assert that it exists,
and to awaken a more intense desire for it and the hope of
achieving it.

It is strange how, at this stage, the soul recalls words from
the Scriptures which it had known for a long time, although
it had not really understood them. Now they open like buds,
showing what they contain, suddenly illuminating and revealing the inner life of the soul. This applies especially to the
psalms and the Canticle of Canticles, that song of love between
God and the soul, which can be crudely misinterpreted, but is
a tenuous endeavor to express what every soul is capable of
experiencing.

In moments of relief from its worst trials the soul may suddenly recall and comprehend the word: "Who is she, who
cometh across the desert, supported by her lover?" (Cant.
8:5). The soul had indeed been in the desert, in an isolated

275]

wilderness; it was lost in aridity and was filled with anguish and bitterness. And now all seems transformed. How did it happen? There is no answer, certainly no explanation; only the fact that again the soul feels that it can breathe freely. No longer is that darkness within, that barren incoherence. All begins to blossom, as when the rains of spring have fallen and enchanting beauty breaks forth from the soil, turning the desert overnight into a paradise. The soul has, so to speak, entered an oasis. Unable to describe its beauty, it yet knows itself to be there. It is as if, in the darkness of its lonely wait, the soul had developed new organs with which to see and to hear in a different way than it had ever known, though it could hardly explain the difference. This cannot be a delusion; everything is too distinct, too intimate for that. This is a new reality, marvelously rich and replete, which proceeds from God, radiates from Him and is, in fact, the soul's Beloved Himself.

It is He who supports the soul. Now it knows with utter clarity that He held it faithfully, protected it in all those terrors, was never absent, but closer to the soul than it was to itself, though He kept hidden. Almost unconsciously and not quite knowing how, the soul had rested upon Him. How else, left to itself, could it have conquered and traversed the desert? Blissfully amazed, the soul now recognizes the exalted power of this love which serves it with unlimited devotion and ardently desires to be united with it forever.

But the soul now sees Him differently than before. It has a clear and profound awareness of His presence, granted in the measure of its sufferings and the purity derived from them and His grace. The soul would rejoice, but hardly can. Looking at Him, words fail. An indescribable joy moves its whole being like a gentle tremor. It leans upon Him as it makes its way, but gazing upon Him now or at least feeling His presence, not with the senses as in the early stages of prayer, but with a totally different perception, purged and entirely spiritual. All sentiment of the emotions has been appeased and no longer disturbs the blessed privacy of spirit meeting Spirit.

As if from a great distance, it vibrates quite gently, like a prelude of that transfiguration through which the body will also share in the glory of the heavenly nuptials. "Winter is gone," a voice within seems to sing (Cant. 2:11), and "the fig tree is in bloom" (Cant. 2:13). "The vines smell sweet" (Cant. 2:15) and everything is pervaded by love's enchantment. What the heart has experienced in pure earthly love as a mere foreboding is here fulfilled. Love re-creates and renews everything; it permeates the remotest corners of the heart and the universe.

"Thou hast widened my heart" (Ps. 118:32)

There are other occasions when, praying or attempting to pray, one has no alternative but to abandon oneself quietly to the will of God and to regard this as the expression of the mutual love between Him and the soul. Though trying to keep its gaze upon God, the soul remains imprisoned and constrained, engulfed by obscurity and a deep sensation of being far removed from the object of its longing. Then an unexpected change occurs. It is as if suddenly a light had been kindled within; as if all heaviness and oppressive weight had fallen away and it could spread its wings. The soul seems to have broken through an impenetrable wall. The heart, formerly chained and compressed, begins to breathe freely, and quietly forms the words: "Thou hast widened my heart" (Ps. 118:32). With astounding speed this poor tormented heart seems to expand, transported by grace. It is transformed into a garden of love and freedom. No prison walls surround it now with their gloom. The darkness has given way and the soul is bathed in light. Not a glaring or piercing light, but spreading gently through the whole of the soul's interior; a light, as it were, vibrating with music.

This has nothing to do with visions or such like; it is far removed from all sensuous perception. It is a wholly spiritual experience, devoid of all images, like floating in space. All gravity has become weightless, all darkness is turned into light, all dejection changes to healing and soothing joy. The soul is delivered from all its cares and sorrows, from its narrowness and its shortsightedness, from prejudice and self-opinionated judgment. Everything has a different look because the soul's viewpoint has been totally changed. In the wonderful expanse of its being as it is now revealed, everything finds its place. The soul understands what is meant by saying that God hates none of the things He created. Together with Him, it loves them, recognizes their beauty and significance and the sublime wisdom that made them. All is part of an order established by the power, wisdom and love of God, and the soul is part of it and actively participates in it. For the first time a truly catholic realization, an all-embracing, all-accepting attitude governs the soul. It has room now for everything—for people and things that hitherto, in spite of an earnest will and serious resolve, it could not tolerate. Effortlessly it can now stretch out its arms to invite them all into its heart or, better, to find them there, commended to its care by Him who loves them all just as He loves the soul.

Even now the soul sees nothing in particular, no detail. It apprehends things in their totality, as an infinite whole, yet in a manner which allows for countless features to stand out and reveal that whole as a structure, an ordered system, though the soul neither analyzes them nor desires to do so. Asked to explain this, one would be nonplussed, for no language offers words to describe such a process. Analogies such as light, ocean, floating rhythms, are apt to mislead anyone not familiar with these experiences, and yet these expressions which are directly and accurately fitting on a lower level must, for lack of other and appropriate terms, be applied on the higher levels as well. There, however, they have a merely indirect value, the equivalence of a parable.

The reality so described cannot be expressed; it must be experienced. But of one thing the soul is certain: this experience is real, a true source of life, a new way of love. These moments or hours endow it with a new sense of values, with different measures of judgment, appreciation and love for the things and people that will soon call upon the soul's care and attention once more. True, these effects do not usually last a long time, since the soul's transformation has not yet reached its deepest level. So the soul slides back every time—or so it would seem—soon to be the same as before. And yet not the same, for those experiences of being dilated gradually exert their influence upon the heart, which will eventually change its whole attitude toward all that exists. That love which gave vision and depth and width, which unites the soul to Him who is Himself love, now teaches the soul to regard everything with kindness, devotion and magnanimous generosity.

"Thou hast given them food at the opportune moment" (Ps. 144:15)

When the darkness is lifted, when the soul emerges from incomprehensible pain which only blind faith in God's wisdom could help it endure, its hunger is satisfied, its thirst is quenched. Could it have borne such desolation much longer? God alone knows the answer. He determines the end of its trials as much as He bids them recur, if so His loving wisdom deems best. Deeply, unquestioningly, the soul now knows that such inner clarity, such spiritual nourishment cannot be extorted by force nor snatched by cunning; it comes directly from God and from Him alone, from His free volition and bountiful grace. Famished, languishing, helpless, agonizing and hardly breathing, incapable of interior movement, the soul experienced something like death, yet it had waited. For He "is able to raise up even from the dead" (Heb. 11:19). Now He has called the soul forth from its tomb and, unlike that other occasion when, having raised Jairus' child from death, "He bid them give her to eat" (Luke 8:55), He will now Himself nourish the soul with that mysterious food which He has prepared from eternity: the food of love which He is Himself. How He will do it, the soul shall never explain, but it knows that gropingly, it had reached the edge of an inexhaustible well and that it now drinks in long draughts from its waters and feels strengthened, refreshed and elated. All its barren land is filled with new life and blossoms; it is reassured of its endurance at a time when more burdens and duties will be imposed.

Now the soul comprehends from a positive angle what, in the painfully growing consciousness of its incapability, it had already begun to see: that its strength is sustained by God alone; that He alone is the source of all that is good, of all life and all action. The measure in which the vital stream of His life imparts itself to the soul is the measure of its vigor to continue in life and being. "At the opportune moment" He gave it food, and the soul gratefully perceives how all that He ever does is right and holy, just and of loving concern.

"I sleep, but my heart waketh" (Cant. 5:2)

When the divine light comes into the soul, invisible yet powerful and convincing, and when the fountain of life has begun to flow, there is deep tranquillity. Though its faculties do not always leave the soul in peace—for they are intruders which are not easily mastered or properly channelled—tranquillity has all the same begun. The faculties—they are called "I" in the verse quoted above—"are asleep"; they hardly stir and will soon be quite still. The soul perceives it, amazed. Just as we sometimes observe the relaxing of the activities of our imagination or memory before we fall asleep, so the soul's powers, too, fall asleep; but its central core is more awake than ever. Its "heart," its innermost substance, that part of the soul which has the most intimate contact with the Beloved, "wakes."

In this wondrous quiet, which can last for longer or shorter periods, nothing at all stirs. Occasionally a fleeting thought may flash across the horizon. A slight animation of the will may be felt for a second. Fundamentally, however, in this condition nothing is said or asked or explained. All is self-evident.

How often the soul had longed to see or to hear Him, to receive from His lips the solution of all its doubts in the dark-

ness that shrouded its vision. Now He has come. In this ineffable silence the soul leans on His heart. What is there to
ask? At the bottom of all the soul's quests there had been only
one: His love, Himself, deep union with Him, the consummation of its own existence in this love. And that quest has now
been fulfilled. There is nothing left to ask, nothing to answer.
The soul was itself the question to which He is Himself the
response. Born of God's love, the soul's essence is love which
returns to its origin. At times in this blessed silence the memory
of its former anxious desire to put forth its questions makes the
soul smile at itself. It knows all the answers. It would not know
what to ask now.

In this state one feels as if he had never been fully awake,
that he had drowsed and dreamed all his life. On the other
hand, he was sure that he had moved and acted in reality. And
so he had, but now he knows a reality of a completely different
and much higher order. Here at last the soul is fully awakened
and given full consciousness of itself. It is centered upon the
Divine Friend whom it loves, and who first loved the soul. This
love alone is final and ultimately decisive reality; to it all things
must lead or else they are nothing.

"It is good for me to adhere to my God"
(Ps. 72:28)

In silence the soul gives itself entirely to God as He gives
Himself to the soul. Unwaveringly, the soul's gaze is fixed
upon His countenance, which it cannot actually see, yet it distinctly perceives in a spiritual perception purified by intense
interior suffering that for His beauty the soul would gladly
renounce all that the world or its own dreams had ever offered.
It is as if the soul had been welded to Him and could never
again be separated. The occasional remembrance that this condition will again be suspended causes a piercing pain, an un-
guarded inclination to resist.

At times, however, individual features or facts emerge quite

naturally from that obscurity which the presence of the Beloved fills with invisible light. Formerly, in the state of meditation, the soul had to trace them consciously and perhaps by
a definite method. Even now this will have to be done when,
for instance, others must be instructed or some theological
point should be expounded. But during contemplative prayer
everything is reversed. God acts, His impulse shows the soul
what to do or to leave. Frequently He merely makes the soul
keep its gaze quietly focused upon Him and does not prompt
it beyond this loving regard. Either His holiness or sweetness
or loving kindness attracts the soul's inner vision. Again it
may, in one flash of comprehension, behold the tender affection with which He turns to the mother of the dead boy from
Naim, or the sovereign authority with which His words, "I
am He" (John 18:5), cast the hostile cohort down to the
ground in Gethsemane. Or again, from the words, "Fear ye
not, little flock, for it hath pleased your Father to give you
a kingdom" (Luke 12:32), an indescribable sense of security
enfolds the soul. Features or words like these may come up in
an instant or may emerge gradually, and their resplendent light
fills the whole soul. It should then continue to dwell on the
material offered, provided this can be done without any violent
effort. There are other occasions when such visions or words
fly past like a sparkling chain, and the soul can neither retain
them nor hold on to them. It only beholds and it knows that
it is His beauty which is there revealed. If, on the other hand,
the soul can succeed to dwell on them further, it should certainly do so and contemplate Him.

Unlike meditation, nothing is analyzed now, nothing examined; the soul beholds divine wisdom as such or some
attribute of the Lord, its Beloved. In this way He engraves into
it, ever more deeply, whatever feature of holiness He thus
demonstrates, to make the soul like to Himself. The more the
soul remains quiet and merely receptive, though ready to receive the divine message with single-minded love, the greater
will be the transforming influence of that communication. Do

we not expose ourselves longer to the sun if we want to receive a more intense effect of its rays? Our spiritual sun operates in a similar way. We must not withdraw from it too soon or be absorbed by other things while that ray still touches the soul. To remain exposed to it is essential to contemplative prayer and that is how the soul cooperates with the grace of contemplation.

To prevent all misinterpretation it is imperative to repeat that the soul will not be given any new or additional "revelation." What we call private revelations, granted to saints or saintly people, is merely a new mode by which truths already revealed are exposed to a better and more profound comprehension. To expect anything else in contemplative prayer would be a fatal error. To experience lovingly the old truths and in vital awareness to participate in them, that is love's final achievement in contemplation.

Seeing that such adherence is decisive in contemplation, one should give oneself over to it whenever a chance might offer: going for a walk, having to wait somewhere, in unexpected spare moments too easily filled up with something like a quick look at a book or a paper or a purposeless fiddling with the radio. The more often the soul joins the Beloved, the sooner and the more perfectly their union will be accomplished.

"Tell me, where have you seen Him?"
(Cant. 3:3)

For a long time the soul's union with the Beloved will be only a temporary experience. Not as if the soul were not by faith always conscious of His inner presence, nor as if He would not permit the soul to find Him with ease whenever it directs its attention to Him. He is present within, and the soul can behold Him always. But there is this distinct alternative: He may either remain utterly silent and as if inactive, or He may approach the soul. This is not easily described. Words like closeness, withdrawal, approximation seem to express it best, if at all. The soul is distinctly aware of His reserve or of an influence from Him. He always waits for the soul to regard Him, but He does not always invite it to greater intimacy, even when the soul looks at His presence and does so for a long time. This can be felt as something ephemeral or in the soul's innermost core, so incredibly close, in fact, that one would never have thought it possible. It is only now that the soul can realize the true meaning of communion.

We shall not speak of those more or less extended periods in which the soul may again have to suffer intensely from being deprived of the interior presence of God. This is part of its sufferings, of the genuine passion of love. And God seems to withdraw, to conceal His countenance from the soul, in order that sorrow and longing for Him might intensify its love, its supplication and its earnest endeavor to please Him. As in earthly love the man leads the bride, so in supernatural love God—and He alone—must reveal the mystery of this unique, holy and eternal love, of which the soul has but a most imperfect knowledge. This is His divine pleasure, and it will soon be the soul's delight. He knows when to conceal His presence and when to vouchsafe for an instant the bliss of His closeness; when to vanish and when to permit the soul to possess Him once more. But the soul must learn the rules of this divine school of love, and in all its trials and tests it must realize that He always returns and that each reunion with Him is richer, deeper and more blessed than before. It begins to dawn upon the soul that an infinitely high summit will have to be reached for the feast of love to be celebrated in a manner worthy of God. There is much that the soul, so immature and foolish, will have to learn from an untiring Master who knows countless methods of instruction, methods with their full measure of both sorrow and bliss.

But let us now consider the alternation of approximation and disappearance of the interior presence which occurs in contemplation. This is not by any means an unfailing experience, since the encounter of love between God and the soul is rich in infinite diversity and full of unexpected changes. The approach and withdrawal seem to succeed one another in a rhythmical sequence. The soul may be visited by most persistent distractions and unable, in spite of every endeavor, to shake them off. Suddenly, right across the distractions, He moves toward it, gently insistent. In happy surprise the soul senses the approach for which it had all the while been hoping, feels the presence grow in intensity and then diminish again as slowly as it had appeared. Involuntary distractions begin to set in again, until the presence seems to have vanished completely. But the approach recurs after a short spell, and the same rhythm is several times repeated, yet in such a way that each new approach makes the encounter more forceful and the intimacy more profound. Then the soul knows that now it will not be led any further; that this was, for today, the culminating offering of the Beloved. This may be the moment in which He communicates the most intimate grace of His love, though of this the soul cannot judge. Soon all recedes; the encounter is over. But there the soul retains the blissful awareness of God's mysterious presence.

All this can happen, of course, without any kind of distractions. But under their impact it is particularly remarkable how the mists of that chaotic confusion are dispersed by the divine approach, and how the soul then feels as if redeemed from their unwanted and unsettling effect. But it would gladly bear them, like everything else, for the love of God if and when He so disposes.

That wonderful rhythm of coming and going appears to the soul at times like a mysterious inhaling and exhaling, or like being lifted with infinite gentleness and then lowered again with equal tenderness. It is as if the Beloved gathered the soul to His heart, soon to release it again, though with most tender love. These are, however, entirely spiritual perceptions, deeper and more distinct as neither the senses nor the nerves are involved, for whenever they are engaged, they are a disturbance rather than a help.

"A cluster of myrrh my Beloved is to me"
(Cant. 1:12)

To arrive is happiness; to depart is sorrow. Who would deny it? The arrival already contains, as it were, the pain of parting. So this, like all other love, brings its own suffering, though in a different measure and with an incomparably firmer hope of a fulfillment. "My Beloved is like a cluster of myrrh resting upon my heart." Myrrh is fragrant, invigorating and healing; but it is also bitter. The Beloved is ineffable happiness to the soul, but there is suffering in this happiness. Embracing Him spiritually, the soul is encompassed by Him, reposes in Him as He reposes in it, yet it knows that this will bring many pains. Pains, though, of a kind which the soul desires, while hitherto it had shunned all manner of hurt. Formerly, one would have preferred to run away when prayer seemed difficult, gloomy and unrewarding. Now the soul accepts it all from His hand without a murmur, and indeed with joy. Love cannot help itself. Should the soul revel in bliss while He is carrying the cross? Should it enjoy sweet repose while, for its sake, His heart is suffering torture? As in His passion the soul recognizes and, deeply shaken, adores the magnitude of His love, so it realizes that its own suffering is the true testimony of its love for Him. And while a great fear often enough assaults it and nature revolts against pain, God has already, through contemplation, trained the soul to be steadfast; to welcome Him who in suffering unites Himself to it; and almost to grieve if He does not concede it a small measure at least of His passion. It knows that without Him it can endure nothing, but does He not always stand by? He gives the soul strength; that suffices.

The mystery of His love, which continues to bring pain and sorrow and is thus brought to its ultimate consummation, fills it with awe. Formerly, the soul would have carefully guarded against suffering; now it accepts it, holding it "like a cluster of myrrh," pressing it to itself, almost jealously. And were one to ask the soul if it would rather be rid of it, the answer would always be: "No, for in this very pain He whom I love is present." And it is only in pain that He is thus present, since this is the law of love as it slowly approaches its glorious consummation. To know this and to know that it can never again fundamentally wish for anything else, causes the soul to suffer much under its natural cowardly fear. But this, too, is one of the offerings of love, another small stalk in the mysterious cluster of myrrh.

Give and take

There is in all this a true reciprocity. The soul not only receives, but there are moments when it is allowed to see itself as one who also gives. Has it not been enriched by divine love? Has not the Holy Ghost become the soul's very own precious possession? He does not merely pretend to give all, He does truly give, as truly as He is the truth. If He does not give in unlimited abundance, it is because the soul could not yet accept it. Again, this is purest love, which does not tax the soul's loving endurance beyond its actual strength. The longing of the Divine Heart would wish to hold back nothing; would desire to shower the soul with the plenitude of the Godhead; but His giving in measured proportions trains the soul to receive better and more.

As the soul reciprocates, its own being widens. This give and take, this receiving and reciprocating happens in the most profound depth of the soul, so softly that it is often hardly perceptible. But the soul learns in a supernatural way that it has been made equal, that its offering is being accepted, and that it is no longer merely patronized like a beggar but honored like a queen. Full of wonder and awe, it comprehends how in this, too, it is called to resemble the Beloved more and more. The soul is permitted to see in great clarity how Christ, too, both as God and as Man, receives everything from the love of the Father—His divine Person by an eternal act of communication of essence; His human nature by an act of creation. Both, however, proceed from divine love, which is the Holy Ghost. And just as the Father imparts everything to the Son, who is His dignity, glory, majesty and beauty, and is Himself truth and grace, so the Son, through the Holy Ghost, eternally gives back to the Father His entire, infinite being. He is less than the Father only in the sense that the Father alone is the primordial source and principle of all manner of being.

The soul is called to participate fully in this mystery. Recipient with the Son and because of Him, it is through Him and with Him able to give in return. It begins to dawn on the soul that this must be the unending bliss of eternal life and that the innermost vision granted by interior prayer must somehow persist even in ordinary daily life. The love of its Lord has so refined the soul that it can now see these things without attributing to itself the faintest shadow of merit. For this reason it had to come face to face with its own nothingness, so that it might realize that it owes its entire being to His love alone. Precisely because of this the whole of its being is purged and thus the soul is restored to its full value in the sight of God.

In this give and take the soul gradually learns that it owns all. It understands St. Paul's words: "He that . . . delivered Him up for us all, how hath He not also, with Him, given us all things?" (Rom. 8:32). If the Father entrusts to the soul His Only-begotten, the eternal reflection of Himself, how could He ever refuse it anything else? Formerly, the soul was permitted to see how everything is good and worthy of love and gratitude in God. Now its vision reaches beyond that level and comprehends that all that is good is a gift bestowed on it by eternal love. Nothing is withheld. True, the soul cannot yet appreciate the immensity of its good fortune. It clasps it to itself as a child would hold a collection of precious stones after having been told that they make him enormously rich and that he must not lose even the smallest. With his little hands tightly clenched, he will be on his way. In like manner the soul possesses all, and of this it is fully aware; but as yet it cannot fully enjoy its great value, and that is just as well. When the soul will have become quite pure, then this too will be permitted. For the present, however, it would merely deflect its attention.

This is where the soul understands the full significance of holy poverty, to which Christ exhorts those who desire to follow Him closely; a way of lofty freedom which, by renouncing some things, conditions the soul to receive all things in exchange. The more willingly the soul allowed itself to be led into poverty—not merely material poverty, but more especially that of the spirit, of which the former, voluntarily chosen, is but a symbol and a very great help—the more the obstacles will disappear which had prevented God from giving the soul what alone is worthy of His boundless love: everything. The soul now knows that in Him, its Lord and its King, all things are being assigned to its dominion. The union of its will with that of its Beloved, and in Him with the all-creative, ever-sustaining and ever-perfecting will of the Father in heaven, confers upon it this right of possession and rule.

Thus it also perceives that man, most beloved creature of God, is given into its care. Purged of its former absurd jealousy, though at times, unfortunately, it is still capable of it outside contemplative prayer, the soul now sees humanity in God, and in Him loves all men with the love that is His. The soul would help each to reach that place in eternity and to attain to that measure of love which God has envisaged for him, even if this were immensely greater than the glory to be vouchsafed to itself. In fact, this aspect hardly arises. For how can he, to whom all has been given, have more or less? And are not all other souls part of that all? Is not the soul made richer by every one of them? In the love of its Beloved the soul knows no boundaries. Unlimited as is its power to receive all that exists, so is its love to give all in return.

This is a new solicitude for others, very different from the soul's former concern about them, which caused it to pray explicitly now for this, now for that person. When asked:

"Please pray for me," it would willingly promise to do so, and do it according to the other person's intention. Now, except for rare occasions, the soul is incapable of this kind of prayer. As a rule, in the offering of itself it will offer them all to God, by whom they were committed to its care and to its being. The soul will expose them, as it were, to the purity of His regard, to the ardor of His heart, so that they may be sanctified and inflamed in precisely the measure which God foresaw. Even when intending to pray for one particular person, the soul will usually find this the only possible manner. To pray for specific intentions is increasingly difficult, since the soul is well aware now that God is always ready to grant whatever will truly benefit us and what His love wishes to grant just now. We need only make ourselves ready in an attitude of compliance. Therefore, when the soul is laid open before God in prayer, it feels at times like a gateway for the stream of God's love to flow into the world to make it His kingdom. And the wider that gate is thrown open, the more certain the coming of God, the more generous His answer to the soul's prayer, to its offering of itself on behalf of the world. This is no longer the impatient petition of former days, and yet it is all this, but condensed into a single act of oblation and dedication. The soul knows that God's grace entering into itself, also enters the others. In like manner, the Blessed Virgin became the salvation of the entire world by her *Ecce ancilla Domini* (Luke 1:38). This is a very blessed experience, by which many anxieties of particular intercession, impatience and worry are conquered. It is enough that the soul, in the single-mindedness of total submission, allow God to enter into it and in complete trust leave it to Him when, how and in whom He will work the perfection which His eternal love has decreed.

Thus the soul here recognizes itself as responsible for all others. Whatever the soul is or does, bears on them, too; on all the brothers and sisters in Christ, the many members of the one mystical body. Therefore the soul not only intercedes for them, but gives thanks and adores in their name, and its own remorse makes reparation for all. No longer does it question the efficacy of its prayer; it knows that it will be effective, because nothing whatever can be in vain, even if neither place nor manner of fulfillment are revealed. To what purpose? Faith, hope and charity will be the purer for not knowing more beyond this undoubted fact.

Formerly the soul could hardly have borne the knowledge of itself being part of all that exists, of its cooperation in the building-up of God's work, of its responsibility in its destruction. Such knowledge would have been crushing. It is quite different now that the soul has been permitted to live this new life in God. For now it perceives that whatever proceeds from its inner being, comes ultimately from God and that whatever arises autonomously in its ego and is consequently void and false, culpable and sinful, must be transformed and sanctified by the same love in which it has its redemption. All is harder now, yet easier, too; all is charged with a responsibility previously unknown, but with a radiance as well, abounding in grace.

"As the servant's eyes watching the hand of her mistress" (Ps. 122:2)

In the soul's loving attention upon the Divine Spouse or, more precisely, by its ready devotion and eager obedience, He not only fashions the heart of His chosen bride but makes it capable of pure and spontaneous union and cooperation with Him. Does it not already will as He wills? To this end it renounced itself or at least tries to become wholly detached from its ego, and it knows that one day it will fully succeed and have no other concern than that of His pleasure. The soul's inner trials and exterior pains have trained it toward this goal; now it has become patient and has learned to wait, to await His calling. Not that He ever speaks in audible words; and the soul would be foolish to look for special signs or communications. But sometimes a call is made, some word is spoken, some letter is written at precisely the opportune moment. All this is mysteriously woven into that mysterious order of divine providence which the soul could neither know in advance nor anticipate in its explicit intentions. But God makes use of the soul, because it is at His bid and call. He permits it to sense the appropriate, since this is what the soul would, in union with Him, long to do.

Again, the soul may be conscious of a delicate impulse. This is not startling and rarely if ever compelling. It is more like the faintest touch, to which God expects the soul to be alert. In the first case one simply acted under the impact of natural thought and judgment, and it proved to be right, because God had already taken possession of the faculties to a degree which brought them spontaneously into full harmony with His will. In the second case there is a definite impulse, an actual indication. Thus the soul senses that some word should be suppressed in a conversation, some glance withheld, or that something should be postponed, to which natural inclination urges just then.

This is different from the time when asceticism was predominant. Then the soul set the task for itself, and it was made to conform to the will of God merely through obedience to spiritual direction. Now all such self-appointing subsides and will one day cease altogether. Then the soul will act solely under the gentle impact that rises from within. Here, too, the soul is wholly under God's guidance. Therefore no violence occurs in this cooperation with Him; nothing alarming, as may so easily attach to the ascetic life. This is quite gentle, tender; it works without effort. Not, though, as if the soul were safe from occasional failure; it does fail and is deeply grieved at its lack of love, which is clearly the cause for its faults. But even these the soul can bear differently now; more patiently, more gently, since it has ceased to wonder at its failings and at its nothingness. It wonders only at Him who always helps, always forgives, and as soon as the soul looks at Him, extends His hand to rescue it from all complexities. When one day, by the grace of contemplation, love will possess the soul's entire being, all its actions will be born in this interior beholding of the Lord. He will then be the measure of all things, and love will be their motive and their goal.

O Sanctissima Trinitas

The soul makes an amazing discovery when in prayer it knows itself admitted into the being of the one it loves. This does not happen every time, nor always in equal intensity. Sometimes, however, interior contemplation is perfect. The soul feels as if its own initiative had been suspended. There is but one activity, absolute and all-embracing. It is as if there were but one prayer, one pleading, one adoration and one thanksgiving. The soul now senses that here must be the key to the strange words of St. Paul: "And I live, now not I; but Christ liveth in me" (Gal. 2:20). The divine-human life has become the life of the soul, without destroying it nor depriving it of its freedom. On the contrary, only now is it completely itself in a freedom beyond all expression. It is integrated completely into the life of Christ. It is permitted now to perceive that the human nature of the Eternal Son adores and worships the Father, that the Son ever remains in perfect submission, humility and love before the Eternal Father, and that in the Son the soul is itself carried into that most holy presence. Unable to comprehend the mystery of the Son's being and acting, the soul is deeply aware of the fact that it participates in both. It need not remain at a distance; together with the Son, it is ever before the Father.

A further experience is vouchsafed. It is the awareness of the indwelling of the Holy Ghost, the "sweet guest of the soul." He is not now like someone distinctly "other," but so fully possessed by the soul that He has become the soul's love, as He is, ever and essentially, the love of the Eternal Son. He is also the love of the Son's human nature, not that Christ was incapable of human love, but that this created love in

Christ is totally permeated by the Holy Ghost. As Divine Love, He ever consecrates the human love of Christ, who even as Man loves the Father entirely in the Holy Ghost, by whom His human power of love is made divine.

The soul recognizes that it participates in this mystery by which its own love is made perfect, like that of Christ. Formerly the soul had been much pained by knowing that its love could never grow enough, since an infinity would forever separate it from what it craved and what alone could be acceptable to God. Now the soul knows that divine love has covered the distance, has filled this last remaining chasm. It recognizes the dignity, the noble adequacy of its love, which responds to that same Holy Spirit of love who had first loved the soul. There is ineffable bliss in this experience. In the most disconsolate hours the remembrance of it will strengthen and animate the soul. When everything seems dead within, one certainty nonetheless persists: that the soul still loves beyond all measure and that even God cannot love more. The soul's tiny human love is permeated by that infinite divine loving and though it cannot keep the pace as yet and often fails, what matter, since the soul loves with the love of God. The Father not only gave it His Eternal Son, but with Him all His love. For this is His love, the giving of the Son, and this is how He loves, that He spares not the Son (Rom. 8:32), that in the Son His love comes to the soul as the Holy Ghost.

This sublime certainty spells deepest peace for the soul whenever prayer carries it to that inner vision. Never will there be more for the soul to give; never will it desire more to give. It knows now that it gives what God Himself, within the soul, gives.

If the soul thus beheld the face of its Beloved and mysteriously savored the sweetness of His Spirit, it will also be given to it to contemplate the Father. True, it had long been certain that in the face of the Son it had seen Him as well. "He that seeth Me, seeth the Father also" (John 14:9). The Father's grace, bounty, solicitude and fidelity are ever reflected in the bounty, solicitude and fidelity of the Son. In the Son it received the Father and held Him as its own. In the Son it could dare to approach Him and feel at home in the Father's house. Yet there had remained an element of remoteness. A delicate veil concealed the Father—precisely in Christ—from the soul's vision. But now it is being admitted into His presence. Not often, perhaps, but when it happens, the soul knows that it is in an immediate union with the Father. The Son has led His bride there, to the place of His constant abode, whence He ever proceeds and where He returns. The veil seems to have lifted; this is the Father! The soul beholds His love and it understands that it is itself entirely received into that love. Its many defects are as if vanished; none of them matter now. It would jubilantly cry out: "My Father!"

The veil, however, will soon be lowered again, and this is as well. Nevertheless, the soul is now fundamentally certain that nothing will be withheld. God desires to give Himself to the ultimate depths of His being, and He will do so. To this end He must further sanctify the soul. An experience of this kind may have caused St. Paul to exclaim: "Nor height, nor depth, nor any other creature shall be able to separate us from the love of God" (Rom. 8:39). Nothing—except ourselves. But shall not our self be consumed by the fires of His love in the life of contemplation?

This is how it is given the soul to unite itself in a particular relationship to each of the three Divine Persons and consciously to live that union. Moreover, under the protective veil of the "invisible light" it may contemplate the Most Holy Trinity as one and three. This may be vouchsafed early or in the later stages of the way, just as God wills. Always, however, the way of contemplation will lead to the center of the divine mystery. The Trinity is the soul's greatest good. It is the beginning and end, origin and consummation of all its loving, adoring, thanksgiving.

The essential interior knowing of the triune mystery can, like the other experiences, rise in the soul like a gentle dawn;

or it can be suddenly impregnated into the soul as if by a supremely powerful hand, as a seal which the soul will now bear, never to lose it again. One cannot describe this, but from then on, the soul's life of prayer and love will resolve around this one central mystery. Whatever inspirations may still be granted the soul, they will be subordinated to and integrated into that most essential and most sublime mystery. This mystery will be engraved on the soul in a purely spiritual manner, free of images, thought or emotion. It fills the soul's essence with strength and humility, love and self-denial. For a long time such an experience usually reverberates strongly in the soul. It does not leave it, but again and again draws the soul into the orbit of love, remains ever present and animates all within. For years this resonance may vibrate in the soul, even though many other experiences may meanwhile be granted and that great experience may have long ceased to be constantly present. But one glance into its depth will suffice for the soul to re-awaken that first experience and to feel its power and beauty with hardly diminished force. This possibility of evoking the inspirations communicated to us by grace distinguishes them fundamentally from those for which our faculties of imagination, reasoning or self-suggestion are responsible.

If before, in its contact with each of the Divine Persons, the soul was predominantly aware of their distinction, now in contemplation of the Trinity it beholds their indivisible unity. Here the soul is no longer as "one" in relation to "Three"; rather, it is as one soul in the presence of the one God. The soul is given over in its entirety and drawn into the entirety of the divine life of love, in a manner which relates each one of the soul's faculties more especially to each of the three Persons in God. This is how the life of the soul arrives at its own miraculous and final perfection in the glorious plenitude of the divine life. For the Persons in God are the modes in which He is inexpressibly alive, infinitely rich, abundantly creative in His one and indivisible essence.